fabulous modern
COOKIES

fabulous modern
COOKIES

Lessons in Better Baking
for Next-Generation Treats

CHRIS TAYLOR
AND PAUL ARGUIN

PHOTOGRAPHS BY
ANDREW THOMAS LEE

The Countryman Press

An Imprint of W. W. Norton & Company
Independent Publishers Since 1923

For information about permission to reproduce selections from this book, write to
Permissions, The Countryman Press, 500 Fifth Avenue, New York, NY 10110

For information about special discounts for bulk purchases, please contact
W. W. Norton Special Sales at specialsales@wwnorton.com or 800-233-4830

Manufacturing by Versa Press
Book design by Allison Chi
Production manager: Devon Zahn

The Countryman Press
www.countrymanpress.com

An imprint of W. W. Norton & Company, Inc.
500 Fifth Avenue, New York, NY 10110
www.wwnorton.com

978-1-68268-659-1 (pbk.)

10 9 8 7 6 5 4 3 2 1

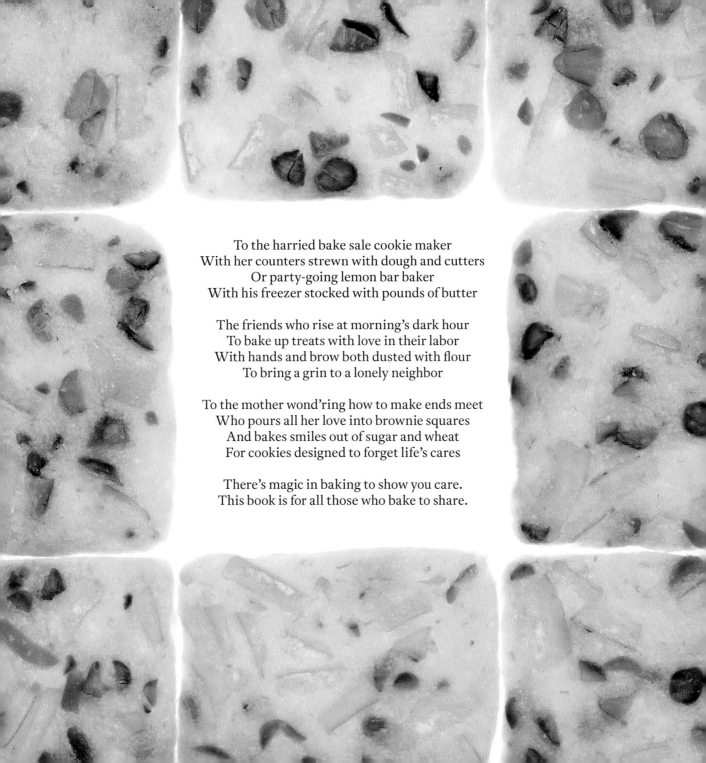

To the harried bake sale cookie maker
With her counters strewn with dough and cutters
Or party-going lemon bar baker
With his freezer stocked with pounds of butter

The friends who rise at morning's dark hour
To bake up treats with love in their labor
With hands and brow both dusted with flour
To bring a grin to a lonely neighbor

To the mother wond'ring how to make ends meet
Who pours all her love into brownie squares
And bakes smiles out of sugar and wheat
For cookies designed to forget life's cares

There's magic in baking to show you care.
This book is for all those who bake to share.

contents

introduction

WHEN WE PUBLISHED our first cookbook, *The New Pie*, we were frequently asked whether pies were the only things that we baked. Of course not! In fact, we have always enjoyed baking almost anything. When we started competing at state fairs more than a decade ago, it wasn't for fame or fortune. (If you've ever entered a county fair and earned a crisp $5 bill for a first-place loaf of bread or a best-in-show brownie, then you know that the joy of competing is not from earning prize money.) Rather, the contests provided us a wonderful outlet to continue to experiment with creating all kinds of baked goods, sweet and savory, with the goal of continuing to learn and grow in the craft of baking. While we have certainly made our fair share of pies (thousands, in fact), we still enjoy baking yeast breads, muffins, biscuits, cakes of all types, pastries, and—of course—cookies.

But why a book on cookies? For one, we love cookies—but that's not the only reason. To us, cookies are the most approachable of all desserts. Because they're small, they're not as fussy as pies or layer cakes can be. Don't get us wrong, pies are heavenly, but a good pie involves a lot of steps: making and rolling pie dough, filling it, baking it, and cooling it *for hours* before cutting and serving. It can be a lot. A drop cookie recipe, like a classic chocolate chip, is dead simple: mix, scoop, bake, cool, and eat (and, honestly, that cooling step is optional for some us). A pie can serve, what, 8, maybe 12 people? One batch of cookies can make three or four *dozen*—and fast. Because of the effort, we like to say pie is for showing someone how much love them. Cookies? Cookies are for making friends.

Portable and already portioned into individual servings, cookies are the perfect sweet snack to share with others. As scientists, we are both mostly introverts, and baking has been a surefire way to meet people and make new friends. Want to meet a new neighbor? Bring them some snickerdoodles. Vying for a promotion at work? A plateful of chewy chocolate chips cookies can't hurt. Need to say you're sorry? A warm brownie can go pretty far in mending fences.

Why cookies? We have a theory. Many families in America grew up with some sort of cookie tradition, and cookies are an indispensable comfort food part of our collective edible conscience.

Even though the two of us grew up in completely different parts of the country, we each grew up eating fairly similar cookies. Near Pittsburgh, Chris's family was influenced by the Pennsylvania Dutch tradition of baking. While he was growing up, his family's cookies would usually be the time-honored Christmastime treats. The occasional family wedding would offer the unique treat of a traditional "cookie table," with dozens and dozens of cookies enjoyed by the guests while the bride and groom posed for photos between the ceremony and reception. The cookies he grew up enjoying were made using classic recipes from his mom's well-worn *Betty Crocker Cookbook* replete with batter-stained pages dotted with handwritten notes. Just as frequently, she would bake from a handful of recipes snipped from glossy magazine pages or empty chocolate chip bags paper-clipped to index cards. During his childhood set more than 1,500 miles away in the sun-soaked Virgin Islands, Paul's mom would bake homemade brownies and lemon bars as her go-to snacks for bake sales and beach picnics. Recipes were pulled from cookbooks published by popular magazines, such as *Better Homes and Gardens* and *Good Housekeeping*. Many of our memories associated with cookies are associated with the feelings we felt when making or eating them. Perched on a stool, helping cut out gingerbread men with chubby preschool fingers. Or sneaking a small bite (or two!) of raw cookie dough from the mixing bowl when our mothers looked away (and long before our careers in public health began). The traditions of cookies are well established throughout the United States. Kids growing up on the white sugar–sand beaches of America's paradise and the snowy steel towns of the Northeast all snacked on many of the same types of cookies at their respective kitchen tables.

While they are certainly comforting, cookies are often very traditional. Many of the same recipes pop up over and over again: the same chocolate chips, peanut butter, sugar cookies, and lemon bars. Comforting? Yes, and there is a potent charm in an unbroken line of recipes handed down from generation to generation. We also honor that tradition, but we have never been fans of strict adherence to tradition solely for tradition's sake. We still have fond memories of beachside lemon bars and Toll House chocolate chip cookies. However, we like to believe that we are not so blinded by convention to see the wonderful possibilities of cookies. Cookies are so amazingly diverse! From simple shortbreads with relatively few ingredients, to easy drop cookies, to cookies that are elaborately decorated, sandwiched around cream or filled with jam, bars, brownies, no-bakes, fried cookies, and on and on and on. Cookies are also amazingly adaptable—simple doughs can be augmented with fun flavors and textures, elevating them to new heights. In recent years, more food bloggers and cookbook authors have started becoming increasingly adventurous with their cookie flavors to reflect more modern flavor combinations, including those from global food traditions that more and more of us are beginning to appreciate as our knowledge of the world of food grows and the boundaries limiting the respectful learning about food cultures fade.

Regardless of the flavors or the traditions behind them, there is something for everyone to like in cookies. For *Fabulous Modern Cookies,* we took the vast universe of cookies and tried to expand it even further. We brought a scientific approach to ensure success in baking regardless of whether you are new to baking or have been elbow-deep in cookie dough for decades. The cookies will still seem familiar (brownies, bars, drop cookies, cookie-cutter cookies, and the like) but with new and exciting flavors (and some really helpful techniques). Throughout this book, we've included Cookie Bytes—bits of bonus information as well as tips and advice on methods, ingredients, and the science of baking. Our goal is to entice and teach fellow cookie lovers and bakers of all stripes to make delicious, foolproof cookies and introduce new flavors that bakers can use to share with friends, wow at parties, and create new memories with their families. No matter if you're a smart cookie, a tough cookie, or even a little bit of a weir-dough, we have something for you.

Happy baking!
Chris Taylor and Paul Arguin
Atlanta, Georgia

getting started

The Philosophy of the Cookie

What *is* a cookie?

We realize that the very definition of cookie can be difficult to nail down. From sugar cookies to shortbread, snickerdoodles to brownies, and roll-outs to rugelach, cookies have a wide range of both flavors and textures. To define what a cookie is, we have to examine what's common among cookies. Easy, right?

Cookies are baked (except when they're not). Sure, cookies generally come out of the oven, but not every cookie needs a trip to the hotbox. Remember Rice Krispies Treats? They were a quick and easy cookie whipped up on the stove, smooshed into a pan, and left to set. Delicious cookies can be cooked on the stove, sizzled in a skillet, or made like a pizzelle on a special electric iron—no oven needed.

Cookies are made with flour (but they don't have to be). Most cookie recipes do call for a cup or two of flour. But flour does not a cookie make. Meringues, those crisp, delicate cookies made with just egg whites and sugar, are naturally free of flour. If wheat flour and the accompanying gluten is not your thing, that doesn't mean that you have to cut cookies out of your life! Gluten-free flour substitutes can take the place of wheat flour in most cookie recipes without batting an eye (see "The Gluten-Free Cookie Lifestyle," page 16). While flour power is nice, it's by no means necessary.

Cookies are round (but they don't have a corner on the market). Drop cookies, such as chocolate chips and snickerdoodles, made by dropping batter from a spoon or scoop, are round, of course. But what about brownies, blondies, and lemon bars? These square snacks are clearly cookies, but rectangles are not the only exception! Cookie cutters can transform dough into any shape imaginable, including gingerbread people, hearts, and cars.

Cookies are soft (sometimes). Linguistically, the word *cookie* comes from the Dutch word *koekje,* meaning "small cake." And while some cookies are like little cakes (for instance, soft, puffy madeleines), that really isn't the best comparison. Not every cookie is fluffy and cakelike. Some cookies are wonderfully chewy. Others are satisfyingly crunchy or delightfully crisp. Of course, if a cookie can be crisp, what about a cracker? Is a graham cracker a cookie? What about a saltine? Which brings us to . . .

Cookies are sweet (but not always). Quick—name a cookie! Chances are that the cookies most of us think of immediately are sweet cookies, such as peanut butter or oatmeal raisin. But who said that a cookie has to be dessert? Our cookie philosophy is broad enough to allow both sweet and savory cookies. In fact, we feel comfortable going so far as saying that a cracker *is* a crisp savory cookie. We love savory cookies so much that we dedicated an entire book chapter to them because savory cookies are every bit as delish as the sweet ones.

So, what is a cookie? Cookies are often round, soft, sweet treats made with flour and baked. But just as often, they're not. Our philosophy is that they are the ultimate portable, sharable, and adaptable finger food. Cookies can be eaten singly when you need just a little something to take the edge off but are also great for bingeing one after another. They're small, so feel free to have just one more.

Okay, maybe just a few more . . .

The Essential Ingredients

These are the essential ingredients that we use throughout the book. We provide this information in case you might have questions about why we might call for one ingredient or another, or what a particular ingredient is if you're not familiar with it. Refer to Sources (page 350) for more information on how to find and purchase ingredients.

The Building Blocks of Cookie Baking

Flour, sugar, butter, eggs, leavening agents (e.g., baking soda and baking powder), and salt are the basic building blocks for baking all types of sweet treats. These six ingredients are not in every cookie recipe, but they are in most.

FLOURS

Nearly every cookie in this book is made with some form of flour. Flour (or a gluten-free flour replacement, see page 16) works to create the structure of a cookie. The structure is held in place through the work of gluten (produced when the proteins in flour are mixed with liquids) and starch (present in both flours and gluten-free flour replacements). Without them, cookies would just be thin blobs with no real shape. Flour also absorbs moisture and helps ingredients mix together, as well as provides flavor.

In America, when we use the word *flour,* it is often used to refer to all-purpose flour made from milled wheat. However, with the numbers of nonwheat flours finding their way into mainstream grocery stores, it's getting easier to incorporate different types of flours into all types of baking. Measuring flour by volume (i.e., by cups) is unreliable because it can settle and pack (see "Weighing the Weight," page 33), so we highly recommend weighing flour using a digital scale. If you do measure flour by cups instead of weight, use the scoop-and-sweep method to help your measurements match as closely as possible the precise ingredient weights that we recommend. First, use the measuring cup to lightly fluff the flour in the bag or container. Scoop the cup measure into the flour and scoop out enough flour to fill the measuring cup. Sweep a flat edge (such as the back of a knife) across the cup to sweep away excess and make the flour even with the rim.

Unbleached all-purpose flour: This is the most commonly used flour in this book. Our brand of choice is King Arthur Baking Company, and this is the flour we used when testing the recipes that call for wheat flour. Other brands will work with minimal differences, but we have found King Arthur to have high-quality products that consistently perform well in our recipes.

Bleached cake flour: We prefer cake flour to be bleached rather than unbleached because bleached cake flour, along with cake flour's lower protein content, makes cookies that are softer and more tender than those made with all-purpose flour.

Whole wheat flour: Unlike refined flours, such as all-purpose or cake flours, whole wheat flour contains the germ, bran, and endosperm of the wheat kernel and provides a nutty, slightly dark flavor.

Rye flour: Derived from a relative of wheat, rye flour gives cookies a subtle nutty flavor. While this lower-protein flour forms less gluten than wheat flour, it is not gluten-free. We recommend rye flours labeled as light or medium for the recipes in this book; dark rye (or pumpernickel) flour is a whole-grain flour that will not work as well in the recipes as written.

Rice flour: Rice flour is a gluten-free flour made from finely ground grains of rice. Using rice flour results in crisper cookies, and it is the key to the wonderful crunchiness of several of our cookies, including the

Whole Wheat: More Isn't Always Better

In an effort to boost a cookie's perceived healthiness, some bakers try to substitute whole wheat flour for white all-purpose or cake flour. Whole wheat flours (which contain more of the whole grain than processed white flours) contain more protein, so they can absorb more moisture in the cookie dough. This can result in a drier dough and, potentially, a drier cookie. If you substitute all of the white flour for whole wheat flour, you could even end up with a dough that is too crumbly to form cookies or too dry to stay together after baking. In addition to absorbing more water, whole wheat flours can impart a grainier texture and earthier flavor to baked goods and can also result in a denser cookie. If you are interested in upping the whole wheat content of your cookies, start by substituting 25 to 50 percent of the white flour in a recipe with whole wheat flour. Whole wheat flours weigh more per cup than white flours, so when substituting we recommend substituting an amount by weight rather than by volume.

Smoked Almond and Caramel Cookie Crunch (page 291). We use white rice flour (made from ground white rice) for the recipes in this book, and all of our recipes calling for rice flour were tested with Bob's Red Mill brand. It can be found with flours or with gluten-free foods in grocery stores.

SUGARS AND OTHER SWEETENERS

The primary function of sugar and sweeteners is exactly what you expect: they contribute sweetness to cookies. However, sweeteners have many more functions in a cookie. In addition to sweetness, some sweeteners (such as honey or brown sugar) provide flavor. During baking, sugars can also melt and brown due to the heat of the oven and create additional flavors through caramelization. Furthermore, when sugar crystals are beaten into softened butter during mixing, small air bubbles are formed that expand in the oven and can help with a cookie's rise (or puff). Additionally, when a cookie is rolled in sugar before baking, the sugar can provide texture by creating a crunchy coating on the outside of the cookie.

All of the sugars and sweeteners we use are available in nearly any grocery store.

Granulated (white) sugar: This is plain, everyday refined white sugar. Don't ask us about substituting artificial sweeteners for sugar in baking. We don't do it, and we can't offer you any advice on how. Many bakers do it without problems, but it's just not something we do.

Brown sugar: In both light and dark varieties, most grocery store brands begin with white sugar and have molasses added to create brown sugar. Brown sugar must be packed into the measuring cup if you are measuring by volume (i.e., cups). Dark brown has about twice as much molasses added than light brown, which results in a more moist and flavorful sugar. The added molasses also makes brown sugars more acidic than granulated sugar.

Turbinado sugar: Also sold as raw sugar, this free-flowing brown sugar has a slight caramel flavor and a coarse texture due to its large sugar crystals.

Confectioners' sugar: Also known as powdered sugar, this is a very finely ground white sugar with a powdery texture. Most confectioners' sugar has cornstarch added to prevent clumping. Some brands of organic confectioners' sugar are made with tapioca starch instead of cornstarch. We prefer tapioca starch–based confectioners' sugar for glazes and fillings because it allows for a more flavorful glaze (see "Starch Madness," page 115).

Honey: A form of sweetener produced naturally by bees. Any mild-flavored honey will do, but those made from clover or orange blossoms are our favorites for baking.

Maple syrup: A liquid sweetener made by concentrating the sap of maple trees. Any grade is fine, but a darker, more robust syrup will provide more maple flavor than a lighter variety. If you store maple syrup in the refrigerator, remember to allow it to come to room temperature, along with other ingredients, before incorporating it into cookie dough or batter.

The Gluten-Free Cookie Lifestyle

A love of cookies should not be hindered by celiac disease, gluten sensitivity, or simply a desire to avoid gluten. As more people have adopted a gluten-free (GF) lifestyle, the need for GF-friendly recipes has dramatically increased over the last decade. As the demand for GF baked goods has increased, manufacturers and bakers have become more aware and developed more ingredients to cater to those with a GF lifestyle.

We do not avoid gluten, and we are certainly not experts in GF baking. However, we have experimented with GF baking products as we developed the recipes for this book.

- We found that the easiest way to adapt a cookie recipe to be GF is through the use of measure-for-measure flour replacement. For testing recipes in this book, we used King Arthur Baking Company's Measure for Measure Flour, but other manufacturers make similar products. King Arthur's product is designed to replace all (or some) of the all-purpose (wheat) flour in equal amounts by volume or weight. We have only used measure-for-measure gluten-free flour substitutes in place of all-purpose (wheat) flours. We cannot recommend substituting gluten-free flour substitutes in these recipes for other flours like whole wheat, cake, or rye, as the baking properties or flavors of those flours differ too widely from all-purpose (wheat) flour to have a one-size-fits-all substitute.

- Cookies made with GF flour replacement are more fragile. They have a crumblier texture compared to the same cookie made with wheat flour. This makes sense because the gluten protein holds baked goods together and provides structure. GF flour replacements can provide some structure but not the exact same texture as those made with gluten-forming wheat flour.

- Cookies made with GF flour replacement tend to spread more. This results in larger cookies but also in thinner and crisper cookies. Bake fewer cookies on a baking sheet (or divide the dough into smaller portions) to prevent cookies from spreading together in the oven.

- Because they are more fragile and spread more, GF cookies are often better when made slightly smaller than what's described in the recipe. In general, try not to cut rolled (cookie cutter) cookies larger than 3 inches across because the cookies can be too delicate to properly move, especially if you plan to decorate them.

- If you are living a GF lifestyle you already know this, but gluten can be hidden in a lot of ingredients other than wheat flour. If you do not have a gluten sensitivity, be sure to read up on all the sometimes surprising places where gluten can be found and how to identify gluten-containing ingredients on a product label before baking for a person who is avoiding gluten.

- If you are a regular GF baker, then you already know this: GF baking products, such as measure-for-measure flour replacement, can be expensive. Measure-for-measure flour is at least three times more expensive per pound than all-purpose (wheat) flour.
- Because of its cost, we did not test every recipe and recipe variation in this book with GF flour replacement. However, we did test all types of cookies that used all-purpose (wheat) flour (bar, drop, rolled, etc.) and had pretty good results with each test. If you are a regular GF baker and want to try adapting our recipes to be GF, start with a GF flour replacement. It's an easy swap (equal amounts by weight), and a pretty reliable method without having to redesign a whole new recipe. Will it always work? Not as well as we would like, but it's an accessible way to ensure that those who can't stomach gluten (literally) can still enjoy a great cookie.

Corn syrup: Light and dark corn syrups often get a bad rap because they are lumped in with the much-maligned high fructose corn syrup (HFCS). Corn syrup from the grocery store is not the same as HFCS. Corn syrup helps prevent crystallization when cooking sugars into candies or caramels and works to keep baked goods moister for longer. We most often find corn syrup sold alongside maple syrup at the grocery store.

A Note on Removing Sugar

Because of all of the purposes that sugar and other sweeteners have (there are several!), reducing sugar in a recipe is not something that we recommend. Less sugar doesn't just mean a less sweet cookie. Reducing sugar could also affect a cookie's taste, texture, and shape.

Golden syrup: Like corn syrup, golden (or refiner's) syrup is a sweetener that resists crystallization. It is light amber in color with a mellow caramel flavor. At our grocery stores, golden syrup is usually stocked with imported foods, as it is often a product imported from the United Kingdom. It's also available online. If you can't find golden syrup, you can substitute dark or light corn syrup.

BUTTER (AND OTHER FATS OF GREAT RENOWN)

Fats, such as butter and oils, make baked goods like cookies tender and prevent toughness. Without fats, cookies would be crisp and dry instead of soft and easy to bite. Simply put, fats get in the way and prevent proteins from forming structures that make a cookie too hard. Of course, this is a delicate balance. If too much fat is added, then the cookie can become too tender and might not even be able to hold together when picked up.

Butter: Many recipes in this book call for some amount of butter, and we have tested recipes with unsalted Grade AA butter. Using salted butter might make your cookies taste too salty, and there's no need for a pricier higher fat European or cultured butter unless we specifically recommend it in a recipe. Likewise, if you substitute vegetable shortening, lard, bacon grease, beef drippings, schmaltz, oil, margarine, spread, spritz, spray, or some other sort of not-quite-butter product sold in a plastic tub, do not be surprised if the recipe doesn't turn out as described.

For many recipes, butter needs to be softened at room temperature to properly mix with other ingredients. Depending on the temperature in your kitchen, butter will take 30 to 60 minutes to come to room temperature. You can speed this up by cutting the butter into pieces. Butter is ready to use when it can be easily pressed with a (clean!) finger or when it reaches between 65° to 75°F on an instant-read thermometer. Don't try to soften butter using a microwave unless you know that you can avoid melting it. Room-temperature butter and melted butter behave differently in recipes.

Some cookies are made with melted, rather than softened, butter. Melted butter should be allowed to cool so it is no longer hot (but still a warm and pourable liquid) before incorporating into a cookie dough. If the butter is too hot when it's added to the dough, it can cause eggs to scramble and form little pieces of cooked egg in the dough (gross!). Hot butter can also warm up cookie dough and make it sticky and difficult to handle. Additionally, warm cookie dough will spread more than intended in the oven, creating thinner and crisper cookies.

To melt butter using a microwave, cut the butter into tablespoon-size chunks and add to a microwave-safe bowl. Heat the butter at high (100%) power, stirring every 30 seconds, until all of the butter is completely melted, 1 to 2 minutes depending on the amount of butter and the wattage of your microwave. Set the bowl aside to cool until the butter is warm and pourable but no longer hot, about 5 minutes.

To melt butter on the stove, cut the butter into tablespoon-size chunks and place in a skillet or saucepan. Heat the mixture over medium heat, occasionally swirling the butter in the pan, until all of the butter is melted. Remove the pan from heat and set the butter

---

Better Baking with Brown Butter

COOKIE BYTE

American butter is about 80 percent fat, 18 percent water, and 2 percent milk solids. This composition can vary by brand and maybe even by season depending on the manufacturer due to changes in a cow's diet. While we treat butter as a fat, it's actually an emulsion with these components all held together in a smooth yellow brick.

Melting butter destroys its emulsion, so the butterfat is now no longer held together with the water and milk solids in one uniform mixture. If you continue to cook the butter after the point of melting, you can create brown butter. This is made by cooking the butter until all of the water has evaporated and the milk solids in the butter have turned amber-colored with a nutty aroma. The browned milk solids impart exceptional flavor, making brown butter a wonderful companion to cookies with toffee or caramel notes. By adding additional milk solids, you can create a delicious, übertasty bronze butter (see page 89).

With the water content cooked off, cookie dough made with brown butter will have less moisture in it than if just regular butter were used. Because butter is about 18 percent water, you lose about 1 tablespoon of water from each stick of butter that is browned. This lost moisture can make a cookie drier, so it's important to consider either adding moisture if you substitute brown butter in a recipe that doesn't call for it or reducing the amount of dry ingredients, such as flour. Because brown butter is melted, it also makes cookies that are chewier rather than puffy and cakier.

aside to cool until the butter is warm and pourable but no longer hot, about 5 minutes.

Vegetable oil: There are many options that can be used when the recipe calls for vegetable oil, including canola, sunflower, and soybean. Choose one that is 100 percent fat, liquid or pourable at room temperature with a neutral flavor profile.

EGGS

In cookies and other baked goods, whole eggs (both the yolk and white) work together to provide several amazing functions. First, eggs act as emulsifiers. This means that adding an egg will allow liquids and fats to mix together when they otherwise wouldn't. Because an egg is about 75 percent water and 10 percent fat, the emulsifiers in the egg (found in the egg yolk) work to make sure that the egg itself can mix together! In baking, emulsifiers help the fat in butter to mix with the water in the egg white and other liquids to form a cohesive mixture. Additionally, eggs can help provide texture to a cookie because they can hold air and their water content converts to steam while baking to contribute to a cookie's puff and spread. Finally, eggs provide structure because their proteins dry and set during baking and allow a cookie to keep its shape.

Recipes in this book were developed using Grade A large eggs. Weighed without its shell, one egg (on average) will weigh about 50 grams per standards set by the United States Department of Agriculture. Eggs are sized based on total weight of one dozen eggs, so slight variations in the weights of individual eggs are expected. However, more and more Americans are gathering eggs that have not been graded or sized from local suppliers in their community. We recommend weighing these eggs to determine whether their size is sufficient for use in these recipes. If the total weight of whole egg, egg yolk, or egg white called for in a recipe is dramatically less than what's stated in the recipe (more than 5 grams per egg), we recommend making up the difference by adding a portion of the appropriate component from an additional egg.

To bring eggs to room temperature (65° to 75°F), remove the eggs from the refrigerator about 30 minutes before you plan to use them. If you are separating eggs into whites and yolks, separate the eggs when they are still cold from the refrigerator. Place the egg whites and yolks in separate bowls and allow the egg components to come to room temperature if instructed. Keep the bowls covered to prevent the egg whites from drying out or the yolks from forming a skin.

BAKING SODA AND BAKING POWDER

Many cookies call for leavening agents, such as baking soda or baking powder, or sometimes a little of each. Leavening is the process of aerating a dough during the baking process. Leavening, sometimes called puff or rise, contributes a lot to a cookie's texture and appearance.

Baking soda reacts with acids in the presence of moisture to create carbon dioxide bubbles during the mixing process. These bubbles are formed before the cookie is placed in the oven. Baking powder is double-acting and produces some bubbles during the mixing process (also reacting with acids) but then reacts again later on in the presence of heat. Once the cookies are in the oven, heat causes these bubbles to expand, lifting up the surrounding dough.

While related, baking soda and baking powder are not the same thing. They react in different ways and at different times during the baking process. Do not substitute one for the other. If you only bake a few times a year, it's a good idea to make sure that your baking soda and baking powder are still active. Add ½ teaspoon of baking soda to a few tablespoons of vinegar, or ½ teaspoon of baking powder to a few tablespoons of hot water. If the mixture bubbles and fizzes, it's still good. If there's no reaction, pick up a fresh one at the grocery store.

SALT

This needs to be said louder for those who haven't heard: salt is not optional when baking! We still meet bakers who don't think they need to put salt in their desserts. Salt, on its own, is not a sweet ingredient. However, salt is not added to sweet foods to add savory flavor. Salt functions to allow your taste buds to experience more flavors. If you don't believe us, make the same recipe with and without salt and compare them. The item made with an appropriate amount of salt will have more flavor.

We most often use plain (noniodized) salt, though fine sea salt will work, too. Occasionally, we prefer to use coarse kosher salt or an even coarser finishing salt, such as Maldon. The recipe will specify when we prefer to use these specialty salts.

Additional Ingredients

ALMOND PASTE

Made from finely ground almonds and sugar, almond paste is a concentrated source of delicate almond flavor. Although similar to (and often sold right next to) marzipan, the latter should not be used as a substitute in these recipes. Once opened, almond paste should be refrigerated in a resealable storage bag or container. Bring the refrigerated almond paste to room temperature before using.

CHOCOLATE AND COCOA

Cookies are chockablock with chocolate in a number of forms, including cocoa powder, cocoa nibs, chopped chocolate chunks, melted chocolate, and chocolate chips. Select a high-quality chocolate, preferably from a brand that lists its cacao percentage on the label.

The microwave oven is our preferred method to melt chocolate. Place finely chopped chocolate in a microwave-safe bowl that is large enough to accommodate the chocolate and some stirring. Melt the chocolate at high (100%) power, stopping to stir every 30 seconds, until about 80 percent of the chocolate is melted. Continue to stir the chocolate to allow the residual heat of the chocolate and bowl to melt any remaining pieces.

Chocolate can also be melted by using a double boiler. Bring about 1 inch of water to a very low simmer in a saucepan over medium heat. Place finely chopped chocolate in a heatproof bowl and set the bowl on the rim of the saucepan, making sure that the bowl does not touch the simmering water. Keeping the water at a low simmer, stir the chocolate frequently until the chocolate is melted. Remove the bowl from the heat, being careful not to splash any water into the melted chocolate. If any water drips into the chocolate, the mixture will seize and become clumpy, and you will need to start over with another batch of chocolate.

Unsweetened chocolate: With no added sugar, unsweetened chocolate has a bitter taste that isn't great for snacking on its own. When included in a cookie, its dark flavor provides fantastic chocolate flavor. Look for brands labeled as 99 or 100 percent cacao.

Bittersweet and semisweet chocolate: There are no laws in the United States that define the cacao content of bittersweet or semisweet chocolate. In general, bittersweet chocolate has less sugar than semisweet. However, one brand's semisweet might have almost the same amount of sugar as another brand's bittersweet. For clarity, we specify a range for cacao content in our recipes.

White chocolate: Despite its name, white chocolate is not a true chocolate because it contains no cacao solids. The best white chocolates have cocoa butter listed first on the ingredients label. We recommend using the highest-quality white chocolate that your budget allows.

Chocolate chips: Chips are designed to be resistant to melting through the addition of fats other than cocoa butter, allowing them to keep their shape while baking. When melted chocolate is called for in a recipe, we prefer bar chocolate, not chips. For cookies where pieces of chocolate are welcome, chopped chocolate or chips can be used (see "Chips Off the Old Block," page 90).

Cocoa nibs: Cocoa nibs, also sold as cacao nibs, are pieces of dried and fermented cacao bean. They have a dark flavor similar to very dark chocolate but with a crunchy coffee bean–like texture. Nibs are used to add deep chocolate flavor and crunch.

Cocoa powder: After cocoa butter is extracted from the fermenting and drying of the cocoa beans, what remains are the dried cacao solids that we call cocoa powder. Cocoa powder can be sold as natural or Dutch-processed. Natural cocoa powders are more acidic. Dutch-processed cocoa powders have been processed (alkalized) to reduce the acidity. Black cocoa powder is a form of Dutch-processed cocoa powder with a dark, Oreo-like flavor that we prefer in some cookies. If you can't find black cocoa powder, you can substitute standard Dutch-processed.

COCONUT

Shredded or flaked coconut is available in both sweetened and unsweetened versions. Be sure to use the correct product specified in the recipe. Shredded coconut is great to use in baking because it provides an amazing coconut flavor without adding additional moisture. When we use coconut, we often like to toast it first to add additional texture (the coconut gets crispy) and additional nutty flavor that pairs well with its tropical taste.

To toast coconut, spread coconut in a single layer across a baking sheet. Bake at 350°F for 8 to 10 minutes, until the coconut is golden brown all over. For the most even browning and perfect golden color, stir the coconut after the first 4 minutes and every minute after that. Make sure when stirring the coconut to move the pieces that are nearest to the rim of the baking sheet to the center of the pan. The frequent stirring might seem tedious, but it is necessary to prevent the coconut from burning in spots. We store toasted coconut for several weeks in a sealed container at room temperature.

DAIRY

Milk and cream: Most baking recipes call for whole milk that is about 3.5 percent fat. If we have tested the recipe with reduced fat or skim (fat-free) milk, that is noted in the recipe's ingredient table. If a recipe calls for heavy cream, use a full-fat cream labeled as "heavy cream" or "heavy whipping cream." Reduced-fat creams, such as light whipping cream or half-and-half, are too thin and will not act as intended in these recipes.

Cream cheese: For baking, use block-style cream cheese, not cream cheese from a tub. It is easier to measure and doesn't have any additives to make it softer or more spreadable. These recipes were developed using full-fat (rather than reduced-fat or fat-free) cream cheese.

Mascarpone: Mascarpone is an Italian cream cheese made from cream. It has a higher fat content than traditional Philadelphia-style cream cheese as well as a softer texture. Mascarpone is sold in tubs, not blocks, and we often find it with fresh cheeses near our supermarket's deli department.

FOOD COLORS

For decorating cookies, we prefer to use gel or paste food colors. These colors have a thicker consistency and produce more concentrated colors than the liquid food colors found in most American supermarkets. The consistency of icing is very important when decorating cookies. Gel and paste colors allow decorators to color icing without thinning it out by adding so much liquid color that it changes its consistency. We prefer gel food colors that come in dropper bottles so that color can be added to icing one drop at a time. Paste colors work as well. Paste colors are usually packaged in small jars and are very thick. Use the tip of a toothpick to add small amounts to icing. An additional option is powdered food colors. They work well, but they are usually more expensive than gel or paste colors and can't be measured as conveniently.

INSTANT ESPRESSO POWDER

This concentrated instant coffee has an intensely dark coffee flavor. Used on its own, it provides the flavor without the added liquid of brewed coffee. It also pairs seamlessly with chocolate. Adding small amounts of instant espresso powder to chocolate produces a bolder chocolate flavor but without a noticeable coffee taste.

NONSTICK BAKING SPRAY

To prevent cookies from sticking to the pans when baking, we use canned nonstick baking spray with flour. We prefer such products as Pam with Flour or Baker's Joy. As an alternative, apply a thin layer of softened butter with a pastry brush and dust with flour. For a few applications in the book, we call for nonstick cooking spray that does not contain flour. Please note that gluten-free cookies should not be baked in pans prepped with a baking spray that contains flour; be sure to use a flour-free spray for those.

NUTS

For most of the recipes in this book, we call for using toasted nuts. Toasting brings out more of the delightful nutty flavor. The nuts have to be toasted and cooled before adding to the cookie dough or batter, or the nuts will lack flavor in the finished cookie. Be mindful that roasted nuts (like most of the canned nuts sold in the supermarket) are not the same as toasted nuts. Commercially roasted nuts often have additional salt and oil added as part of the roasting process. Toasted nuts are raw nuts that are toasted to a light golden brown.

To toast nuts, spread raw nuts in an even layer on a baking sheet. Bake at 350°F until the nuts are fragrant and light brown, about 7 minutes. Nuts can also be toasted in a skillet on the stovetop over medium heat.

OATS

We most often use old-fashioned rolled oats in our cookie recipes. A few recipes might call for quick-cooking oats. Be sure not to use steel-cut oats, as these oats will not soften to an enjoyable texture and will have the texture of gritty pellets even after baking. If measuring oats by volume (i.e., cups), scoop the oats from the can or bag into the measuring cup and level the top. If the recipe needs to be made gluten-free, be sure to use oats that have been certified gluten-free.

PEANUT BUTTER

For baking, always use a commercial peanut butter that does not require stirring. Natural peanut butters (which are often made from just nuts and salt) will not work in the recipes in the book.

SPECULOOS COOKIE BUTTER

This soft, lightly spiced flavor spread is usually marketed as speculoos butter, spiced cookie butter, or Biscoff spread. It is a paste made mostly from crushed speculoos cookies (Biscoff brand is popular). Because of the additional fats and sugars added, cookie butter acts similarly to peanut butter for baking applications. (We have also used it as a substitute for peanut butter when making fudge.) We find it stocked alongside peanut butter in our neighborhood supermarkets in both creamy and crunchy varieties, but we prefer to use creamy.

SPICES AND HERBS

After they are ground, dried spices and herbs can lose their flavor quickly. For the most flavorful cookies, freshly grind whole spices if you can. Otherwise, make sure to buy the freshest spices (and herbs) that you can find.

VANILLA EXTRACT

We use pure vanilla bean extract when baking. Purchase the highest-quality vanilla extract that your budget will allow.

ZEST

The outer rind of lemons, limes, grapefruits, and oranges is a concentrated source of citrus oils perfect for bringing those bright flavors to cookies. Use a rasp-style grater to remove only the thinnest outer layer of the fruit (e.g., the orange part of the orange rind), making sure not to grate off any of the underlying bitter white pith. Remember to remove the zest from fruits before cutting or juicing the fruits. If possible, zest your citrus fruits directly over your mixing bowl to capture all of the flavorful oils that might spray from the surface of the fruit while you are grating it. We usually do not measure zest with teaspoons but most often prefer to incorporate all of the zest from a whole fruit. Occasionally, only the zest from a half of a fruit is needed. In these cases, do not cut the fruit in half before zesting! Rather, grate the zest from only half of the fruit. To prevent fruits with their zest removed from drying out, wrap them, and store in the refrigerator.

The Essential Equipment

Most cookies are not terribly complicated to make, and they don't require much special equipment outside what you might already have in your home if you are an occasional baker. This book is organized by chapter, and each chapter begins with some specific equipment that we recommend for that chapter's cookie type: cake pans for bar cookies, rolling pins for rolled cookies, and things like that. But in general, this is the basic equipment that we recommend for any home baker to have. Refer to Sources (page 350) for more information on how to find and purchase equipment.

COOKIE BYTE

Live Your Zest Life

To draw out the flavorful oils, we will often smoosh the zest and the sugar in the recipe between our fingers. The sharp edges of the sugar crystals rough up the surface of the zest and leach the oils into the sugar. This mixture is called an oleo-saccharum (o-lee-o sack-uh-rum). The sugar will often change color as the zest is rubbed into it. This mixture can be made the day before preparing the cookie dough or batter and left, covered, at room temperature.

Measuring Equipment

Digital scale: When we bake, we weigh nearly all of our ingredients by using a digital scale. A digital scale can provide weights in ounces or grams, and we provide grams for almost all of the ingredients in this book. Why not all of the ingredients? Most digital kitchen scales are not very accurate with items weighing less than 10 grams. Basically, anything under about 2 tablespoons is easier to measure by volume (with a measuring cup or spoon) than by using a digital kitchen scale. You can use another scale (sometimes called a gram scale) that is more accurate for lighter items (such as small amounts of baking soda), but we don't find that level of precision is necessary for the cookies in this book. If we don't give a weight for a particular ingredient, measure it by using the volume measurement provided.

Measuring spoons: A set of spoons used to measure small amounts of dry or liquid ingredients by volume. We recommend the standard sizes commonly found in most sets (1 tablespoon, 1 teaspoon, ½ teaspoon, and ¼ teaspoon). Although not as common, we strongly recommend a ⅛ teaspoon measure, as well. If you can find them, a ¹⁄₁₆ teaspoon (sometimes labeled "pinch") and a 2-teaspoon measure are staples in our kitchen, but you can get by without them. For an accurate measure of dry ingredients, fill the bowl of the spoon completely and use a flat edge (such as the back of a knife) to scrape away any mounded ingredients for a level measure.

Liquid measuring cups: These are often clear glass or plastic cups with spouts and graduated measurements on the side. While we do use liquid measuring cups, we don't use them to measure ingredients by volume. Often, we'll weigh ingredients into cups with spouts to enable pouring. If you do use liquid measuring cups to measure liquids, be sure to read the measurement at the bottom of the meniscus, the curved surface of the liquid. It is often helpful to squat down so that your eye is at the same level as the measurement markings for an accurate reading.

Dry Measuring Cups

We still keep several perfectly fine sets of cups that look like small saucepans with flat edges and handles, but we rarely use them. We don't have much need because we rely on weighing our ingredients. If you can't bring yourself to give them up, please use a quality set that is accurate. America's Test Kitchen frequently rates dry measuring cups and has found that some brands can be up to nearly 20 percent off in their measurement.

Equipment for Mixing and Preparing

Whisk: These are used to whisk hot items on the stove or combine dry ingredients in a bowl. We like to have several sizes nearby so we're not stuck using a tiny whisk with a short handle over a hot pan.

Mixing bowls: We use both glass and metal bowls. Metal bowls from the restaurant supply store are really inexpensive and don't break if you drop them, whereas tempered glass bowls, such as Pyrex, can be used in a microwave. When it matters, we try to suggest a size of bowl you might need for certain steps throughout the book: small (4 cups), medium (6 cups), and large (10 cups or larger, including the bowl of a stand mixer).

Silicone spatulas: These are also sometimes referred to as silicone scrapers. These are invaluable for scraping the last bit of cookie dough out of bowls or ensuring every morsel of brownie batter has been transferred to a pan. Most often, silicone scrapers have a flat, flexible head and a wooden handle that can be pulled apart for cleaning. If you can find them, we like the one-piece silicone spatulas that can be tossed right into the dishwasher. While we were growing up, our mothers referred to these as rubber spatulas, but they haven't been made from rubber in years.

No Food Processor?

For recipes where ingredients are chopped very finely in the food processor, use a knife (and a lot of elbow grease) to chop the ingredients. You might have to gently knead some of the doughs to get them to come together. For recipes where the cookie dough is mixed in the processor using cold butter, you will need to blend the dry ingredients and butter together, using a pastry blender or two butter knives as you would when making pie dough. Really, though, a food processor is really the best tool for the job and is a staple in our baking kitchen.

Mixer: For most of the ingredients in this book, we mention a stand mixer in the instructions. However, if you don't have a stand mixer, you can use an electric hand mixer and a large bowl. There are a few recipes where the amount of ingredients is too small for a stand mixer to mix properly, and we do suggest using hand mixers in those recipes.

Food processor: We love our food processor, and we recommend using one for several recipes. Because the processor is a real workhorse in our kitchen, we have a 12-cup capacity model. You can get away with something closer to 8 cups for these recipes. If you don't have a food processor, you can still be successful making those cookies, but it may be a lot more work for some recipes.

Mesh Sieves　　　　　　　*Rasp-Style Grater*

Pastry brush: A food-safe brush is necessary for dusting flour, applying egg wash, and a handful of other tasks in the kitchen. Either a 1-inch-wide natural boar's hair brush or one with silicone bristles will work.

Mesh sieve: Metal sieves are great for sifting away clumps from cocoa powder or straining lumps out of custards cooked on the stove. Sieves generally have two different sizes of holes. We recommend having at least one standard mesh sieve (with holes that measure about 1.5 mm) and one fine-mesh sieve (with 1 mm holes). We use sieves with larger holes for sifting flour and cocoa. We use the sieves with finer holes for straining egg-based mixtures for silky smooth custards.

Rasp-style grater: A rasp-style grater is the only tool we need to produce finely grated zest from citrus fruits, such as lemons and limes. Rasp-style graters, such as those made by Microplane, are similar in appearance to other graters but with much smaller holes (sometimes even small slits) to allow for the removal of only the thinnest layer of flavorful zest without cutting into the bitter pith that lies just beneath.

Ruler: Terrific for ensuring that your brownies are evenly cut, your dough is evenly rolled, and your dough is uniformly divided. Any material is fine, but keep a separate one for kitchen tasks. You don't want a ruler used for glue-and-glitter craft projects around your food.

Thermometer: An instant-read thermometer is a great tool for making sure that your ingredients are at room temperature, heating egg whites on the stove for meringues, candying fruits, and checking the doneness of baked custards, such as our Whiskey-Lemon Sweet Potato Squares (page 58). We rely on our thermometer a lot, and it is has become a necessary tool in our baking kitchen.

Baking Equipment

Oven: A must for baking! We're not going to recommend a particular oven, but we do have some tips for working with the oven that you have.

- Get to know your oven. Use an oven thermometer and make sure that it's accurate. If you heat your oven to 350°F, it should really heat to 350°F and not 275°F or 425°F. If the temperature is dramatically off, your baking times will be off, too.

- Preheat your oven sufficiently. We preheat every oven we use for at least 15 minutes. The oven has to be sufficiently hot to be able to bake as well as sustain its heat when the door is opened to put the cookies inside. Some ovens claim to preheat in 3 or 4 minutes. Don't believe it. That might be enough time to heat the air in the oven, but not enough time to sufficiently heat the metal walls of the oven for proper even baking.

- Cookies can be baked one or two sheets at a time, depending on the recipe. When baking one pan at a time, position the oven rack in the middle of the oven so that it divides the oven in half. If baking two sheets at a time, position racks in the upper- and lower-middle of the oven so that the racks divide the oven into thirds.
- Prevent hot spots by rotating pans halfway through baking. Each pan should be spun around so that the part of the pan at the back of the oven now faces the front. When baking two pans at one time, in addition to spinning the pans, switch the upper pan to the lower rack and vice versa. Many ovens have hot spots where the heat is more intense, and these turns prevent cookies from overbaking.
- Our recipes are based on times and temperatures for standard ovens. If you are baking cookies in a convection oven, reduce the temperature in the recipe by 25°F. You may also need to reduce the time needed to bake the cookies.

Baking sheets: Most cookies in this book bake on aluminum 18-by-13-inch baking sheets. Since "full sheet" pans measure 26 by 18 inches, 18-by-13-inch pans are often described as "half sheet pans" or "half sheets."

Baking sheets have 1-inch-high rims on all four sides that allow multiple pans to nest inside one another for stacking. We prefer rimmed baking sheets to cookie sheets. Cookie sheets only have a rim on one or two sides. Baking sheets are less expensive and easier for us to store. If you can, seek out a restaurant supply store. We buy baking sheets by the dozen, and we don't pay more than a few dollars per pan. The pans that we bake on have a light-colored finish. If your pans are darker, you might have to make some changes to the baking time and temperature (see "The Dark Side of Baking Sheets" below).

In addition to 18-by-13-inch baking sheets, we do also use a 15-by-10-inch pan with a 1-inch-high rim, also known as a jelly roll pan. Based on the measurements, a jelly roll pan is essentially one-third the size of a full sheet pan, but it is never marketed that way.

Regardless of the size, baking sheets need to be at room temperature before placing unbaked dough on them. If a baking sheet is too warm, dough will start to

The Dark Side of Baking Sheets

Dark gray or black baking sheets can bake cookies faster than those with a lighter gray or silver finish because they can absorb more heat. If your baking sheets are dark in color, reduce the baking temperature by 25°F and check on your cookies a few minutes sooner to prevent the bottoms from burning.

melt and misshape before it's even placed in the oven. This will result in more spread and thinner, crisper cookies. We recommend owning *at least* four sheet pans so that if you have two pans in the oven, you can portion the dough onto two other pans that can go right into the oven after the first two are removed. Otherwise, you will have to wait until the two pans have cooled before baking more cookies.

Parchment paper: Parchment is paper coated in silicone to help prevent sticking when baking on baking sheets. Parchment is often sold in rolls, but we find the constant curling of the cut paper to be a nuisance. If your parchment paper is curled, place it curved side down on the baking sheet. The paper will stop curling once a few unbaked portions of dough are placed on top.

We prefer precut parchment sheets instead of rolls. Half sheets are nice, but we save money by purchasing larger full sheets and cutting them in half ourselves. Most brands of parchment paper can be baked on several times before the sheets need to be discarded. Remember—parchment paper is not the same as waxed paper. Waxed paper is not meant to be used in the heat of the oven.

Silicone baking mats: Silicone baking mats can be used instead of parchment paper to prevent cookies from sticking directly to baking sheets. Unlike parchment paper that you can just throw out, silicone mats can be washed so they are less wasteful. A proper cleaning of hot, soapy water is needed after each use (and some brands can be tossed into the dishwasher). They can be used over and over again,

Silicone Baking Mats

and provided you show them a little care, will last many years. They are pricey, though, so if you do a lot of baking and want enough to cover all of your baking sheets, it will be an investment. Silicone mats can absorb odors, so keep mats used for baking cookies separate from mats used for roasting savory foods, such as meat or fish.

There are two types of silicone baking mats: solid and perforated. Most of the ones you can find are solid. Perforated baking mats are sometimes marketed as crisping mats. We like perforated mats for baking rolled cookie cutter cookies, but they're not required.

Thin Spatulas

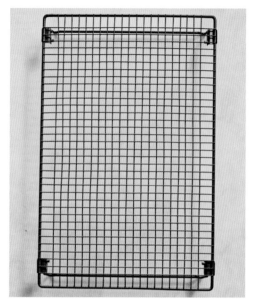

Wire Rack

Thin spatulas: Use these for lifting cookies from sheet pans and transferring them to a wire rack or for removing individual bar cookies once they've been cut. Our favorites have a very thin metal blade. A small one with a 1-inch-wide blade is great for bar cookies, but you will also want a slightly wider one (closer to 3 inches) for better support when picking up soft cookies.

Wire racks: Cookies need time to cool and set before they can be served, stacked, or stored in containers.

Although we let some cookies cool directly on the baking sheet, many cookies are removed from their baking sheets after about 5 minutes and transferred to a wire rack. We let uncut bar cookies (still in their pan) cool on them, too. The wire rack allows air to circulate around the cookies to promote cooling. We prefer all-metal racks ("dishwasher-safe" is our love language) with grid designs to support the cookies. We also buy these at a restaurant supply store because they are used a lot by restaurants and are less expensive there than practically anywhere else.

Weighing the Weight

We have a fairly extensive cookbook library. As bakers without formal training at a cooking or pastry school, cookbooks have been our textbooks as well as a source for entertainment, weekly menu planning, and research. All of our favorites, especially among the baking books, provide weights for ingredients in the recipes. Of course, savory cookbooks are less likely to include weights because savory cooking is generally not considered as precise as baking. However, for baking cookbooks, we at least expect to see a description indicating their method for determining 1 cup of flour.

Flour is such an important part of baking, but it can weigh differently depending on how it's measured. Some authors prefer to spoon-and-sweep flour while others prefer to dip-and-sweep. Without one of these benchmarks, a baking cookbook is really kind of unreliable.

- Sifting flour into a 1-cup dry measuring cup and leveling the top will make a cup of flour that weighs about 4 ounces (113 grams).
- Lightly spooning flour into a 1-cup dry measuring cup and leveling off the top will create a cup of flour that will weigh about 4.25 ounces (120 grams).
- Dipping a 1-cup dry measuring cup into a bin of flour and leveling the top (our preferred method) will create a cup of flour weighing 5 ounces (142 grams)—a 25 percent difference across the three methods.

If the recipe author used a 4-ounce cup when developing the recipes and you scoop up a 5-ounce cup, you will be left wondering why your cookies are so hard and dry. On the other hand, if you know that 1 cup of flour is supposed to be 5 ounces (142 grams), you can weigh that amount directly into your bowl and have the correct amount every time. No guesswork necessary.

If you're a few grams off one way or another in a recipe, will you still make a darn good cookie? Absolutely. We're not persnickety about weighing ingredients simply for accuracy's sake. One of the most valuable benefits of weighing ingredients is consistency. Knowing that you include the exact same amount of ingredients in your cookies time after time means that you will have more reliable results every time you make your favorite cookies.

In addition to improving your baking accuracy, weighing your ingredients is also a cleaner way to bake, especially when you consider ingredients beyond just the flour. It is so much easier to pour an exact amount of a sticky ingredient, such as molasses, directly into the bowl set on a scale, rather than trying to measure by volume into a cup then struggling to scrape out all of the sticky molasses with a spatula and *then* having to wash all of those extra implements (as well as your hands!) and the countertop (because it always manages to drip somewhere). Weighing your ingredients is the most important advice we can give to you.

The Essential Rules for Playing with Your Food

As recipe writers, we have the advantage in deciding how our cookies taste. But more than taste, each recipe also defines the texture of the cookie. We choose which cookies we like to be chewy and which cookies we want to be crisp. If we want a cookie to be crisp, we refine the recipe until it's crisp enough. Or, if we want a cakey bar cookie, we change the ingredients and techniques until it's the perfect fluffy square of our dreams. We like all kinds of cookie textures, from delightfully chewy to shatteringly crisp to soft and cakelike, but our tastes determine which cookies are chewy and which are crisp or cakey. For example, we *love* a chewy chocolate chip cookie. You, too? Maybe, or perhaps you prefer them thin and crispy. Well, if our recipe is for a chewy one, what can you do? Well, you can work to change it! Recipes aren't written in stone, and cookies are ripe for experimentation. Baking is a science, and you have to know The Rules before you go into the Cookie Lab.

Rule #1

Try a recipe before you start making changes. That seems obvious, but you don't want to start changing a recipe unless you know what the recipe is and what kind of cookie it makes. Make a recipe at least once with no substitutions or changes before you start tinkering with it. You might like it just as it is. Once you know that a recipe makes a chewy/crispy/cakey cookie, then you can get to work on editing it to fit your tastes.

Rule #2

Each ingredient in a cookie contributes not only to the cookie's final taste but also to its texture. Sometimes changing one ingredient is enough to get the texture that you like. Sometimes you have to change several ingredients or even the shape, baking time, or oven temperature to get exactly what you want. It can be hard work and sometimes frustrating—believe us! This is the process that we use to develop recipes, and it can sometimes take a half dozen times or more to get a cookie to exactly where you want it to be.

Rule #3

This is a big one: make only one change to a recipe at a time. That's good science. You might think that making several changes at one time will get you to your desired outcome faster, which might be true—if your experiment works. However, if your cookie experiment isn't exactly what you want (or worse, is a flaming hot disaster), then it makes it much more difficult to know what to change to fix it. Additionally, changing one ingredient can affect how other ingredients react while baking. Take notes on each change so the next time you want to make changes, you know what you did, which can guide you in what to do next.

Rule #4

We developed these recipes, but please—unless you make the recipes as written, don't fault us for your failed experiments. Experimentation is good—that's how we can grow and learn! With experimentation, however, can come failure. Sometimes things just don't work out how you expected. Failures can teach us so much, and they are sometimes the best way to learn. However, failure can hurt. It can make us feel stupid and mess up our confidence. Life advice: it's never a failure if you learn something from it.

How Does a Cookie Bake?

Now that you know The Rules, it's important to know what happens as a cookie is made, using a basic chocolate chip cookie as an example. After measuring the ingredients:

- Room-temperature butter and sugar are creamed together until the mixture is light and fluffy. The rough edges of the sugar cut into the butter, helping to create little pockets of air as they are mixed together.
- Eggs are then beaten into the batter, one at a time, to help emulsify the fat and liquid components of the batter. Adding the eggs (which are mostly water) all at once can cause a mixture to separate.

Finally, the flour, leavening, salt, and chips are stirred in. The dough is dropped onto prepared baking sheets and placed in a preheated oven. At this point, there's no going back. Everything that's been done to the dough is finished, and good mixing technique combined with quality, well-measured ingredients come together in the heat of the oven. When the dough hits the heat of the oven, several physical and chemical changes begin:

- The butter begins to melt, causing the cookie to spread, get thinner at the edges, and flatten in the middle.
- The leavening in the dough reacts and gives off gas bubbles that fill the air pockets created from creaming the butter and sugar, and the cookie begins to puff with some assistance from the eggs.
- As it gets hotter, any bacteria present in the raw ingredients will be killed or pasteurized, making the cookie safe to eat.
- At some point, the continuous heat from the oven begins to set the edges of the cookie and prevents the cookie from spreading farther.
- After enough time has passed, sugars in the cookie begin to caramelize, and the proteins in the eggs and flour begin to set and brown, completing the transformation from pliable dough to rigid cookie.

The exact rates of how this all occurs depends on the size of the cookie dough portions, the baking temperature, the baking time, and the placement of the sheet of cookies in the oven. Remember that although baking is a science, you don't have to be a scientist to bake. Because we've used scientific principles to develop these recipes, if you follow the recipes, the science will happen whether you understand it or not.

CHAPTER ONE
bar cookies

Bar cookies can be some of the simplest cookies to make: usually one (or two) layers baked in a pan and cut into equal pieces. One-step bars, like brownies, are the fastest to make because they are one layer of batter prepared and baked. Two-step bars, such as bars with a shortbread crust layer baked topped with jam, take just a little more work. Once baked and cooled, the cookie is cut into equal-size bars. While we recommend how many bars each recipe makes, you can cut them into bigger or smaller pieces as you see fit. In fact, while we typically cut brownies into twenty-four 2-inch squares, cutting the brownies even smaller is a great idea for party bites or as snacks for those with little fingers. Conversely, a 3-inch brownie square is a particularly generous treat when you need some chocolate therapy to soothe away the stress of the day.

Helpful Tools

- **Cake pans.**
- **Aluminum foil or parchment paper.** Create a lining that can be used to lift the baked uncut bars out of the cake pan for easy cutting.
- **Offset spatula.** Spread batters and fillings in even layers across the pan.
- **Ruler.** Optional, but nice to use to measure equally sized bars before cutting.
- **Knife.** Cut the uncut bars into individual portions.

Tips and Techniques

Proper pan proportions: We call for three different pan sizes throughout this chapter: 13-by-9-inch rectangle, 9-inch square, and 8-inch square. While 8- and 9-inch pans might seem similar in size, do not be tempted to substitute one for the other. A 9-inch square pan is 25 percent larger than an 8-inch pan. This means that a recipe meant for an 8-inch pan would be thinner and would bake for a shorter time than what's described in the recipe. Conversely, baking a recipe meant for a 9-inch pan in one measuring 8 inches would result in a thicker cookie that will take longer to fully bake in the center, which could lead to dry edges. All three sizes of pans should have 2-inch-deep sides to hold the cookie components without overflowing. We bake all of our bar cookies in metal pans with a light-colored finish. Pans with a black finish can bake the cookies too fast and dry out the edges.

Silver linings: For bars, we line the bottom and sides of our pans with aluminum foil. We use a trick we learned from cookbook author David Lebovitz: First, turn the pan upside down and gently press the foil over the bottom and sides to shape the foil. Turn the pan right side up and gently push the molded foil into the pan, using the corners of the pan as a guide. Fold the overhanging edges of the foil over the outside edges of the pan. For best results, we always spray the aluminum foil lining with nonstick baking spray (nonstick spray with flour).

Do the two-step: Some bars have crusts that are baked before the rest of the filling. For these crusts, press the mixture evenly over the entire bottom of the pan, being sure that the mixture gets into all four corners. Tamp the mixture down with the flat bottom of a dry measuring cup or drinking glass.

All about even spread: To spread batters evenly in pans, we turn to a 4-inch offset spatula. The blade is offset (angled) to keep the handle (and your hand) above the mixture while spreading. It's important that that the batters are spread evenly across the pan because if the batter is mounded in the center with less at the edges, the bars will bake unevenly.

Cut it out: We prefer to remove all of our bars from the pans before cutting. This makes cutting easier because you can cut the bars with a knife without having to worry about the pan edges getting in the way. Additionally, it can help extend the life of your pan by not having a sharp knife create scratches over the bottom and sides of your pan. Use the aluminum foil lining to lift the uncut bars from the pan and transfer to a cutting board. For the easiest transfer, allow the cookies to cool completely before moving them. Warm bar cookies will bend and might break if lifted from

Rectangular Cake Pan

Square Cake Pans

Offset Spatulas

Knives

the pan while still warm. If you can slide away the aluminum foil before cutting, that's great. Be sure that no pieces of foil stick to the bottom of your bars.

Portion control: To get equal-size bars, use a ruler to make notches along the edge of the bar before you pick up your knife. It might seem picky, but don't be afraid of a little precision if you want equal-size cookies. See "How to Cut a Batch" at right for help on dividing the bars for perfect portions every time.

Get your knives out: For most bars, a sharp metal knife will work great. However, for brownies and soft bar cookies, we insist on using a plastic knife. This can be a large plastic lettuce knife or even a small disposable knife picked up from your visit to a drive-thru restaurant. Whereas brownies will often stick to a metal knife blade, the slick texture of a plastic knife glides easily and cleanly through the brownie's fudgy interior.

How to Cut a Batch

Cutting bars into equal-size cookies isn't brain surgery, but it may be the closest thing there is to cookie surgery. Making that first slice into an uncut bar can be intimidating for some, and it's nice to have a guide so you know you can get perfectly sized pieces every time.

13–by–9–inch pan

Size: 3–inch squares
Yield: 12 (4 x 3)
1. Position the uncut bars with the longer side facing you. Cut in half vertically.
2. Cut each half in half again to create four 3–inch strips.
3. Rotate the whole batch one-quarter turn and cut into thirds.

Size: 2–inch squares
Yield: 24 (6 x 4)
1. Position the uncut bars with the longer side facing you. Cut in half vertically.

2. Cut each half into thirds to create six 2-inch strips.
3. Rotate the whole batch one-quarter turn and cut in half.
4. Cut each half in half again.

Size: 3–by–1–inch fingers
Yield: 36 (9 x 4)
1. Position the uncut bars with the longer side facing you. Cut in half vertically.
2. Cut each half in half again to make four 3-inch strips.
3. Rotate the whole batch one-quarter turn and cut into thirds.
4. Cut each third into thirds again.

8–inch square pan

Size: 2–inch squares
Yield: 16 (4 x 4)
1. Cut the square in half.
2. Cut both pieces in half again in the same direction to make four 2–inch strips.
3. Rotate the whole batch one-quarter turn and repeat.

9–inch square pan

Size: 2¼–inch squares
Yield: 16 (4 x 4)
1. Cut the square in half.
2. Cut both pieces in half again in the same direction to make four 2¼-inch strips.
3. Rotate the whole batch one-quarter turn and repeat.

Size: 3–by–1½– inch fingers
Yield: 18 (6 x 3)
1. Cut the batch into three 3-inch strips.
2. Rotate the whole batch one-quarter turn and cut each strip into thirds to create three 3–inch squares.
3. Cut each square in half.

Size: 1¾–inch squares
Yield: 25 (5 x 5)
1. Cut the batch into five 1¾-inch strips (and there is no shame in using a ruler!).
2. Rotate the whole batch one-quarter turn and repeat.

10–by–15–inch pan

Size: 3–by–1½–inch fingers
Yield: 27 (9 x 3)
1. Position the bars with the longer side facing you. Cut into thirds vertically.
2. Cut each third into thirds in the same direction to create nine strips about 1½ inches wide.
3. Rotate the whole batch one-quarter turn. Cut the strips crosswise into thirds.

Size: 2½–inch squares
Yield: 24 (6 x 4)
1. Position the bars with the longer side facing you. Cut in half vertically.
2. Cut each half into thirds to create six 2½-inch strips.
3. Rotate the whole batch one-quarter turn and cut the strips crosswise in half, then in half again.

Fudgy Cloud Brownies

MAKES 2 DOZEN (2-INCH) BROWNIES

To us, brownies should be fudgy and richly chocolaty, *never* cakey, and certainly not gooey or so stodgy that you need a glug of milk to wash it down. These are our perfect brownies—thick, delectably fudgy, but with a texture that is somehow both dense and light at once. The paradox comes from making these with a Swiss meringue, where egg whites and sugar are gently heated over a double boiler. The extra step of making the meringue is entirely worth it to create a treat that is deeply satisfying without being gooey or underbaked.

INGREDIENT	VOLUME	WEIGHT
Unbleached all-purpose flour	1 cup	142 grams
Dutch-processed cocoa powder	1¼ cups	106 grams
Salt	¾ teaspoon	
Unsalted butter, cut into chunks	21 tablespoons	298 grams
Unsweetened chocolate, finely chopped		142 grams (5 ounces)
Light brown sugar	Packed 1½ cups	300 grams
Granulated sugar	1 cup	200 grams
Eggs, separated, at room temperature	6 large	90 grams yolks 210 grams whites
Instant espresso powder	2 teaspoons	
Pure vanilla extract	2 teaspoons	
Semisweet chocolate chips	1 cup	142 grams
Confectioners' sugar (optional)	3 tablespoons	21 grams

1. Position a rack in the center of the oven and preheat to 325°F. Line the bottom and sides of a 13-by-9-inch baking pan with aluminum foil. Lightly spray the foil with nonstick baking spray.

2. Whisk together the flour, cocoa powder, and salt in a medium bowl; set aside.

3. Melt the butter and unsweetened chocolate, in a microwave-safe bowl, in a microwave at medium (50%) power, stirring occasionally. Alternatively, melt in a double boiler or large heatproof bowl set over a pan of barely simmering water, being sure that the bowl does not touch the hot water (see "Double Boiler: Toil and Trouble?," page 44). Stir in 1 cup (200 grams) of the brown sugar and set aside to cool.

4. Whisk together the remaining ½ cup (100 grams) of brown sugar, granulated sugar, egg whites, and espresso powder in the heatproof bowl of a stand

(continued)

mixer. Place the bowl over a pan of barely simmering water (being sure that the bowl does not touch the hot water). Whisking constantly, heat until the sugar is dissolved and the hot mixture reaches 165°F on an instant-read thermometer. Remove the bowl from the heat and transfer to a stand mixer fitted with a whisk attachment. Beat the mixture on medium-high speed until it has cooled to room temperature and the bottom of the bowl no longer feels warm to the touch, 6 to 8 minutes.

5. Reduce the mixer speed to medium-low. Beat in the egg yolks, one at a time, and the melted chocolate mixture until uniformly incorporated. Beat in the vanilla. Stir in the cocoa mixture and chocolate chips by hand just until no dry flour is visible. Scrape the sides of the bowl with a silicone spatula to make sure all ingredients have been incorporated.

6. Spread the brownie batter in the prepared pan, making sure the pan corners are filled and the top is smooth and level (a small offset spatula makes this easy). Bake until a toothpick inserted into the center comes out with moist crumbs (but no gooey batter) attached, 33 to 37 minutes. Halfway through baking, rotate the pan from front to back. The brownies will crack and puff in a few places but will fall as they cool.

7. Remove from the oven and let cool to room temperature in the pan on a wire rack. Use the overhanging foil to lift and remove the uncut brownies from the pan before cutting into 2-inch squares (see "How to Cut a Batch," page 40). Use a fine-mesh sieve to sprinkle the confectioners' sugar (if using) over the brownies before serving. The brownies can be stored in an airtight container at room temperature for several days or well wrapped and frozen for several months.

Double Boiler: Toil and Trouble?

At its simplest, a double boiler is two pots with one set atop the other. The larger, bottom pot contains water that is brought to a simmer. The heat from the simmering water is used to warm whatever is in the smaller pot on top. It is a gentler method of cooking that helps prevent overcooking and burning compared to cooking something in a pan set directly on a hot burner. This method of gentle heating can be used for making lemon curd, melting chocolate, or slowly cooking egg whites and sugar for Swiss meringues.

While you can buy a traditional pot-in-a-pot double boiler, it's probably easier to assemble a makeshift one with your own pot and bowl. To make your own, you need a saucepan that can safely hold at least 2 to 3 cups of water, plus a heatproof bowl that is wider than the pan. The goal is to be able to add about 1 inch of water to the bottom of the saucepan, heat the water, and set the bowl on top so that the bottom of the bowl doesn't touch the water. If the bowl touches the water, it will create a hot spot on the bowl and heat unevenly. You might have to experiment with a couple of pots or bowls until you get the right combination. Be sure to check on the water level occasionally and add more water to prevent the pan from going dry.

Variation: Tuxedo Brownies

Tart cherries and sweet, smooth white chocolate are natural pairs for dark chocolate desserts.

For the best texture, plump the dried cherries first. Cover 1½ cups (213 grams) of dried tart (a.k.a. sour) cherries with boiling water in a medium heatproof bowl. Cover the bowl and set aside for at least 15 minutes (or up to 1 hour). Drain away the water, blot the cherries dry, and set aside. Make the brownies as directed but decrease the amount of vanilla to 1 teaspoon and add 2 tablespoons of cherry liqueur (we prefer Heering Cherry) in Step 5. Substitute an equal amount of white chocolate chips for the semisweet chips and fold the chips and plumped cherries into the batter in Step 6. Bake as directed until a toothpick inserted into the center comes out with moist crumbs (but no gooey batter). Because of the additional moisture in the cherries, these brownies might need a few more minutes in the oven.

Variation: Streusel Crown Brownies

We're not fans of nuts *in* brownies. More often than not, the nuts are not crisp and the chocolate flavor overwhelms their nutty nature. However, by adding the nuts as part of a topping, it's the best of both worlds. This streusel makes a crisp layer that nicely contrasts our brownie's velvety texture and packs enough nutty flavor to stand shoulder to shoulder with the fudgy chocolaty goodness. We use commercially roasted and salted mixed nuts because the combination of nut flavors really shines against the brownie's deep chocolatiness, but any nut can be substituted.

To prepare, preheat the oven to 350°F (instead of 325°F). Create a streusel topping by stirring together 1 cup (142 grams) of unbleached all-purpose flour, a packed ½ cup (100 grams) of light brown sugar, and ¼ teaspoon of salt in a medium bowl. Stir in 6 tablespoons (85 grams) of melted unsalted butter to create a sandy mixture. Stir in 1 cup (142 grams) of chopped roasted mixed nuts; set aside. Prepare the brownie batter and spread in the pan as instructed. Sprinkle the nut streusel evenly over the top of the brownie batter and gently press it into the very top of the batter to help it adhere. Bake as directed, increasing the baking time to 45 to 50 minutes. Although we recommend cutting brownies with a plastic knife, that can be a little tricky with the nutty streusel. We like to use a serrated knife to gently saw through the top layer of streusel, then cut through the brownies with a plastic knife.

Infinity Brownies

MAKES 16 (2-INCH) BROWNIES

Everyone has their opinion on the brownie. While you may have staked your claim on cakey versus fudgy, the true Great Brownie Debate is actually middle piece versus edge piece. We confess—we are totally #TeamMiddle. Don't get us wrong—*any* brownie is better than *no* brownie, but give us all the fudgiest middle pieces, please! Because these brownies are baked in a water bath, they bake up smooth and fudgy throughout with no edge or corner pieces to be had. For the water bath, you will need a small roasting pan that can hold the 8-inch square baking pan without touching the sides. You will also need about 6 cups of boiling water (depending on the size of your roasting pan).

INGREDIENT	VOLUME	WEIGHT
Unbleached all-purpose flour	½ cup plus 2 tablespoons	89 grams
Unsweetened (natural) cocoa powder	1 cup	85 grams
Salt	½ teaspoon	
Unsalted butter, melted and cooled but still pourable	10 tablespoons	142 grams
Light brown sugar	Packed ⅔ cup	133 grams
Granulated sugar	½ cup	100 grams
Eggs, at room temperature	2 large	100 grams (weighed without shells)
Pure vanilla extract	1½ teaspoons	

1. Position a rack in the center of the oven and preheat to 300°F. Line the bottom and sides of an 8-inch square baking pan with aluminum foil (see Note). Lightly spray the foil inside the pan with nonstick baking spray.

2. Whisk together the flour, cocoa powder, and salt in a medium bowl; set aside.

3. Whisk together the melted butter, brown sugar, and granulated sugar in a large bowl. (If the mixture [or bowl] is still hot, set it aside to cool for 10 minutes to prevent the eggs from scrambling in the next step).

4. Whisk in the eggs, one at a time, and the vanilla. Stir in the cocoa mixture until no dry flour is visible. Spread the brownie batter in the prepared pan, making sure the pan corners are filled and the top is smooth and level (a small offset spatula makes this easy).

5. Place the brownie pan inside the roasting pan and transfer to the oven. Carefully pour boiling water into the roasting pan until it comes about 1 inch up the sides of the brownie pan. The pan might float, but that's okay.

6. Bake until a toothpick inserted into the center comes out clean, 35 to 40 minutes. Lay a kitchen towel over the open oven door to protect the glass. Remove the brownie pan from the water bath and place on a second dry kitchen towel on a heatproof surface to catch any dripping water. (It's easier to lift the brownie pan out of the water bath separately instead of trying to move the roasting pan, water, and brownie pan out all at once because it can be rather heavy. Don't forget to remove the towel covering the oven door glass!) Remove the brownie pan from the outer layer of foil (if using) and let the uncut brownies cool to room temperature in the pan on a wire rack for about 2 hours. Use the foil to lift and remove from the pan before cutting into 2-inch squares (see "How to Cut a Batch," page 40). The cookies can be stored in an airtight container at room temperature for several days or well wrapped and frozen for several months.

NOTE: If your 8-inch square metal pan has seams, line the outer bottom and sides of the pan with foil to prevent water from leaking into the batter while baking. This is in addition to the greased foil lining the inside of the pan.

Middle Brownie Syndrome

COOKIE BYTE

In proportion to edge and corner pieces, middle brownie pieces might be rarer than you realize. For standard 2-inch brownies, an 8-inch square baking pan of 16 brownies will produce just 4 middle pieces versus 12 edges and corners. A 13-by-9-inch baking pan of 24 brownies will make just 8 middle pieces compared to 16 edges and corners. It would take a whopping 18-by-13-inch baking sheet filled with batter to deliver 24 middle pieces, but alongside an equal number of edges and corners. While things might seem bleak to those of us who love the middles, a little sympathy for those who love the corners—there are only four of those per batch, no matter how you cut it.

(continued)

Variation: Midnight in Seville (Orange) Brownies

The addition of both freshly grated zest and liqueur delivers dark chocolate brownies with a lively and sophisticated orange flavor. We prefer to use Grand Marnier for this variation because its cognac base provides deep flavor notes along with the brightness of the bitter Seville oranges that flavor the liqueur. (Alternatively, a triple sec, such as Cointreau, can be used.) Add the finely grated orange zest from 1 medium navel orange to the granulated sugar. Rub the zest and sugar between your thumbs and fingertips until the sugar is fragrant and light orange in color (see "Live Your Zest Life," page 25). Prepare the brownies as directed, adding the orange-infused sugar to the butter in Step 3. Decrease the amount of vanilla to ½ teaspoon and add 1 tablespoon of orange liqueur with the vanilla in Step 4. Bake and let cool as directed.

COOKIE BYTE

Baking in the Bath

Baking the Infinity Brownies in a water bath ensures that the texture of the brownie is smooth and uniform throughout. In traditional baking, the metal pan heats up quickly, causing the brownie batter to cook from the edges inward. By the time the middle of the brownies has finished baking, the sides have become slightly drier, producing those characteristic edge and corner pieces. However, the middle of the brownies cooks slower and remains fudgy because it is insulated by the rest of the brownie batter. The water bath acts as an extra insulating layer. It is effective because water can't get hotter than its boiling point of 212°F—much lower than the temperature of the oven. Because the bottom and sides of the brownie pan are surrounded by water, the low-and-slow baking approach prevents the edges of the brownie from heating up to the temperature of the oven (usually at least 300°F). This method takes longer because the heat is lower, but it results in a magnificently fudgy brownie from edge to edge.

You can bake these brownies without a water bath at 300°F for 25 to 30 minutes. They won't have a perfectly fudgy texture from edge to edge, but they will still be a heckuva good brownie with a little less fuss.

Grahammies

MAKES 16 (2-INCH) SQUARES

As a former zoologist, I always find it exciting to hear news reports of a previously undiscovered animal species somewhere in the world. Whether it is a new butterfly in the Amazon or an Australian jellyfish, it's fun to learn about new discoveries of the animal kingdom that have been here all along but we're just hearing about now. While zoologists certainly deserve their glory, we are very proud to announce our latesft cookie discovery—the Grahammie! This fudgy bar cookie made with whole wheat flour and golden syrup is a cross between a chewy blondie and a delicately spiced graham cracker. Don't expect these beauties to be featured on the cover of *National Geographic* any time soon, but like its relative, the brownie, this new creature will be right at home in your lunch box or in a small stack next to a glass of cold milk. —*P.A.*

INGREDIENT	VOLUME	WEIGHT
Whole wheat flour	1½ cups	234 grams
Salt	1 teaspoon	
Ground cinnamon	⅛ teaspoon	
Sugar	1 cup	200 grams
Unsalted butter, at room temperature	8 tablespoons	113 grams
Golden syrup (see page 18)	⅓ cup	112 grams
Eggs, at room temperature	2 large	100 grams (weighed without shells)
Pure vanilla extract	1 teaspoon	

1. Position a rack in the center of the oven and preheat to 350°F. Line the bottom and sides of an 8-inch square baking pan with aluminum foil. Lightly spray the foil with nonstick baking spray.

2. Whisk together the flour, salt, and cinnamon in a medium bowl; set aside.

3. Depending on the capacity of your stand mixer, this might be more convenient to mix using an electric hand mixer. Combine the sugar, butter, and golden syrup in a large bowl and mix on medium speed until smooth and creamy, 1 to 2 minutes. Beat in the eggs, one at a time, followed by the vanilla until the mixture is uniform.

4. Beat in the flour mixture on low speed until no dry flour is visible. Scrape the sides of the bowl with a silicone spatula to make sure all ingredients have been incorporated.

(continued)

5. Spread the batter in the prepared pan, making sure the pan corners are filled and the top is smooth and level, using a silicone or small offset spatula.

6. Bake until a toothpick inserted into the center comes out with moist crumbs (but no gooey batter) attached, 25 to 35 minutes. Remove from the oven and let cool to room temperature in the pan on a wire rack for about 2 hours. Use the foil to remove from the pan before cutting into 2-inch squares (see "How to Cut a Batch," page 40). They can be stored in an airtight container at room temperature for several days or well wrapped and frozen for several months.

NOTE: Want to dress up your Grahammies a bit? Spread a batch of Salted Caramel Ganache (page 337) over the top of the uncut bars once they have cooled.

COOKIE BYTE

The Truth about True Cinnamon

The suggestion to use regular cinnamon in the Grahammies and Ceylon (Sri Lankan) cinnamon in the Portland Portland Pie Squares might seem oddly particular. Over the years, we've had the opportunity to smell and taste several cinnamons side by side, and the differences are quite striking. Ceylon cinnamon *(Cinnamomum verum)*, or true cinnamon, has a mild, more subtle flavor with hints of citrus and floral notes. Most cinnamon sold and consumed throughout the world is the more assertive, almost peppery, cassia *(Cinnamomum cassia)*. Unless it's labeled as Ceylon cinnamon, what's in your spice cabinet is probably cassia. Cassia cinnamon will also work in this recipe, but for the Portland Pie Squares the subtle flavor of true cinnamon is preferred.

Portland Pie Squares

MAKES 25 (1¾-INCH) SQUARES

Although Paul lived in Portland, Oregon, for a few years, I had not visited until a couple years ago, when we drove down after a book event in Seattle. I was struck by the lush magnificence of its evergreen landscape. In addition to providing its verdant beauty, Oregon's climate (particularly in the Willamette Valley) is ideal for growing wine grapes, hazelnuts, and sweet cherries, including Bing and Rainier varieties. In addition to its agriculture, Portland (in particular) is known for its coffee culture and has a history of roasting and selling coffee since 1900—long before baristas in green aprons appeared on the scene. Taking some liberties, we paired sour cherries (the traditional fruit for cherry pies) with crunchy hazelnuts for a streusel-topped bar that's made even more special with the addition of instant espresso powder. While it doesn't add a definite coffee flavor, it provides a complex dark undercurrent that highlights the cherry's tart bite. —C.T.

INGREDIENT	VOLUME	WEIGHT
TART CHERRY FILLING		
Canned red tart (a.k.a. sour) cherries, packed in water	Two 15-ounce cans	850 grams
Granulated sugar	¼ cup	50 grams
Cornstarch	1½ tablespoons	12 grams
Salt	⅛ teaspoon	
Dried tart (a.k.a. sour) cherries, chopped	¾ cup	106 grams
Instant espresso powder	4 teaspoons	
Almond extract	⅛ teaspoon	
BROWN SUGAR–HAZELNUT CRUST AND TOPPING		
Unbleached all-purpose flour	1¾ cups	248 grams
Light brown sugar	Packed 1 cup	200 grams
Old-fashioned rolled oats	1 cup	100 grams
Salt	½ teaspoon	
Ground cinnamon, preferably Ceylon (see "The Truth about True Cinnamon," page 50)	¼ teaspoon	
Unsalted butter, melted and cooled but still pourable	12 tablespoons	170 grams
Hazelnut liqueur, such as Frangelico (or substitute ½ teaspoon hazelnut extract)	2 teaspoons	
Hazelnuts, toasted, cooled, and chopped (see page 24)	½ cup	62 grams

(continued)

1. Make the Tart Cherry Filling: Drain the canned cherries, reserving ½ cup (121 grams) of the liquid. Whisk together the reserved liquid, granulated sugar, cornstarch, and salt in a medium saucepan until the cornstarch has dissolved. Stir in the cherries.

2. Bring the mixture to a boil over medium heat. Lower the heat to maintain a slow boil and continue to cook, stirring frequently to prevent sticking and pressing on the cherries to help break them down. Simmer until the mixture has the consistency of applesauce and mostly holds a trail when a spoon is dragged across the bottom of the pan, about 30 minutes. You will have about 1¼ cups (330 grams) of filling.

3. Remove the pan from heat and stir in the dried cherries, espresso powder, and almond extract. Transfer the filling to a bowl and leave to cool completely, about 2 hours.

4. Once the cherry filling has completely cooled, position a rack in the center of the oven and preheat to 350°F. Line the bottom and sides of a 9-inch square baking pan with aluminum foil and lightly spray with nonstick baking spray.

5. Make the Crust and Topping: Combine the flour, brown sugar, oats, salt, and cinnamon in a stand mixer fitted with a flat beater, and beat on low speed. While still mixing, slowly drizzle in the melted butter and hazelnut liqueur. Continue to mix until uniform and no dry flour remains on the bottom of the bowl.

6. Press about 2½ cups (about 450 grams) of the flour mixture across the bottom of the prepared pan. The flat bottom of a drinking glass or dry measuring cup can be helpful in pressing the crust into a flat and even layer.

7. Bake until the crust is starting to turn golden brown all over and is firm when pressed in the center, 20 to 25 minutes. Remove from the oven and let cool in the pan on a wire rack for 10 minutes.

8. Spread the cherry filling in an even layer over the warm crust, using a small offset spatula.

9. Mix the hazelnuts into the remaining flour mixture. Firmly squeeze small handfuls of the topping in your hand (sort of like a rubber stress ball); open your hand and break the piece into marble-size pieces of topping over the top of the filling. Repeat with the remaining topping and sprinkle the filling with remaining bits. Gently press the topping into the cherry filling.

10. Return the pan to the oven and continue to bake until the topping is beginning to brown along the top, 35 to 40 minutes. The edges of the filling might also begin to bubble.

11. Remove from the oven and let cool to room temperature in the pan on a wire rack. Use the foil to lift and remove from the pan before cutting into 1¾-inch squares (see "How to Cut a Batch," page 40). The squares can be stored in an airtight container at room temperature for several days or well wrapped and frozen for several months.

Dandy Cake Bars

MAKES 27 (3-BY-1½-INCH) BARS

One of the cookies that my mom frequently baked when I was a child was a retro tandy cake from a well-worn recipe she had been using since the 1970s. If you don't know, the classic tandy cake is a soft vanilla sponge crowned with a coating of smooth peanut butter and a veneer of milk chocolate. I updated her traditional recipe by adding brown sugar and espresso powder to the cake for a richer, deeper flavor. Swapping the milk chocolate and peanut butter for bittersweet chocolate and lightly spiced speculoos cookie butter (see page 24) creates a marvelous modern treat. For a decorative look, the chocolate can be spread over a silicone texture mat and chilled (see "Impress-ive Chocolate," page 56). —C.T.

INGREDIENT	VOLUME	WEIGHT
Unbleached all-purpose flour	¾ cup plus 2 tablespoons	124 grams
Baking powder	½ teaspoon	
Salt	⅛ teaspoon	
Whole milk	½ cup	121 grams
Unsalted butter	4 tablespoons	57 grams
Instant espresso powder (optional; see Note)	1½ teaspoons	
Pure vanilla extract	1 teaspoon	
Eggs, at room temperature	2 large	100 grams (weighed without shells)
Granulated sugar	½ cup	100 grams
Light brown sugar	Packed ½ cup	100 grams
Speculoos cookie butter, such as Biscoff (see page 24)	1½ cups	360 grams
Bittersweet chocolate, preferably 60 to 63 percent cacao, finely chopped		227 grams (8 ounces)

1. Position a rack in the center of the oven and preheat to 350°F. Line a 15-by-10-inch baking sheet with aluminum foil. Lightly spray the foil with nonstick baking spray.

2. Whisk together the flour, baking powder, and salt in a medium bowl; set aside.

3. Heat the milk and 2 tablespoons (28 grams) of the butter in a small saucepan or, in a microwave-safe bowl, in a microwave at medium (50%) power, stirring occasionally, until the mixture is hot (but not boiling) and the butter has melted. Whisk in the espresso powder and vanilla. Set aside but keep warm.

(continued)

4. Combine the eggs, granulated sugar, and brown sugar in the bowl of a stand mixer fitted with a whisk attachment. Beat on medium-high speed until the mixture is lighter in color, thick, and it forms a ribbon when the mixture falls from the whisk, 3 to 5 minutes. Reduce the mixer speed to medium-low and slowly pour in the warm milk mixture. Once incorporated, reduce the mixer speed to low and mix in half of the flour mixture until most of the flour is incorporated. Mix in the remaining flour until no white streaks of flour remain.

5. Scrape the sides and bottom of the bowl with a silicone spatula to ensure all of the mixture is incorporated. Pour the batter into the prepared pan.

6. Bake until the top is lightly browned and the center springs back when gently pressed, 20 to 25 minutes. Remove from the oven and let cool in the pan on a wire rack for 7 minutes.

7. Dollop the cookie butter over the top of the warm cookie and leave it to begin to soften for about 2 minutes. Slather the cookie butter evenly across, using a small offset spatula. Set aside to cool completely. If you have a warm kitchen and your cookie butter hasn't fully set after 2 hours, refrigerate the pan for about 10 minutes to allow the cookie butter to set.

8. Melt the remaining 2 tablespoons (28 grams) of butter and chopped chocolate in a heatproof bowl set over a pan of barely simmering water (being sure that the bowl does not touch the hot water) or, in a microwave-safe bowl, in a microwave at medium (50%) power, stirring occasionally.

9. Spread the melted chocolate over the set layer of cookie butter. Refrigerate until the chocolate is firm and set, about 30 minutes. Use the foil to lift from the pan before cutting into bars (see "How to Cut a Batch," page 40). For the neatest cuts, run a metal knife under hot water before each slice so it can cleanly cut through the chocolate. Clean the knife after each cut and rewarm it with hot water before the next slice. Depending on how you prefer the texture of the chocolate, store the bars in a covered container at room temperature (for softer chocolate) or in the refrigerator (for firmer chocolate) for up to 5 days.

NOTE: The dark flavor of the espresso powder adds wonderful bass notes that nicely complement both the lightly spiced cookie butter and dark chocolate. If that's not your thing, reduce the amount or leave it out entirely.

COOKIE BYTE

Impress-ive Chocolate

To create an especially beautiful chocolate topping, use a silicone texture mat (see Sources, page 350). To create, melt the chocolate and butter as directed. Pour the chocolate mixture over a 15-by-10-inch rectangle area of silicone texture mat set in a baking sheet. Chill the chocolate in the refrigerator until it is cold and firm, at least 2 hours. Flip the chocolate over (with the mat) and lay onto the layer of cookie butter. Gently peel off the texture mat. Any overhangs of chocolate can be trimmed away with a hot knife.

Variation: Tandy Cake Bars

To make our take on the original tandy cakes with chocolate and peanut butter, omit the instant espresso powder from the cake. Prepare and bake as directed, but substitute smooth peanut butter for the speculoos cookie butter. Use an equal amount of semisweet chocolate for a slightly sweeter taste, if desired.

Whiskey-Lemon Sweet Potato Squares

MAKES 25 (1¾-INCH) SQUARES

Situated on Commercial Street within earshot of Cape Cod Bay's lapping waves, the Provincetown Portuguese Bakery is one of our favorite spots to enjoy breakfast when we vacation in P-town, Massachusetts. The bakery makes pastries filled with a sweet potato puree and flavored with whiskey, lemon, and cinnamon. While sweet potato pies are traditionally very autumnal and spice-forward, we really liked the flavor of the sweet potato filling with a lemony brightness. For these squares, we add whiskey, a hint of cinnamon, and both lemon zest and juice to a velvety sweet potato pie filling. Capped with a crunchy crumb topping, these cookies can be enjoyed at the beach or when a long vacation's just out of reach. The summery flavors allow the sweet potato to shine and honor its seaside inspiration.

INGREDIENT	VOLUME	WEIGHT
LEMON-INFUSED SUGAR		
Sugar	1¾ cups	350 grams
Lemon zest, freshly grated	1 large lemon	
CRUST		
Unbleached all-purpose flour	1¾ cups	248 grams
Salt	½ teaspoon	
Unsalted butter, melted and cooled but still pourable	11 tablespoons	156 grams
SWEET POTATO FILLING		
Sweet potatoes, baked and cool enough to handle (see "Baking Sweet Potatoes," page 61)	2 large	about 800 grams (about 1¾ pounds), weighed before cooking
Unsalted butter, melted and cooled but still pourable	3 tablespoons	43 grams
Salt	½ teaspoon	
Eggs, at room temperature	3 large	150 grams (weighed without shells)
Sour cream (full fat), at room temperature	⅔ cup	161 grams
Whiskey (see Note)	2 tablespoons	25 grams
Lemon juice, freshly squeezed	2 tablespoons	28 grams
Ground cinnamon	½ teaspoon	

CRUNCHY CRUMB TOPPING

Panko bread crumbs (unseasoned)	1½ cups	85 grams
Lemon juice, freshly squeezed	1 teaspoon	
Whiskey (see Note)	1 teaspoon	
Ground cinnamon	¼ teaspoon	
Salt	⅛ teaspoon	
Unsalted butter, melted and cooled but still pourable	6 tablespoons	85 grams

1. Make the Lemon-Infused Sugar: Combine the sugar and lemon zest in a medium bowl. To extract the most lemon flavor, rub the zest and sugar between your thumbs and fingertips until the sugar is fragrant, very light yellow in color, and has a texture like wet sand (see "Live Your Zest Life," page 25). This sugar is used in the crust, filling, and topping and can be prepared the day before baking the squares.

2. Make the Crust: Position a rack in the center of the oven and preheat to 350°F. Line the bottom and sides of a 9-inch square baking pan with aluminum foil. The finished squares are almost 1½ inches deep, so be sure that the foil covers most of your pan's sides. Lightly spray the foil with nonstick baking spray.

3. Stir together ¼ cup plus 2 tablespoons (75 grams) of lemon-infused sugar, the flour, and salt in a large bowl. Stir in the melted butter until a dough forms. Keep working the dough with a spoon or silicone spatula until no more little bits of white flour are visible. Press the dough evenly into the bottom of the prepared pan and prick all over with a fork.

4. Bake until the crust is light brown all over and firm to the touch, 25 to 30 minutes. Halfway through baking, rotate the pan from front to back and use a fork to prick any large bubbles that might have appeared. Remove from the oven and let cool on a wire rack while preparing the filling. Keep the oven at 350°F.

5. Make the Sweet Potato Filling: Combine 2 cups (482 grams) of peeled, roasted sweet potatoes, 1 cup (200 grams) of lemon-infused sugar, the melted butter, and the salt in a food processor. Process until the mixture is smooth, five to ten 1-second pulses. Scrape the sides of the food processor bowl.

6. Add the eggs and process until they are incorporated, about five 1-second pulses. Stop the machine and scrape the sides of the bowl. Add the sour cream, whiskey, lemon juice, and cinnamon and process continuously until the mixture is smooth and creamy, 10 to 15 seconds. Pour the mixture over the warm crust. Bake for 15 minutes.

7. While the squares are baking, make the Crunchy Crumb Topping: Combine the remaining ¼ cup plus 2 tablespoons of lemon-infused sugar, panko, lemon juice, whiskey, cinnamon, and salt in a medium bowl. Stir in the melted butter until the crumbs have all been coated.

(continued)

8. After the filled crust has baked for 15 minutes, remove from the oven and place the pan on a wire rack. Sprinkle the crumb topping evenly over the top of the sweet potato filling.

9. Return the pan to the oven and continue to bake until the edges have slightly puffed, the crumb topping is beginning to lightly brown all over, the center is nearly set but jiggles slightly when gently shaken, and an instant-read thermometer reads 165°F when inserted into the center of the sweet potato filling, an additional 18 to 22 minutes. Remove from the oven and let cool completely in the pan on a wire rack. For easiest cutting, refrigerate until the filling is cold throughout, at least 2 hours. Use the foil to lift and remove from the pan before cutting into 25 squares (see "How to Cut a Batch," page 40). The bars can be stored in an airtight container in the refrigerator for several days, but the crunchy topping will begin to soften after about a day.

NOTE: We particularly like these when made with bourbon, but rye or a blended whiskey will work just fine. If you don't keep bourbon on hand at your house, one 50-milliliter "airline"-size bottle holds enough liquor for this recipe.

Baking Sweet Potatoes

When we are using them for baking, we prefer to cook whole sweet potatoes in a microwave because they cook much faster without any noticeable difference in the taste or texture of the orange flesh. However, you can bake them in the oven, too. **Microwave Method**: Poke the sweet potatoes all over with a fork. Microwave the potatoes on high (100%) power on a microwave-safe plate for 5 minutes. Flip the potatoes over and continue to cook for an additional 3 to 5 minutes, until tender and a sharp knife can easily pierce the center of the potatoes and be removed without resistance. **Oven Method**: Preheat the oven to 425°F. Poke the sweet potatoes all over with a fork. Line a baking sheet with parchment paper or lightly greased aluminum foil. Bake the sweet potatoes on the lined baking sheet for 40 to 45 minutes, until tender and a sharp knife can easily pierce the center of the potatoes and be removed without resistance. If you are using the same oven to make the squares, remember to reduce the oven temperature to 350°F before baking the crust.

Crumb On

COOKIE BYTE

Panko is a Japanese-style dry and crunchy bread crumb most commonly used in savory cooking as part of a crispy baked or fried coating. Individual crumbs are pretty large and flaky, providing an attractive nubbly appearance and textural interest to those coated foods. Because panko has such a neutral and mild flavor profile, it can also be easily co-opted for use in desserts. The addition of butter, sugar, spices, and other flavorings transforms this pantry staple into a modern sweet and crunchy crumb topping.

Where's Waldorfs

MAKES 16 (2-INCH) SQUARES

Where's Waldorf? Waldorf salad, if you don't remember it, is an old-school dish made with raw celery, apple chunks, raisins (or grapes), and walnuts and tossed with a tangy dressing. When made well, it is delicious with a satisfying mix of flavors and textures. In recent years, it seems to have faded from most menus and dining room tables. We wanted to bring Waldorf back, and we paired those crisp, bright flavors with a brown sugar blondie base heady with warm toffee notes and vanilla. We ditched the dressings of its namesake but added some subtle tang with a smooth layer of cream cheese frosting. We know that if we're going to make you put fresh celery into a cookie, that it had better be a pretty frikkin' amazing cookie. Trust us—these *are*. Besides, botanically speaking, celery is in the same family as carrots, so just think of it as making a variation on carrot cake in cookie form, okay?

INGREDIENT	VOLUME	WEIGHT
WALDORF BLONDIES		
Celery, diced into ¼-inch pieces (from 2 stalks)	⅔ cup	75 grams
Granulated sugar	2 teaspoons	
Unsalted butter, melted and cooled but still pourable	8 tablespoons	113 grams
Light brown sugar	Packed 1 cup	200 grams
Celery salt (see Note)	1 teaspoon	
Cream of tartar	½ teaspoon	
Egg, at room temperature	1 large	50 grams (weighed without shell)
Pure vanilla extract	½ teaspoon	
Unbleached all-purpose flour	1¼ cups	177 grams
Dried apple, diced into ¼-inch pieces	¾ cup	63 grams
Raisins (dark or golden), chopped	½ cup	75 grams
Walnut pieces, toasted, cooled, and chopped (see page 24)	½ cup	57 grams
CREAM CHEESE FROSTING		
Cream cheese (full fat), at room temperature		85 grams (3 ounces)
Unsalted butter, at room temperature	3 tablespoons	43 grams
Confectioners' sugar	1½ cups	170 grams
Pure vanilla extract	1 teaspoon	
Salt	Pinch	

1. Make the Waldorf Blondies: Toss together the diced celery and granulated sugar in a bowl. Cover the bowl and set it aside at room temperature for 30 minutes to allow the celery to macerate. The sugar will draw out excess moisture that will be drained away before baking.

2. Position two racks to divide the oven into thirds and preheat to 350°F. Line the bottom and sides of an 8-inch square baking pan with aluminum foil. Lightly spray the foil with nonstick baking spray.

3. Once the celery is done macerating, drain and discard the liquid that has been drawn out of the celery (there will probably be a tablespoon or two). Use a paper towel or lint-free cotton towel to blot away any liquid still clinging to the celery.

4. Whisk together the melted butter, brown sugar, celery salt, and cream of tartar in a large bowl. Whisk in the egg and vanilla until the mixture is uniform.

5. Gently fold in the flour with a silicone spatula until just a few streaks of flour remain visible. Fold in the blotted celery, dried apple pieces, and chopped raisins, being sure to scrape the sides and bottom of the bowl until all white streaks of flour are gone. The mixture will be thick.

6. Smooth the batter into an even layer in the prepared baking pan, using a small offset spatula. Scatter the walnut pieces over the top and gently press the nuts into the surface of the batter. This ensures that the nuts don't break off as the bars are cut into squares.

7. Bake on the lower rack positioned in the bottom third of the oven until a toothpick inserted into the center comes out with just a few moist crumbs (and no wet batter) attached, 30 to 40 minutes. Halfway through baking, rotate the pan from front to back. Do not underbake these or the texture will be gummy.

8. Remove from the oven and let cool to room temperature in the pan on a wire rack. The blondie layer must be completely cool before frosting.

9. Make the Cream Cheese Frosting: Place the cream cheese and butter in a stand mixer fitted with a flat beater and cream on medium speed until creamy and combined. Scrape the sides and bottom of the bowl.

10. Reduce the mixer speed to medium-low and beat in the confectioners' sugar, vanilla, and salt. Once the sugar is incorporated, increase the speed to medium-high and beat until the frosting has lightened and is very creamy, about 3 minutes.

11. Spread the frosting over the top of the blondie layer. You can cut and serve immediately after frosting, but the bars will cut more neatly after chilling in the refrigerator until the frosting is firm, about 2 hours. Use the foil to lift and remove from the pan before cutting into 2-inch squares (see "How to Cut a Batch," page 40). The bars can be stored in an airtight container in the refrigerator for several days. They will taste best when removed from the refrigerator and allowed to come to room temperature before serving, about 30 minutes.

NOTE: If you don't have celery salt, substitute ½ teaspoon of salt plus ½ teaspoon of celery seeds.

Black-Bottom Lemon Squares

MAKES 16 (2-INCH) SQUARES

For years, we scoffed at the thought of mixing the fresh sharpness of lemon with the creamy duskiness of dark chocolate. Those two flavor powerhouses seemed too far apart to be compatible. When we finally tried it, we wished we had not waited so long. Of course, our worries were irrational because we already loved the combo of chocolate paired with the bright zing of orange! The marriage of tangy citrus and rich cocoa is a wondrous pairing, and this updated lemon bar brings the happy couple together again with a creamy layer of fresh tart lemon atop a rich chocolate base.

INGREDIENT	VOLUME	WEIGHT
CHOCOLATE CRUST		
Unbleached all-purpose flour	1 cup	142 grams
Dutch-processed cocoa powder	¼ cup plus 3 tablespoons	37 grams
Confectioners' sugar	½ cup	57 grams
Salt	Pinch	
Unsalted butter, cold, cut into 12 pieces	12 tablespoons	170 grams
CHOCOLATE GANACHE LAYER		
Bittersweet chocolate, preferably 60 to 63 percent cacao, finely chopped		57 grams (2 ounces)
Heavy cream	¼ cup	58 grams
LEMON LAYER		
Egg yolks, at room temperature	3 large	45 grams
Sweetened condensed milk	One 14-ounce can	396 grams
Salt	Pinch	
Lemon juice, freshly squeezed (from about 2 large lemons)	½ cup	113 grams

1.   Make the Chocolate Crust: Position a rack in the center of the oven and preheat to 350°F. Line the bottom and sides of an 8-inch square baking pan with aluminum foil. Lightly spray the foil with nonstick baking spray.

2.   Place the flour, cocoa powder, confectioners' sugar, and salt in the bowl of a food processor. Pulse the ingredients once or twice to combine them.

3.   Scatter the cold butter pieces across the flour mixture and pulse the mixture until the butter is in very small pieces and the mixture begins to look sandy,

(continued)

eight to ten 1-second pulses depending on the power of your machine. Once the butter is incorporated, process the mixture continuously just until a ball of dough forms. Press the dough evenly over the bottom of the prepared pan. Prick the dough all over with a fork to prevent it from puffing too much. Bake the crust until it is dry and firm, 28 to 32 minutes. Remove from the oven and let cool on a wire rack for 10 minutes.

4. Make the Chocolate Ganache Layer: Place the chopped chocolate in a medium bowl. Heat the cream to a simmer, in a microwave-safe bowl, in a microwave at high (100%) power or in a small saucepan over medium heat. The cream should just begin to bubble around the edges.

5. Pour the hot cream over the chopped chocolate and gently shake the bowl to ensure that the hot cream is in contact with all of the chocolate. Set it aside for 30 seconds.

6. Whisk the chocolate and cream together until the mixture is smooth and uniform. Pour the chocolate mixture over the warm crust and spread it into an even layer with a small offset spatula. Set it aside until the chocolate mixture is set, about 1 hour. (You can turn the oven off while the crust cools, but make sure it is preheated at 350°F before continuing with baking the lemon layer.)

7. Make the Lemon Layer: Whisk together the egg yolks, sweetened condensed milk, and salt in a medium bowl. Whisk in the lemon juice; the mixture will begin to thicken. Gently ladle the lemon mixture over the chocolate layer (so as to not disturb it). Spread the lemon layer evenly with an offset spatula, if necessary.

8. Bake until the center is set and no longer wobbles when jostled, 10 to 15 minutes. Remove from the oven and let cool completely in the pan. For easiest cutting, refrigerate the bars in the pan until cold throughout, at least 2 hours. Use the foil to remove from the pan before cutting into sixteen 2-inch squares (see "How to Cut a Batch," page 40). Store the bars in an airtight container in the refrigerator for up to 3 days.

Custard from a Can

COOKIE BYTE

Sweetened condensed milk is a canned dairy product made from milk that has been cooked down and concentrated along with added sugar. Originally developed as a way to safely preserve shelf-stable milk, it has become a staple of dessert-making worldwide, most notably in the making of simple custards. With the addition of eggs and an alcohol or an acid, such as citrus juice, the sweetened condensed milk mixture will begin to thicken and set into a creamy custard. Using pasteurized eggs or gently baking the custard will also make it safe to eat. Be sure not to confuse it with evaporated milk (which is thinner and unsweetened). Coconut milk-based condensed milk is now sold in similar-looking cans on the same shelf in the store but will not thicken properly in this recipe.

New-School Banana Puddin' Squares

MAKES 16 (2-INCH) SQUARES

Old-school banana pudding, with its banana slices, meringue, and southern charms, certainly has its place. To make these portable puddin' squares, we had to set tradition aside to create cookies with a new-school twist. We transformed conventional banana pudding by tossing the banana slices (which get slimy in a few days) and infused fresh banana flavor right into the cream. We also ditched the sugary-sweet meringue and replaced the one-note vanilla wafer crust with a sweet-and-salty version made with frosted cornflake breakfast cereal. For some culinary purists, messing with Tradition (with a capital T) is a capital offense, but these phenomenal modern squares are so delicious, we would gladly serve our time in the culinary clink.

INGREDIENT	VOLUME	WEIGHT
BANANA CREAM		
Banana	1 medium	
Heavy cream	1 cup	232 grams
Sugar	⅔ cup	133 grams
Mascarpone, cold	1 cup	227 grams
CEREAL CRUST		
Sugar-frosted cornflake cereal, such as Frosted Flakes	7¼ cups	200 grams
Unsalted butter, melted and cooled but still pourable	6 tablespoons	85 grams
Sugar	2 tablespoons	25 grams
Salt	½ teaspoon	

1. Start the Banana Cream: Peel and slice the banana into 1-inch chunks. Bring the cream and the sugar to a boil in a small saucepan, stirring with a silicone spatula to ensure that the sugar is all dissolved. Add the banana chunks, cover the saucepan, and remove it from the heat. Let cool to room temperature in the pan (about 1 hour) before refrigerating until cold (at least 2 additional hours, or overnight).

2. Make the Cereal Crust: Line the bottom and sides of an 8-inch square baking pan with aluminum foil. Lightly spray the foil with nonstick baking spray. Pour the cereal into the bowl of a food processor. Process in 1-second pulses until finely ground. Alternatively, place the cereal in a resealable storage bag and crush the cereal to fine crumbs, using a rolling pin or the bottom of a saucepan.

(continued)

3. Add the melted butter, sugar, and salt to the crumbs and process in 1-second pulses until the crumbs are moistened throughout, resembling wet sand. Transfer the crumb mixture to the prepared pan. Using your fingertips, press the crumbs into an even layer. Place the pan in the freezer for 15 minutes.

4. While the crust is chilling, position a rack in the center of the oven and preheat to 350°F.

5. Bake the cereal crust until it is just starting to brown at the edges and smelling toasty, about 15 minutes. Place on a wire rack and cool completely.

6. Finish the Banana Cream: Pour the cold banana mixture through a fine-mesh sieve (don't press on the bananas; discard them after straining). Keep 1⅛ cups (306 grams) of the cream in a medium bowl.

7. Depending on the capacity of your stand mixer, this might be more convenient to mix using an electric hand mixer. Add the mascarpone to the cold banana cream and beat on high speed until the mixture has thickened and holds stiff peaks, 3 to 5 minutes. Spread or decoratively pipe the filling onto the cooled cereal crust.

8. Unmold the whole cookie by carefully lifting it from the pan, using the aluminum foil. Transfer it to a cutting board and cut it into sixteen 2-inch squares (see "How to Cut a Batch," page 40).

9. The cookies can be stored in an airtight container in the refrigerator for several days, but the delicious crisp crust is best within a day or two of baking.

Peanut Butter Humdinger Fingers

MAKES 3 DOZEN (3-INCH) FINGERS

These chewy peanut butter blondies slathered with a creamy, peanut butter glaze could not have more peanut-y goodness in them! With no jam, no jelly, and no chocolate to be found, these purely peanut treats have it all. Peanut butter? Gobs of it. Roasted, salted peanuts? They're in here. Peanut butter chips? Absolutely. *More* peanut butter? Sure, why not? In a nutshell, these bars are the ultimate indulgence for the True Peanut Butter Lover™!

INGREDIENT	VOLUME	WEIGHT
PEANUT BUTTER BLONDIE		
Unbleached all-purpose flour	1¾ cups	248 grams
Baking powder	2 teaspoons	
Salt	¾ teaspoon	
Creamy peanut butter	½ cup	135 grams
Unsalted butter, melted and cooled but still pourable	4 tablespoons	57 grams
Granulated sugar	1¾ cups	350 grams
Light brown sugar	Packed ½ cup	100 grams
Eggs, at room temperature	3 large	150 grams (weighed without shells)
Pure vanilla extract	1¼ teaspoons	
Peanut butter baking chips	½ cup	85 grams
Roasted salted peanuts, coarsely chopped	½ cup	75 grams
PEANUT BUTTER GLAZE		
Creamy peanut butter	1 cup	270 grams
Unsalted butter, at room temperature	6 tablespoons	85 grams
Confectioners' sugar	1½ cups	170 grams
Whole or reduced-fat (not nonfat) milk	2 tablespoons	30 grams
Pure vanilla extract	¼ teaspoon	
Salt	⅛ teaspoon	

1. Position a rack in the center of the oven and preheat to 350°F. Line the bottom and sides of a 13-by-9-inch baking pan with aluminum foil. Lightly spray the foil with nonstick baking spray.

2. Make the Peanut Butter Blondie: Whisk together the flour, baking powder, and salt in a medium bowl; set aside.

3. Combine the peanut butter and melted butter in a large bowl, using a whisk or an electric mixer on medium speed, until smooth and well blended. Beat in the granulated sugar and brown sugar. The mixture will seem dry and crumbly.

4. Beat in the eggs, one at a time, waiting for each egg to fully incorporate before adding the next. Beat in the vanilla with the last egg. The mixture will be smooth but will appear a little grainy because of the sugar.

5. Reduce the mixer speed to low and mix in half of the flour mixture until it's mostly incorporated. Stop mixing and scrape down the sides of the bowl with a silicone spatula. Mix in the remaining flour mixture just until no dry flour is visible. Scrape the sides of the bowl and stir in the peanut butter chips and peanuts.

6. Transfer the batter to the prepared pan. The batter will be quite thick. Use a small offset spatula or lightly wet your fingertips and coax the mixture into an even layer.

7. Bake until a toothpick inserted in the center comes out with moist crumbs (but no wet batter) attached, 23 to 27 minutes. The bars will be shiny and lightly golden brown all over. Halfway through baking, rotate the pan from front to back.

8. Make the Peanut Butter Glaze: While the bars are baking, beat the peanut butter and butter until smooth and creamy, using a stand mixer on medium speed. Beat in the confectioners' sugar, milk, vanilla, and salt on low speed until the sugar is incorporated and no longer visible. Increase the mixer speed to medium until the glaze is smooth and creamy. Set aside until the blondie is done baking.

9. Remove the pan from the oven and set on a wire rack to cool for 5 minutes. Dollop the Peanut Butter Glaze all over the warm uncut blondie. The glaze will start to melt (this is good). Let the glaze melt for 1 to 2 minutes, then use a small offset spatula to spread the glaze into an even layer.

10. Let the glazed uncut blondie cool completely in the pan on a wire rack. Use the foil to lift and remove from the pan. To cut into 3-by-1-inch fingers, first divide lengthwise into thirds. Cut each 3-inch-wide strip into fourths to make four 3-inch squares. Cut each square into three 1-inch bars (see "How to Cut a Batch," page 40). The bars can be stored in an airtight container in the refrigerator for several days. The bars will taste best when removed from the refrigerator and allowed to come to room temperature before serving, about 30 minutes.

Drunken Date Bars

MAKES 2 DOZEN (2-INCH) SQUARES

Simmering soft, sweet dates in fragrant sherry creates a jam with notes of dried fruits (from the sherry) and toffee (from the dates) in an elevated interpretation of rum-raisin. Sandwiched between a brown sugar oatmeal crust and a crunchy almond streusel, this dark, sticky jam is worlds apart from the store-bought spreads destined for slathering on cottony white bread. Although much of the alcohol is cooked out of the filling, the glaze topping has a gentle kick from the raw sherry, so keep that in mind. These are great for an after-dinner nibble with friends, but donating "Drunken Date Bars" to the next PTA bake sale might not earn you any brownie points.

INGREDIENT	VOLUME	WEIGHT
DRUNKEN DATE FILLING		
Dates, pitted and quartered (see Note)		454 grams (16 ounces)
Cream sherry	1 cup	264 grams
Ground cinnamon	½ teaspoon	
Ground cardamom	¼ teaspoon	
Salt	¼ teaspoon	
Pure vanilla extract	1 teaspoon	
BROWN SUGAR–ALMOND CRUST AND TOPPING		
Unbleached all-purpose flour	2½ cups	354 grams
Light brown sugar	1½ packed cups	300 grams
Old-fashioned rolled oats	1½ cups	150 grams
Salt	¾ teaspoon	
Ground cinnamon	¼ teaspoon	
Ground cardamom	¼ teaspoon	
Unsalted butter, melted and cooled but still pourable	18 tablespoons	255 grams
Pure vanilla extract	1 teaspoon	
Slivered almonds, toasted and cooled (see page 24)	¾ cup	96 grams
GLAZE		
Confectioners' sugar, preferably made with tapioca starch (see "Starch Madness," page 115)	1½ cups	170 grams
Cream sherry	2 to 4 tablespoons	33 to 66 grams
Salt	Small pinch	

1. Position a rack in the center of the oven and preheat to 350°F. Line the bottom and sides of a 13-by-9-inch baking pan with aluminum foil and lightly spray with nonstick baking spray.

2. Make the Drunken Date Filling: Combine the dates, sherry, cinnamon, cardamom, and salt in a medium saucepan. Bring to a boil over medium heat, stirring occasionally. Lower the heat to medium-low and allow the mixture to simmer for about 5 minutes, or until the mixture is softened and thickened. Remove the pan from the heat. Stir in the vanilla and set aside to cool for 10 minutes.

3. Transfer the date mixture to the bowl of a food processor. Process in 1-second pulses until the mixture is broken down into a spreadable consistency. Set aside.

4. Make the Crust and Topping: Combine the flour, brown sugar, oats, salt, cinnamon, and cardamom in a stand mixer fitted with a flat beater, and beat on low speed. While still mixing, slowly drizzle in the melted butter and vanilla. Continue to mix until uniform and no dry flour remains in the bottom of the bowl.

5. Press 400 grams (about 4 cups) of the flour mixture across the bottom of the prepared pan. The flat bottom of a drinking glass or dry measuring cup can be helpful in pressing the crust into a flat and even layer.

6. Bake until the crust turns golden brown at the edges and is firm when pressed in the center, 20 to 25 minutes. Remove from the oven and let cool on a wire rack for 10 minutes. Leave the oven on.

7. Spread an even layer of the date filling over warm crust, using a small offset spatula.

8. Mix the almonds into the remaining flour mixture. Firmly squeeze small handfuls of the topping in your hand (sort of like a rubber stress ball); open your hand and break the piece into marble-size pieces of topping over the top of the filling. Repeat with the remaining topping and sprinkle on any remaining bits. Gently press the topping into the date filling.

9. Return the pan to the oven and continue to bake until the topping is beginning to brown along the top, 35 to 40 minutes. The edges of the filling might also begin to bubble.

10. Remove from the oven and let cool to room temperature in the pan on a wire rack.

11. Make the Glaze: Whisk together the confectioners' sugar, 2 tablespoons of sherry, and salt. Add more sherry, ½ teaspoon at a time, until the mixture has the consistency of honey. If the icing gets too thin, whisk in additional confectioners' sugar, one spoonful at a time, to thicken it up. Drizzle the glaze over the top of the filling. Leave the glaze to set for about 30 minutes before cutting.

12. Use the foil to lift and remove from the pan before cutting into 2-inch squares (see "How to Cut a Batch," page 40). The squares can be stored in an airtight container at room temperature for several days or well wrapped and frozen for several months.

NOTE: Quarter the dates with a sharp knife and remove the pits. If you purchased pitted dates, quartering allows the chance to remove any pits that were missed during the commercial pitting process. Don't make it a whole production—they will be pureed in a food processor later on, but when you find your first pit, you will be grateful for taking the time to do this.

Thai Coconut Macaroon Bars

MAKES 18 (3-INCH) BARS

Makrut lime leaves feature in cuisines throughout South and Southeast Asia. Before making these cookies, we had only experienced the flavor in savory dishes like soups and curries, where it was often paired with coconut. The flavor combination works incredibly well in sweet baked goods, as well! The sharpness of the lime leaf with the cooling flavor of coconut and a welcome crunch of cashews really make these bars pop!

INGREDIENT	VOLUME	WEIGHT
CRUST		
Unbleached all-purpose flour	1¾ cups	248 grams
Sugar	⅓ cup	67 grams
Salt	½ teaspoon	
Unsalted butter, melted and cooled but still pourable	11 tablespoons	156 grams
COCONUT FILLING		
Cream of coconut, well stirred (see "Going Coconuts," page 76)	¾ cup	225 grams
Eggs, at room temperature	2 large	100 grams (weighed without shells)
Fresh makrut lime leaves, finely chopped (see Note)	Four 2–inch leaves	
Salt	½ teaspoon	
Unbleached all-purpose flour	2 tablespoons	18 grams
Sweetened shredded coconut, toasted and cooled (see page 22)	4⅔ cups (One 14-ounce bag)	396 grams (weighed before toasting)
Roasted unsalted cashews, split into halves	½ cup	57 grams

1. Position a rack in the center of the oven and preheat to 350°F. Line the bottom and sides of a 9-inch square baking pan with aluminum foil. Lightly spray the foil with nonstick baking spray.

2. Make the Crust: Stir together the flour, sugar, and salt in a medium bowl. Stir in the melted butter until all of the dry ingredients are moistened, a soft dough forms, and the mixture is uniform.

3. Press the dough evenly over the bottom of the prepared pan. Prick the dough all over with a fork to prevent it from puffing too much. Bake the crust until golden brown, 25 to 35 minutes. Remove from the oven and transfer to a wire rack to cool in the pan while you make the Coconut Filling. Leave the oven on.

4. Make the Coconut Filling: Whisk together the cream of coconut, eggs, chopped lime leaves, and salt until combined. Whisk in the flour until incorporated.

(continued)

Use a silicone spatula to stir in the toasted coconut and the cashews. Spread this mixture on the warm crust, smoothing the top with a silicone spatula or offset spatula.

5. Return the pan to the oven and bake until the topping is set and golden brown, about 25 additional minutes. Remove from the oven and let cool completely in the pan on a wire rack. Use the foil to transfer the filled crust from the pan to a cutting board. Slide the foil away before using a sharp knife to cut it into eighteen 1½-by-3-inch bars (see "How to Cut a Batch," page 40). Store the bars in an airtight container at room temperature.

NOTE: If you can't find them in your supermarket, fresh makrut lime leaves can often be found in specialty Asian grocery stores as well as online. If you have extra leaves left after baking these bars, keep them stored in a resealable storage bag in the freezer. Their unique flavor is definitely worth seeking out. While you still can make the cookie without them or by substituting lime zest, you'll be missing out.

COOKIE BYTE

Going Coconuts

Coconut product names can be confusing. There is coconut water, coconut milk, and coconut cream, all of which are pure coconut. Cream of coconut (not to be confused with coconut cream) is sweetened with additional sugar and has the thick consistency of condensed milk. It has a thick creamy layer on top that needs to be stirred in with a small silicone spatula or whisk before measuring or using. This thick, sweet cream of coconut is what you need for this recipe. Coco López is a popular brand. If you can't find it with the canned milks in your supermarket, check by the drink mixers. Cream of coconut is an essential ingredient in piña coladas (and gives you a good idea of what to do with any leftovers).

Mango Sunshine Bars

MAKES 16 (2¼-INCH) SQUARES

Although winter weather in Atlanta is pretty mild, we do get our share of unusually cold and gray days. Even after putting on wool socks, bumping up the thermostat, and sipping some hot tea, sometimes I still need something more summery to summon up some cold-weather comfort. These summertime mango bars always do the trick! With a sandy graham cracker base topped with a bright and tropical custard, it's sort of like if a lemon bar went on a Caribbean cruise. Even with a cloudy sky and snow in the forecast, I can close my eyes and let one bite of these bars transport me to a sun-soaked beach with my toes covered with warm sand and the sounds of lazy sapphire waves rolling ashore. It may be winter now, but I can start to feel that spring thaw coming. —P.A.

INGREDIENT	VOLUME	WEIGHT
CRUST		
Unbleached all-purpose flour	1¼ cups	177 grams
Graham cracker crumbs	½ cup	64 grams
Light brown sugar	Packed ⅓ cup	65 grams
Salt	½ teaspoon	
Unsalted butter, melted and cooled but still pourable	10 tablespoons	142 grams
MANGO LAYER		
Mango puree (see Note)	1¼ cups	375 grams
Lime juice, freshly squeezed	¼ cup	57 grams
Cornstarch	¼ cup	30 grams
Sweetened condensed milk	One 14-ounce can	397 grams
Egg yolks	3 large	45 grams
Dried spearmint (see Additional Note)	1 teaspoon	
Salt	Pinch	
Unsalted butter	2 tablespoons	28 grams

1. Position a rack in the center of the oven and preheat to 350°F. Line the bottom and sides of a 9-inch square baking pan with aluminum foil. Lightly spray the foil with nonstick baking spray.

2. Make the Crust: Stir together the flour, graham cracker crumbs, sugar, and salt in a bowl, using a silicone spatula. Stir in the melted butter until all of the dry ingredients are uniformly moistened. Press the

(continued)

dough evenly over the bottom of the prepared pan. Prick the dough all over with a fork to prevent it from puffing too much. Bake the crust until golden brown, about 30 minutes. Remove from the oven and let cool in the pan on a wire rack.

3. Make the Mango Layer: Whisk together the mango puree, lime juice, and cornstarch in a medium saucepan until completely dissolved. Whisk in the sweetened condensed milk, egg yolks, spearmint, and salt. Bring the mixture to a boil over medium heat, whisking constantly. Once the liquid starts to boil and bubbles appear all over the surface, set a timer for 60 seconds and whisk vigorously to prevent clumps.

4. Remove the saucepan from the heat and whisk in the butter. Pour the mixture through a fine-mesh sieve onto the cooled crust and smooth the top. Refrigerate until cold and firm throughout, at least 2 hours.

5. Use the foil to transfer the filled crust from the pan to a cutting board. Slide the foil away before using a sharp knife to cut it into sixteen 2¼-inch squares (see "How to Cut a Batch," page 40). Store the squares in an airtight container in the refrigerator.

NOTE: We use commercially available mango puree, which can often be found in the frozen food section of the grocery store year-round. You can also make your own from fresh mangoes when they are in season by pureeing peeled and seeded mangoes.

ADDITIONAL NOTE: Do not be tempted to "upgrade" the dried spearmint to fresh—even if you have tons of it growing in your garden. We've tried it, and it does not perform as well. The cooked fresh mint imparts an undesirable grassy, almost spinachlike flavor, to the mango. The dried herb, however, reliably provides the pure mint flavor we are after.

Speaking of Enzymes

COOKIE BYTE

Fresh tropical fruits, such as mango, papaya, and pineapple, can be difficult to incorporate into desserts. You've probably seen recipes, usually for gelatin-based desserts, that include a warning to avoid these fruits altogether. The reason for this is that the fruits contain enzymes, including actinidain, papain, and bromelain, that break down gelatin bonds, preventing the gelatin from setting. Fortunately, these enzymes can all be inactivated by heat (between 140° and 200°F depending on the enzyme). So, as a rule of thumb, if your recipe allows you to boil your fruit, you can use gelatin to set it. Additionally, amylase, an enzyme in egg yolks, can break down the mixtures set by cornstarch (like this one). (If you've ever made a lemon meringue pie that never quite set right, it's probably due to amylase.) While it's important to bring cornstarch to a boil to ensure that it fully thickens the mango custard, it also helps destroy the amylase enzyme.

drop cookies

Drop cookies include some of the most iconic American cookies, such as peanut butter, oatmeal raisin, and chocolate chip. They are some of the simplest cookies to make and require very few tools. They are made by portioning cookie dough, one cookie at a time, and dropping the dough onto a baking sheet from a spoon or scoop. Heat from the oven spreads the portioned dough, resulting in round (or almost round) cookies. Drop cookie dough can be made ahead and kept frozen.

Helpful Tools

- **Cookie scoops.** Portion dough (or ice cream!) quickly and evenly. Also known as portion scoops or dishers. We prefer scoops that dispense dough with a "trigger" operated by pressing on a lever with your thumb or by squeezing the handle with your palm.
- **Round metal cookie cutter.** Optional, but a great way to keep cookies round for a picture-perfect look.

General Tips and Techniques

All things being equal. We have found that scoops are the easiest way to portion drop cookie doughs evenly and efficiently. Of course, our mothers did fine scooping cookie dough with two spoons out of the silverware drawer, but the speed, ease, and accuracy of the scoop can't be beat. All of the drop cookie recipes in this chapter describe the amount of dough that each cookie uses and include a recommended scoop size. Scoops come in a variety of sizes, and most brands specify the size of the scoop with a number or a colored handle (or both).

- Numbers on a scoop usually range from 100 to 4. The *larger* the number, the *smaller* the scoop because the number indicates the number of scoops needed to make 1 quart. A #4 scoop would take 4 scoops of cookie dough to make 1 quart. A #100 scoop would take 100 scoops

to make 1 quart. The number can be found in a variety of places on the scoop, including on the metal bowl or the handle, so look carefully!
- Most scoop manufacturers use a standardized color scheme to display the size of the scoop. This makes using them in a commercial setting easy because you can very quickly see what size a scoop is instead of squinting all over the scoop, looking for a number. Because they are often made for commercial use, scoops (or dishers, as they are often called in professional kitchens) are durable and relatively inexpensive. These are the scoop sizes that are most appropriate for making cookies:

SCOOP HANDLE COLOR	NUMBER (PORTIONS PER QUART)	VOLUME
Black*	#30	2 tablespoons
Orchid (Purple)	#40	1½ tablespoons
Pink	#60	1 tablespoon
Orange	#100	2 teaspoons

* Be careful when looking for black-handled scoops! Some brands have black handles on all of their scoops. It is important to try to find out the size of the scoop that you have.

- We also use a small 1 teaspoon (#200) scoop. This is not a typical size that commercial manufacturers make, but it is usually the smallest scoop size that you can find. There is no corresponding color, and the 1-teaspoon scoops we have are all metal.

Cookie Scoops

Round Metal Cookie Cutters

- For any of these scoops, if you don't have one (or don't want to buy one), you can use measuring spoons instead or portion dough using the weights provided for each portion of dough in the recipe instructions (see "Weigh it out," which follows).
- If you have a scoop and don't know its size, fill it up with water 1 teaspoon at a time until the scoop is full. Make a note of its volume so you remember when you need to use it again.

Weigh it out. Another way to get equal-size cookies is to weigh out portions of dough, using a scale. As you know, we are proud proponents of weighing when baking, but weighing each scoop of dough can be a bit tedious—especially when you are scooping out dozens at one time. It works fine, but we like the scoops better.

Rollin' dough. While scoops are great at evenly portioning dough, we also often roll drop cookie portions in our hands before baking them. This smooths the cookie dough balls and makes for more even spreading in the oven and a more regularly shaped cookie. In other words, it helps prevent cookies with blobby, amoeba shapes.

Spread the love. If you've ever had several cookies (or a whole panful!) merge into one large megacookie, then you know the importance of properly spacing cookies on a baking sheet. As cookies bake in the oven, they can spread and become larger. It's important to position cookie dough portions far enough apart so they stay individual cookies once baked. Each drop cookie recipe says how far apart cookies should be placed on the standard 18-by-13-inch baking sheet. Refer to "Proper Portion Placement Primer" (page 86) for more information.

Press on. As cookies bake, the heat from the oven melts the butter and causes the cookie to spread. We often recommend flattening the dough balls to help achieve the desired shape for that specific cookie. Flattening encourages spread and results in a less domed cookie. To flatten, simply press on the top of the dough portion with two or three fingers (or a flat-bottom drinking glass). If the dough is sticky, spritz your fingers (or the bottom of the glass) with a bit of nonstick cooking spray.

Well-rounded education. If you have portioned the cookie, rolled the dough into balls, and properly spaced the dough on the cookie sheet, you've already done a lot to create beautiful, equal-size cookies. However, sometimes cookies have a mind of their own and bake up a little wonkier than what you'd like. If you act fast, you can fix it using a metal circle-shaped cookie cutter. Immediately after the cookies are removed from the oven, place a cutter large enough to fit around the hot cookie and move the cutter in small circles around the cookie, shimmying the edges of the dough back into a more even circle. Actually, you don't have to wait until the cookies are done baking to do this trick. We will often do it at the halfway point when we rotate the pans. The trick is that the edges of the cookie must be somewhat set (or soft, unbaked dough will gunk up the cookie cutter) but before the cookie is fully set and can't be reshaped. Remember: This will only work with a metal cutter—a plastic cutter will melt!

Let it rest. Immediately after baking, cookies can be soft and fragile. Generally, we recommend leaving cookies to cool directly on the cookie sheets for about 5 minutes before transferring them to a wire rack. This allows the cookies to cool slightly and firm up. Some-times we recommend cooling cookies completely on their baking sheets. This is especially true for large cookies or cookies that bake best by using the residual heat of the baking sheet to bake through completely.

Planning ahead. All of the drop cookies in this chapter can be made ahead in some way. Unbaked dough can be portioned, rolled, shaped (as instructed in the recipe), and positioned as close as possible to each other (without touching) on a baking sheet and frozen for about 4 hours. Once the dough balls are frozen, transfer them to a heavy-duty resealable storage bag. When stored properly, the dough will keep for at least 3 months. To bake, arrange the cookies on a baking sheet and bake as directed, adding a few additional minutes, if needed. Additionally, baked cookies can be wrapped in foil, placed in a heavy-duty resealable storage bag or container, and frozen. When stored properly, the cookies will keep for at least 3 months. Leave cookies wrapped and allow them to thaw to room temperature before enjoying.

Proper Portion Placement Primer

For all of our recipes where cookies are baked on a sheet pan, we tell you how many portions to arrange on the pan. It's essential to place unbaked cookie dough portions correctly if you want to avoid megacookies, where multiple cookies merge together into giant blobs. The merging makes for unattractive misshaped cookies. In addition to appearances, cookie blobs might not properly bake and can result in doughy middles or dry edges.

These configurations maximize baking sheet real estate by fitting—not arranging—cookies in perfect grid patterns. For our recipes, we recommend one of five different configurations based on how large the cookies are and how much they spread. These arrangements are based on (1) the use of an 18-by-13-inch baking sheet, and (2) the portion sizes prescribed in the recipe.

6 cookies per sheet (arranged in 2 rows of 3 cookies)

8 cookies per sheet (arranged in a 3–2–3 pattern)

13 cookies per sheet (arranged in a 3–2–3–2–3 pattern)

18 cookies per sheet (arranged in a 4–3–4–3–4 pattern)

24 cookies per sheet (arranged in 4 rows of 6 cookies)

Bronze Butter Chocolate Chip Cookies

MAKES 36 (3-INCH) COOKIES

We would argue that the chocolate chip cookie, invented in the 1930s, is *the* quintessential American cookie. Our version includes a few tweaks, but it isn't worlds apart from Ruth Wakefield's original Toll House recipe. To enhance the toffee flavors of the brown sugar batter, we brown the butter with dry milk powder to create a supercharged version of brown butter that we call bronze butter (see "Bronze Butter" page 89). While browning the butter is an additional step compared to Ruth's original recipe, the rich flavor is undeniably worth the effort. The deep, toasty flavor is balanced marvelously by the dark chocolate, a generous glug of vanilla, and the welcomed crunch of toasted pecans. As a bonus, these cookies come together great by hand with no need for an electric mixer.

INGREDIENT	VOLUME	WEIGHT
Unbleached all-purpose flour	2 cups	284 grams
Salt	1¼ teaspoons	
Baking soda	¾ teaspoon	
Unsalted butter, cut into chunks	16 tablespoons	227 grams
Nonfat dry milk powder, strained of lumps through a fine mesh sieve	½ cup	46 grams
Light brown sugar	Packed 1 cup	200 grams
Granulated sugar	½ cup	100 grams
Instant espresso powder	1 teaspoon	
Eggs, at room temperature	2 large	100 grams (weighed without shells)
Pure vanilla extract	1 tablespoon	
Chocolate chips or chopped chocolate, preferably 60 to 70 percent cacao (see "Chips Off the Old Block," page 90)	2 cups	340 grams (12 ounces)
Pecan pieces, toasted and cooled (optional; see page 24)	1 cup	113 grams

1. Whisk together the flour, salt, and baking soda in a medium bowl; set aside.

2. To make bronze butter, melt the butter in a small saucepan with a light-colored bottom (so you will be able to see the butter browning) over medium-low heat. Whisk the milk powder into the melted butter. The milk powder will clump and float on the surface of the butter. Bring to a boil, whisking occasionally. When the mixture starts to boil, begin whisking constantly until the bubbling has slowed, the mixture smells nutty, and all of the solids have become chestnut brown, about 5 minutes.

(continued)

3. Remove the saucepan from the heat, and immediately whisk the brown sugar, granulated sugar, and espresso powder into the melted butter, being sure to scrape up all the flavorful bits on the bottom of the pan. Transfer the mixture to a large bowl and let cool until the mixture is barely warm, about 30 minutes. (The mixture will appear separated because there is no liquid left in the butter to dissolve the sugar. It might also start to appear hard and crystalline—this will change once the eggs and vanilla are mixed in.)

4. While the mixture is cooling, position two racks to divide the oven into thirds and preheat to 350°F. Line two 18-by-13-inch baking sheets with parchment paper (or silicone baking mats).

5. Whisk the eggs, one at a time, and vanilla into the butter mixture until the mixture is uniform and no clumps remain. Make sure that the mixture is no longer hot—excess heat will give you scrambled eggs!

6. Switch out the whisk for a silicone spatula, and stir in the flour mixture, chocolate chips, and pecans (if using) just until no dry flour is visible.

7. Portion 2 tablespoons (37 grams) of dough, using a #30 scoop, and roll into a ball. Place the balls 3 inches apart on the prepared baking sheets (you can fit eight on each pan; see page 86). Gently press on the balls to flatten them slightly.

8. Bake until the cookies are light golden brown, set at the edges, and still puffed in the middle, 12 to 15 minutes. Halfway through baking, rotate the pans from front to back and top to bottom. Remove from the oven and let cool for 5 minutes on the baking sheet before transferring to a wire rack to cool completely. Repeat with the remaining dough once the baking sheets have completely cooled, or prepare additional baking sheets.

After cooling, the cookies can be stored in an airtight container at room temperature for several days.

Bronze Butter

COOKIE BYTE

Brown butter (see page 19) is made when the milk solids in butter cook and become browned and flavorful. While a very small portion of butter is milk solids (only 1 to 2 percent), brown butter is still remarkably flavorful. We wondered if it was possible to create even more flavor by adding additional milk solids to brown. (Spoiler alert: Yes.)

It turns out, we weren't the first to think about the advantage of using additional milk solids to amplify flavor. On their blog, *Ideas in Food*, authors Aki Kamozawa and H. Alexander Talbot describe a technique first presented by Chef Cory Barrett for adding additional milk solids to butter and browning it for added nutty flavor. It's a fabulous idea! Adding and browning an additional ¼ cup of nonfat dry milk (which is essentially all milk solids) with each stick (½ cup) of butter increases the milk solids content tenfold. Those additional toasted milk solids create what we called bronze butter, a supercharged version of brown butter.

To maximize the flavor, don't strain the toasted milk solids from the butter. The addition of those browned solids to the dough creates a deep, nutty flavor more wonderful than simple brown butter and results in the most delicious cookies that we have ever dreamed.

Chips Off the Old Block

In this recipe, you can choose to use either chips or chopped chocolate.

There is no right or wrong choice, but both options do affect the flavor and structure of the cookie more than you might realize.

Chocolate chips are real chocolate, but they have been manufactured with less cocoa butter, so they hold their shape instead of melting into puddles when baked. When we take extra steps to boost the flavor of the batter with bronze butter, we tend to prefer chips in these cookies. Because the pockets of chocolate are more discrete, larger areas of the flavorful bronze butter dough can shine through uninterrupted by chocolate. It's the best of both worlds—chocolate and the toffeelike flavors of the bronze butter batter. Because the chocolate chips remain unified, the cookie has more structure and a magnificently chewy texture. However, chocolate chips have fewer options to select from compared to bar chocolate. Although Nestlé Toll House semisweet chips are the ones we both grew up with, we now prefer a slightly less sweet chocolate chip. Companies who also make delicious bar chocolate, such as Ghirardelli and Guittard, make delicious semisweet and darker bittersweet chips with cacao percentages around 60 percent. However, if you are in the mood for an especially dark chocolate (something 70 percent cacao or higher), then you'll have to use bar chocolate.

Bar chocolate is available in many varieties, cacao percentages, styles, and origins that create many more options for creating a signature chocolate chip cookie with a unique flavor. While we aim for chopped chocolate pieces between ¼ and ½ inch in size, shards and slivers chip off during chopping. When these chips and shards and slivers are added, it results in chocolate being more evenly distributed throughout the dough. Although chocolate chips retain their shape, chopped chocolate pieces surrender to the heat of the oven and create puddles of chocolate throughout the cookie. The melting of the chocolate during baking, especially these small pieces, affects not only the shape but also the texture of the entire cookie. Cookies will bake up slightly flatter with a softer and less chewy texture compared to a cookie made with chocolate chips, because the structure is weakened by small pockets of chocolate interrupting the structure of the dough. Additionally, cookies made with chopped chocolate have more chocolate flavor because the chocolate is speckled throughout the dough. When we want to use bar chocolate, we sift away the smallest pieces of chocolate through a colander or other sieve with approximately ¼-inch holes. Pans or baskets made for cooking on barbecue grills work well for this. You will have to chop closer to 454 grams (1 pound) of chocolate to get 12 ounces of larger chunks to add to the dough. Save the smaller pieces of chocolate for other uses.

Go ahead and experiment. You can even divide the dough in half and add 1 cup of chips to one half and chopped chocolate to the other. When the cookies are cool, you can sit down and nibble away with a cookie in each hand, trying to determine your favorite. If anyone asks why you're double-fisting chocolate chip cookies, just let them know that it's all in the name of science.

Salted Caramel Sugar Cookies

MAKES 2½ DOZEN (3-INCH) COOKIES

In the cookie world, caramel is often relegated to a supporting role. Whether drizzled over a brownie or sandwiched as a filling, she is a welcome addition to almost any cast but never seems to get star treatment. Well, it's caramel's turn to be the leading lady. These sugar cookies are infused with an intense brown butter–boosted caramel sauce that is incorporated directly into the dough. Portions are rolled in a mixture of salt and sugar, creating a svelte, award-worthy, chewy sugar cookie packed with caramel flavor.

INGREDIENT	VOLUME	WEIGHT
Granulated sugar	1¼ cups	250 grams
Unsalted butter, cut into 8 pieces	8 tablespoons	113 grams
Unbleached all-purpose flour	2¼ cups	319 grams
Baking powder	1 teaspoon	
Baking soda	½ teaspoon	
Salt	1½ teaspoons	
Light brown sugar	Packed ½ cup	100 grams
Sour cream (full fat), cold from the refrigerator	¼ cup plus 1 tablespoon	75 grams
Vegetable oil	¼ cup	50 grams
Egg, cold from the refrigerator	1 large	50 grams (weighed without shell)
Pure vanilla extract	1 tablespoon	

1. Place ½ cup (100 grams) of the granulated sugar in a medium saucepan with high sides (see "Hot Stuff," page 92) over medium-high heat. Once the sugar starts to melt, swirl the pan occasionally, encouraging any dry sugar to fall into the liquid parts, until it has all melted and started to turn golden brown or caramelize. You can also stir the mixture with a long-handled silicone spatula instead of swirling, if you prefer. Let the caramelization go on until it is an amber color resembling maple syrup. Chris likes a medium amber caramel, but Paul likes a very dark brown caramel with more intense flavor. Feel free to take it as dark as you like—just don't burn it.

2. When the caramel is the color you desire, immediately remove the saucepan from the heat and add the butter (the mixture might bubble ferociously—be careful). Once the butter is melted, after about 15 seconds, whisk gently to make sure that the caramel mixture is not sticking to the sides of the pan. Set aside to cool in the pan for 10 minutes.

(continued)

3. Whisk together the flour, baking powder, baking soda, and ½ teaspoon of the salt in a bowl; set aside.

4. Whisk together ½ cup (100 grams) of the granulated sugar, the brown sugar, sour cream, and vegetable oil in a large bowl. Whisk in the cooled caramel sauce until the mixture is smooth. Whisk in the egg and vanilla until the mixture is uniform. Using a silicone spatula, stir in the flour mixture until all of the dry ingredients have been incorporated and a smooth, soft dough forms. Let the dough cool and firm up a bit for 15 minutes while preheating the oven.

5. Position two racks to divide the oven into thirds and preheat to 350°F. Line two 18-by-13-inch baking sheets with parchment paper or silicone baking mats.

6. Stir together the remaining ¼ cup of granulated sugar and the remaining 1 teaspoon of salt in a small, shallow bowl. Portion 2 tablespoons (30 grams) of dough, using a #30 scoop, and roll into balls. Drop the balls into the sugar mixture, roll to coat, and place them on the prepared baking sheets about 3 inches apart (you can fit eight per sheet; see page 86). Use the flat bottom of a drinking glass to gently flatten the balls to about 2 inches in diameter. (These cookies will spread, so don't overcrowd the pan.)

7. Bake until the edges are set and the cookies are evenly browned, 13 to 15 minutes. Halfway through baking, rotate the pans from front to back and top to bottom. Remove from the oven and let cool for 5 minutes on the baking sheets before transferring to a wire rack to cool completely. Repeat with the remaining dough once the baking sheets have completely cooled, or prepare additional baking sheets. After cooling, the cookies can be stored in an airtight container at room temperature for several days.

Hot Stuff

Don't be intimidated by making caramel! While it might seem like a bit of kitchen witchcraft, it's a reliable scientific reaction that is really quite simple. As sugar is heated, chemical bonds are broken, the crystalline structure falls apart, and the sugar crystals begin to melt. As the sugar gets hotter, it starts to brown, becoming less sweet and generating tons of rich and complex flavors. However, this is not the time to try to multitask! Caramel reaches temperatures of more than 300°F, and it can create a nasty burn if you're distracted, so keep your attention focused on that pan of sugar at all times. If you turn away for even a few seconds, your caramel can burn. For these cookies, butter is added to help stop the caramel from continuing to cook and to start to cool down the mixture. Because of the high temperature of the caramel, when the butter is added, it will instantly begin to brown, producing an intense flavor base for this thin and chewy sugar cookie.

We prefer to use a dry method for making caramel. This means that no water is added to the pot and the sugar melts more quickly. If you're new to making caramel, you might find it easier to start with a mixture of water and sugar. The water dissolves the sugar and then is boiled off, allowing the caramelization reaction to occur more slowly. This process takes longer, but a slow-and-steady approach will get you to the same finish line. For this recipe, you can add 2 tablespoons of water to the sugar in Step 1.

Variation: Chewy Malted Vanilla Sugar Cookies

The vanilla sugar cookie, a hallmark of our lunchtimes in school cafeterias, might be one of the most ordinary cookies in the world. But not these. The addition of the malted milk powder to the chewy sugar cookie base adds depth and an almost umami-like interest to these satisfyingly large cookies. Note that malted milk powder contains gluten (from its origins in barley) and should not be included in cookies that need to be made gluten-free.

In Step 1, instead of making a caramel sauce, simply melt the butter and let it cool slightly. In Step 4, omit the brown sugar, increase the granulated sugar to 1½ cups (300 grams), and add ½ cup (57 grams) of malted milk powder. Omit the 1 teaspoon of salt from the ¼ cup (50 grams) of rolling sugar. Because they spread a little more, these should be baked six cookies per baking sheet (see page 86) until the edges are set and just beginning to lightly brown, 10 to 12 minutes. This makes about 2 dozen (3½-inch) cookies.

Next-Gen Peanut Butter Cookies

MAKES 4½ DOZEN (1½-INCH) COOKIES

Any baker worth their butter knows that coffee adds a magical boost to the flavor of dark chocolate. In these cookies, we use toasted sesame oil to perform that same wizardry with peanut butter. While we are more familiar with toasted sesame oil as a component in savory dishes, its dark warm flavor perfectly amplifies peanut butter's roasted nuttiness in our modern take on the classic peanut butter cookie. We also used brown butter and dark brown sugar for additional intensity, ditched the fork crosshatch, and added a coating of coarse sugar to create a supremely crunchy cookie.

INGREDIENT	VOLUME	WEIGHT
Unbleached all-purpose flour	1⅓ cups	189 grams
Baking soda	1 teaspoon	
Salt	½ teaspoon	
Unsalted butter	7 tablespoons	99 grams
Dark brown sugar	Packed 1 cup	200 grams
Toasted sesame oil (see Note)	4 teaspoons	18 grams
Creamy peanut butter	½ cup	135 grams
Water	1 tablespoon	
Egg, at room temperature	1 large	50 grams (weighed without shell)
Turbinado sugar	½ cup	100 grams

1. Position two racks to divide the oven into thirds and preheat to 300°F. Line two 18-by-13-inch baking sheets with parchment paper or silicone baking mats.

2. Whisk together the flour, baking soda, and salt in a medium bowl; set aside.

3. To make brown butter (see "Better Baking with Brown Butter," page 19), melt the butter in a small saucepan with a light-colored bottom (so you will be able to see the butter browning) over medium heat. Continue to cook and it will start to bubble noisily as the water boils off. Once the bubbling begins to quiet down, swirl the pan constantly for about 1 minute, or until the milk solids at the bottom of the pan have turned golden brown and the butter has a nutty aroma. Remove the pan from the heat and add the brown sugar. Stir with a whisk or silicone spatula, making sure you scrape all of those luscious, browned bits off the bottom of the pan. Stir in the sesame oil and transfer the mixture to the bowl of your stand mixer to cool completely to room temperature.

4. Add the peanut butter to the bowl and, fitting the mixer with a flat beater, beat on medium speed until the peanut butter and sugar mixture is well mixed, 1 to 2 minutes. Add the water and egg and mix until the egg is fully incorporated. Reduce the mixer speed to low and stir in the flour mixture. Scrape the sides of the bowl and the beater with a silicone spatula to make sure that all of the ingredients are incorporated and no dry flour is visible.

5. Place the turbinado sugar in a small, shallow bowl. Portion 2 teaspoons (12 grams) of dough, using a #100 scoop, and roll them in the turbinado sugar, placing 18 on each baking sheet (see page 86).

6. Bake until the cookie edges are set and just beginning to brown, 18 to 22 minutes. Halfway through baking, rotate the pans from front to back and top to bottom. Remove from the oven and let cool for 5 minutes on the sheet before transferring to a wire rack to cool completely. Repeat with the remaining dough once the baking sheets have completely cooled, or prepare additional baking sheets. After cooling, the cookies can be stored in an airtight container at room temperature for several days.

NOTE: While we use it in all kinds of foods to impart delicious nutty flavor, we most often find toasted sesame oil in the international or Asian food sections of our grocery store.

COOKIE BYTE

Water Works

When developing these cookies, we knew we wanted to have lots of peanut butter flavor along with the flavor boosts from the toasted sesame oil and browned butter. Those three components contribute a fair amount of fat to the cookie, but not much water. Once the rest of the ingredients were added, we found that we could produce a tasty cookie, but the dough was rather crumbly and difficult to handle. The dough needed just a bit of water to help hold it together. By mixing the water in with the egg, the liquids and fats are easily emulsified, producing a smooth and cohesive dough.

Speckle and Spice Softies

MAKES 2½ DOZEN (3¼-INCH) COOKIES

These cookies are our take on the flavors of *bara brith*, a traditional Welsh tea cake whose name translates to "speckled bread." In both the bread and these cookies, the speckles are a mix of dried fruits that have been plumped in strongly brewed tea. Tea leaves in the dough and a tea-infused glaze drizzled over the tops add another level of flavor that pairs well with the fragrant spices. While some recipes for the spiced and tea-studded loaf call for candied citrus peel, we prefer freshly grated lemon and orange zest for a brightness that counters the husky sweetness of the plump fruits. If you can find it, you can replace all seven spices with 1 teaspoon of mixed spice, a spice blend used in the United Kingdom.

INGREDIENT	VOLUME	WEIGHT
Dried fruit, such as raisins, cherries, cranberries, or chopped apricots or prunes (we prefer a mixture)	1 cup	170 grams
Plain, unflavored black tea (decaffeinated is fine)	8 tea bags, or 3 tablespoons loose-leaf tea	
Boiling water	2 cups	473 grams
Unbleached all-purpose flour	2¼ cups	319 grams
Baking soda	½ teaspoon	
Baking powder	¼ teaspoon	
Salt	½ teaspoon plus a pinch	
Ground allspice	¼ teaspoon	
Ground cinnamon	¼ teaspoon	
Ground nutmeg	¼ teaspoon	
Ground ginger	⅛ teaspoon	
Ground mace	⅛ teaspoon	
Ground cloves	Pinch	
Ground coriander	Pinch	
Unsalted butter, melted and cooled but still pourable	12 tablespoons	170 grams
Granulated sugar	½ cup	100 grams
Lemon zest, freshly grated	1 medium lemon	
Orange zest, freshly grated	Half of 1 medium orange	

(continued)

Light brown sugar	Packed 1¼ cups	250 grams
Egg, at room temperature	1 large	50 grams (weighed without shell)
Egg yolk, at room temperature	1 large	15 grams
Pure vanilla extract	1 teaspoon	
Confectioners' sugar, preferably made with tapioca starch (see "Starch Madness," page 115)	1¼ cups	142 grams

1. Place the dried fruits in a medium heatproof bowl. Brew three tea bags (or 1 tablespoon of loose-leaf tea) in the boiling water for 6 minutes to create a strong tea. Discard the brewed tea bags (or loose tea) and pour the hot tea over the fruits. Cover and set aside until the mixture has cooled to room temperature, at least 30 minutes (see Note).

2. Position two racks to divide the oven into thirds and preheat to 350°F. Line two 18-by-13-inch baking sheets with parchment paper or silicone baking mats.

3. Whisk together the flour, baking soda, baking powder, ½ teaspoon of salt, allspice, cinnamon, nutmeg, ginger, mace, cloves, and coriander in a medium bowl; set aside.

4. If using tea bags, empty the tea from the five remaining tea bags. Your tea might already be finely ground. If you are using loose-leaf tea (or your tea bags were made with larger pieces of tea leaf), finely grind the tea in a spice grinder or with a mortar and pestle. Stir the tea powder into the melted butter.

5. Place the granulated sugar and the lemon, and orange zest in the bowl of your stand mixer. To extract the most citrus flavor, rub the zest and sugar between your thumbs and fingertips until the sugar is fragrant,

pale orange in color, and has a texture like wet sand (see "Live Your Zest Life," page 25).

6. Add the brown sugar and melted butter mixture to the zest mixture in the stand mixer, fit the mixer with a flat beater, and beat on medium speed until combined, about 1 minute. Beat in the egg, egg yolk, and vanilla until the mixture is creamy.

7. Reduce the mixer speed to low and beat in the flour mixture just until everything is well combined and no streaks of white flour are visible. Stop mixing and scrape down the sides of the bowl and the beater with a silicone spatula.

8. Drain the tea from the dried fruits, reserving about ½ cup of this soaking liquid to make the glaze; set aside. Fold the fruits into the batter. The dough will be soft. Let the dough sit at room temperature for 10 minutes to allow it to firm up.

9. Portion 2 tablespoons (36 grams) of dough (using a #30 scoop makes this easy). Place scoops 3 inches apart on the prepared baking sheets (you can fit eight on each pan; see page 86). Gently press down on the mounds to flatten the tops.

10. Bake until the edges are set and light golden brown, and the centers are still soft but no longer puffy, 13 to

15 minutes. Halfway through baking, rotate the pans from front to back and top to bottom. Remove from the oven and let cool for 5 minutes on the baking sheets before transferring to a wire rack to cool completely. Repeat with the remaining dough once the baking sheets have completely cooled, or prepare additional baking sheets.

11. For the glaze, combine the remaining pinch of salt and confectioners' sugar in a medium bowl. Whisk in 2 tablespoons of the reserved soaking liquid. Whisk in additional soaking liquid ½ teaspoon at a time until the mixture is a smooth, pourable glaze. (If you went too far and made the mixture too thin, whisk in additional confectioners' sugar.)

12. Use a spoon or a piping bag fitted with a small round piping tip to drizzle the glaze over the cookies. After the glaze sets for about 2 hours, the cookies can be stacked and stored in an airtight container at room temperature. The cookies will keep for several days, but their chewy texture is best within two days of baking.

NOTE: The dried fruits can be left to soak in the tea overnight. Keep the fruits covered, but there's no need to refrigerate them.

Gingerbread Bogs

MAKES 3½ DOZEN (2½-INCH)
COOKIES

I'm not usually a fan of flavored coffees, but I do look forward to my annual gingerbread latte in December. With that in hand, I'm ready to hit the stores for some serious Christmas shopping. While there are so many flavors of the season (English toffee! Eggnog! Peppermint! Fruitcake!), for me, gingerbread is my holiday ride-or-die. Besides the season's first airing of the Elizabeth Taylor White Diamonds TV commercial, my first gingerbread sighting is my trigger to let me know that it is holiday season go-time. While gingerbread is often seen in many forms, including people-shaped cookies and houses, cakes and even gingerbread pie, its flavors can sometimes be overwhelmingly spicy, or worse: woefully plain. For our version, we've balanced the sharp spices and added some sweet-tart dried cranberries to a soft and chewy cookie for the perfect way to kick-start your winter holidays. —P.A.

INGREDIENT	VOLUME	WEIGHT
Unbleached all-purpose flour	2¼ cups	319 grams
Ground ginger	1½ teaspoons	
Ground cinnamon	1 teaspoon	
Baking powder	1 teaspoon	
Baking soda	½ teaspoon	
Salt	½ teaspoon	
Ground cloves	¼ teaspoon	
Sugar	1¼ cups	250 grams
Molasses	¼ cup	85 grams
Sour cream (full fat), cold from the refrigerator	¼ cup	60 grams
Vegetable oil	¼ cup	50 grams
Unsalted butter, melted and cooled but still pourable	8 tablespoons	113 grams
Egg, cold from the refrigerator	1 large	50 grams (weighed without shell)
Dried cranberries	½ cup	60 grams
Crystallized ginger, finely chopped	¼ cup	40 grams
Orange zest, freshly grated	1 small orange	

1. Whisk together the flour, ginger, cinnamon, baking powder, baking soda, salt, and cloves in a medium bowl; set aside.

2. Whisk together 1 cup (200 grams) of the sugar and the molasses, sour cream, and vegetable oil in a large bowl. Whisk in the cooled butter, followed by the egg, until the egg is incorporated and the mixture is uniform. Using a silicone spatula, stir in the flour mixture until all of the dry ingredients have been incorporated and a smooth soft dough forms. Stir in the cranberries, ginger, and orange zest. Let the dough rest for 10 to 15 minutes while preheating the oven.

3. Position two racks to divide the oven into thirds and preheat to 350°F. Line two 18-by-13-inch baking sheets with parchment paper or silicone baking mats.

4. Place the remaining ¼ cup of granulated sugar in a small, shallow bowl. Portion 1½ tablespoons (23 grams) of dough, using a #40 scoop. Roll the portions between your palms into balls. Roll the balls in the sugar and place them on the prepared cookie sheets (you can fit 13 per sheet; see page 86).

5. Bake until the edges are set and just beginning to turn a darker shade of brown, 12 to 14 minutes. Halfway through baking, rotate the pans from front to back and top to bottom. Remove from the oven and let cool for 5 minutes on the baking sheets before transferring to a wire rack to cool completely. Repeat with the remaining dough once the baking sheets have completely cooled, or prepare additional baking sheets. After cooling, the cookies can be stored in an airtight container at room temperature for several days.

Variation: Honey Whole Wheat Bogs

When the holidays are over and you are ready to bring those visions of dancing sugar plums back down to earth, you can transform that wintertime gingerbread into a more homespun everyday cookie. A few easy swaps produces a soft and chewy treat that you will want to enjoy year-round. In Step 1, decrease the unbleached all-purpose flour to 1⅛ cups (159 grams) and add 1⅛ cups of whole wheat flour (176 grams). Omit the ginger, cinnamon, and cloves. In Step 2, replace the molasses with an equal amount of honey plus 2 teaspoons of pure vanilla extract. Replace the cranberries with ¾ cup (100 grams) of raisins and omit the crystallized ginger and orange zest. This also makes about 3½ dozen (2½-inch) cookies.

Escapes (The Piña Colada Oatmeal Cookies)

MAKES 2 DOZEN (3-INCH) COOKIES

In his 1979 hit song, singer-songwriter Rupert Holmes's "Escape" charmed us with lyrics about piña coladas and getting caught in the rain. Remembered as "The Piña Colada Song," Holmes's hit recounts the joy of finding new happiness in something old and familiar. While he was crooning about a reenergized relationship, we have the same philosophy for cookies. If you've grown tired of the same old, dull routine of oatmeal cookies, plan your escape with these cocktail-inspired treats. Chewy and made with sweet roasted pineapple, toasted coconut, and crunchy macadamia nuts, these might be the (cookie) love that you've looked for.

INGREDIENT	VOLUME	WEIGHT
Fresh pineapple, trimmed, cored, and cut into chunks no larger than ½ inch	1 large	454 grams (1 pound)
Unbleached all-purpose flour	1 cup	142 grams
Baking soda	½ teaspoon	
Salt	½ teaspoon	
Unsalted butter, melted and cooled but still pourable	4 tablespoons	57 grams
Light brown sugar	Packed ¾ cup	150 grams
Granulated sugar	½ cup	100 grams
Eggs, at room temperature	2 large	100 grams (weighed without shells)
Pure vanilla extract	1 teaspoon	
Coconut rum or dark rum	1 tablespoon	
Old-fashioned rolled oats	2½ cups	250 grams
Sweetened coconut flakes, toasted and cooled (see page 22)	⅔ cup	57 grams
Roasted salted macadamia nuts, coarsely chopped	⅔ cup	75 grams

1. Position a rack in the center of the oven and heat the broiler. Line an 18-by-13-inch baking sheet with aluminum foil. Spread the pineapple pieces over the foil in a single layer. Broil the pineapple, stirring every 5 minutes, until half of the pineapple pieces have begun to brown at the edges, about 15 minutes.

Once the first pieces begin to brown, begin stirring every 3 minutes to prevent burning. Leave the roasted chunks on the baking sheet to cool completely and turn off the oven. You will have about 1 cup (170 grams) of roasted pineapple. The pineapple can be roasted up to 2 days before baking the cookies (see Make Ahead). We

(continued)

find that positioning the baking sheet on the middle rack of the oven allows a little more control over the browning. If you can't position your baking sheet that far away from the broiler, be sure to check on and stir the pineapple more often because it will cook faster.

2. Position two racks to divide the oven into thirds and preheat to 350°F. Line two 18-by-13-inch baking sheets with parchment paper or silicone baking mats.

3. Whisk together the flour, baking soda, and salt in a medium bowl; set aside.

4. Combine the melted butter, brown sugar, and granulated sugar in a stand mixer fitted with a flat beater, and beat together on medium speed until well mixed, 1 to 2 minutes. Beat in the eggs, one at a time, followed by the vanilla and coconut rum, until the mixture is uniform.

5. Reduce the mixer speed to low, and stir in the flour mixture until it's mostly incorporated. Stop mixing and scrape down the sides of the bowl and the beater with a silicone spatula. Mix in the oats, coconut, macadamia nuts, and roasted pineapple on low speed.

Remove the bowl from the mixer and scrape the sides to make sure that everything is evenly distributed throughout.

6. Portion 2 tablespoons (44 grams) of dough, using a #30 scoop, and place directly on the prepared baking sheets 2 inches apart (you can fit 13 on each pan; see page 86). The dough is sticky, so do not try to roll this dough in your palms. Use lightly moistened fingers to press down the tops of the scoops by ½ inch to form a thick disk.

7. Bake until the edges of the cookies are lightly browned but the centers are still pale in the middle, 11 to 14 minutes. Halfway through baking, rotate the pans from front to back and top to bottom. Remove from the oven, place the baking sheets on wire racks, and leave the cookies on the pans to cool completely and allow the centers to finish cooking through. Repeat with the remaining dough once the baking sheets have completely cooled, or prepare additional baking sheets. After cooling, the cookies can be stored in an airtight container at room temperature for several days.

MAKE AHEAD: The roasted pineapple can be stored in the refrigerator for up to 2 days. Bring it to room temperature along with the eggs.

Mocksies

MAKES 22 (1½-INCH) COOKIES

At one time, boxes of Ritz crackers always had a recipe card on the back for mock apple pie. The recipe's claim was that you could boil(!) some buttery crackers in water and add cream of tartar and a few spices to create a faux apple pie that was nearly as good as the original. As devoted (and award-winning) pie bakers, that claim seemed absurd to us. Could this possibly be true? How could a pile of wet crackers create the illusion of apple pie? The secret is in the cream of tartar. We keep that white powder in our pantries for adding just a pinch to our stiff-peaked egg whites. Turns out that when used in larger quantities, it is not only a convenient source of acid but a flavoring agent that is close enough to the taste of a tart apple to provide an ideal basis for the deception. With the addition of some nuts and a sprinkling of fall spices, the mirage is . . . close flavorwise, but should never actually fool anyone who is remotely familiar with an actual apple pie. Here we used this surprisingly effective deception to make mock apple pie cookies. With a satisfying crunch, we've transformed this back-of-the box sorcery into a 21st-century delight.

INGREDIENT	VOLUME	WEIGHT
Ritz crackers	40 crackers	133 grams
Pecan halves, toasted and cooled (see page 24)	¾ cup	71 grams
Light brown sugar	Packed ½ cup	100 grams
Cream of tartar	½ teaspoon	
Ground cinnamon	¼ teaspoon	
Ground nutmeg	¼ teaspoon	
Egg white	1 large	35 grams
Lemon juice, freshly squeezed	1 tablespoon	
Unsalted butter, melted and cooled but still pourable	4 tablespoons	57 grams

1. Position two racks to divide the oven into thirds and preheat to 350°F. Line two 18-by-13-inch baking sheets with parchment paper or silicone baking mats.

2. Place the crackers in the bowl of a food processor and pulse until they are small crumbs. Transfer the crumbs to a bowl. Add the pecans to the food processor and coarsely grind them as well. Add the ground nuts to the bowl with the cracker crumbs. (Alternatively, the crackers can be crushed by hand directly in the bowl and the pecans can be chopped by hand.)

(continued)

3. Add the brown sugar, cream of tartar, cinnamon, and nutmeg to the bowl. Mix these dry ingredients together by hand, using a silicone spatula. Add the egg white, lemon juice, and melted butter and mix until the dry ingredients have all been moistened and the mixture has formed into a cohesive clump. Let the mixture rest for 15 minutes before scooping.

4. Portion 1 tablespoon (18 grams) of dough, using a #60 scoop, roll into balls, and evenly arrange 13 portions on the first baking sheet (see page 86). Flatten the balls slightly with your fingertips. Repeat with the remaining dough and arrange on the second baking sheet.

5. Bake until cookie edges are set and just beginning to brown, 13 to 17 minutes. Halfway through baking, rotate the pans from front to back and top to bottom. Remove from the oven and let cool for 5 minutes on the baking sheets before transferring to a wire rack to cool completely. After cooling, the cookies can be stored in an airtight container at room temperature for several days.

Crispy Chocolate Five-Spice Oatmeal Cookies

MAKES 39 (2½-INCH) COOKIES

In the world of cookies, chocolate and spice are an overlooked flavor combination. Several spices can hold their own with its dark bittersweetness, but chocolate and five-spice powder are a particularly harmonious combination. If you're not familiar (and you should be), five-spice powder is a spice blend used in East Asian cuisines, including those of China, Taiwan, and Vietnam. Not all five-spice powders are the same (in fact, some varieties have more than five spices!), but they can include variations on cinnamon, cloves, star anise, fennel seeds, and Szechuan peppercorns, as well as versions made with anise, ginger, or white pepper. In these crisp oatmeal cookies, the spice blend brings a sultry warmth that doesn't overwhelm the seductive richness of its cocoa powder dance partner.

INGREDIENT	VOLUME	WEIGHT
Unbleached all-purpose flour	¾ cup	106 grams
Dutch-processed cocoa powder	¼ cup	21 grams
Five-spice powder, preferably McCormick or Simply Organic brand (see Note)	1¾ teaspoons	
Baking powder	¾ teaspoon	
Baking soda	½ teaspoon	
Salt	½ teaspoon	
Unsalted butter, at room temperature	16 tablespoons	227 grams
Granulated sugar	1 cup	200 grams
Light brown sugar	Packed ¼ cup	50 grams
Egg, at room temperature	1 large	50 grams (weighed without shell)
Pure vanilla extract	1 teaspoon	
Old-fashioned rolled oats	2¾ cups	275 grams

1. Position two racks to divide the oven into thirds and preheat to 350°F. Line two 18-by-13-inch baking sheets with parchment paper or silicone baking mats.

2. Whisk together the flour, cocoa powder, five-spice powder, baking powder, baking soda, and salt in a medium bowl; set aside.

3. Combine the butter, granulated sugar, and brown sugar in a stand mixer fitted with a flat beater, and beat together on medium speed until creamy, 1 to 2 minutes. Beat in the egg and vanilla.

4. Reduce the mixer speed to low and stir in the flour mixture until combined. Stop mixing and scrape down the sides of the bowl and the beater with a silicone spatula. Stir in the oats until the mixture is combined.

5. Portion 1½ tablespoons (23 grams) of dough, using a #40 scoop or heaping tablespoon measure, and roll into a ball. Place the balls 3 inches apart on the prepared baking sheets (you can fit eight on each pan; see page 86). Press the balls to a 2-inch-wide circle, using a flat-bottomed cup or your fingers. (If the dough sticks to the glass, spritz it with a quick shot of nonstick cooking spray.)

6. Bake until the edges are set and centers are firm when gently pressed, 14 to 18 minutes. Halfway through baking, rotate the pans from front to back and top to bottom. Remove from the oven and let cool for 5 minutes on the baking sheets before transferring to a wire rack to cool completely. Repeat with the remaining dough once the baking sheets have completely cooled, or prepare additional baking sheets. After cooling, the cookies can be stored in a closed container at room temperature for several days.

NOTE: Full disclosure: We have not tried every five-spice powder available for sale. However, among those we have tried, we prefer both McCormick and Simply Organic brands. In our opinion, they are widely available and their spice blends pair very well with both sweet and savory foods. Some blends with white pepper or Szechuan peppercorns are too assertive for these cookies.

Everybody Ryes

MAKES 4 DOZEN (2-INCH) COOKIES

Many may be mindful of the myriad mass-market musicals with sometimes saccharine sentimentality and syrupy sweet storylines. However, a Stephen Sondheim musical—peppered with penetrating prose, purposeful polyphony, and ornamental alliteration—is no walk in the park with sappy song-and-dance numbers. Mr. Sondheim's stunning catalog of cunning dialogue brims with storylines of well-timed rhymes that bring his often all-too-human characters to life. They are darkly tinged and multilayered stories of men and women who face impossible odds; seek lost love, redemption, or even revenge; and sing about it in elaborate and soaring emotional masterpieces that only he can devise. For our cookie honoring the life and work of Stephen Sondheim, we choose to combine the darker and complex notes of rye flour with the subtle sweetness of honey and a slightly salty edge. If you are still here or just being alive, these cookies are suitable for taking into the woods or serving to the ladies who lunch. Sing it with us:

A toast to these most flavorful treats!
With honey and rye flour (no wheat),
Soft and chewy, but subtly sweet!,
Everybody Ryes!

INGREDIENT	VOLUME	WEIGHT
Rye flour (see Note)	1¾ cups	198 grams
Baking soda	½ teaspoon	
Salt	1¾ teaspoons	
Ground cinnamon	⅛ teaspoon	
Unsalted butter, at room temperature	8 tablespoons	113 grams
Light brown sugar	Packed ¼ cup	50 grams
Honey (see Note)	½ cup	170 grams
Pure vanilla extract	½ teaspoon	
Granulated sugar	½ cup	100 grams

1. Position two racks to divide the oven into thirds and preheat to 300°F. Line two 18-by-13-inch baking sheets with parchment paper or silicone baking mats.

2. Whisk together the rye flour, baking soda, ¼ teaspoon of the salt, and the cinnamon in a medium bowl; set aside.

3. Combine the butter and brown sugar in a stand mixer fitted with a flat beater, and beat together until smooth, 1 to 2 minutes. Beat in the honey and vanilla.

4. Reduce the mixer speed to low, and mix in the flour mixture just until no more white flecks of flour are visible. Scrape the sides of the bowl and the beater to make sure that everything is mixed in and no little clumps of butter or flour are hiding out at the bottom of the bowl. The dough will be soft.

5. Stir together the remaining 1½ teaspoons of salt and the granulated sugar in a pie plate or shallow bowl.

6. Portion 1½ teaspoons (11 grams) of dough (use a #100 scoop if you have one) and drop directly onto the sugar mixture. Roll each ball in the sugar mixture and place the balls about 1½ inches apart on the prepared baking sheets (you can fit 18 on each pan; see page 86).

7. Bake until the cookies have puffed and the edges are set just and beginning to lightly brown, 13 to 16 minutes. Halfway through baking, rotate the pans from front to back and top to bottom. Remove from the oven and let cool for 5 minutes on the baking sheets before transferring to a wire rack to cool completely. (The cookies will slightly fall as they cool.) Repeat with the remaining dough once the baking sheets have completely cooled, or prepare additional baking sheets. After cooling, the cookies can be stored in an airtight container at room temperature for several days.

NOTE: For baking, we prefer to use a mild-tasting honey, such as one made from clover or orange blossoms. Remember that rye flour is lower in gluten than wheat flour, but it is not gluten-free.

Blush and Bashfuls

MAKES 24 (2¾-INCH) COOKIES

These two-tone treats are variations of the classic black-and-white cookies found everywhere now but especially ubiquitous in New York City. Scented with almond and vanilla, they are so light and puffy that they could pass as cakes. Instead of the traditional chocolate and vanilla coating, we glaze these with fresh strawberry and rhubarb icings in two shades of pink (one is much deeper than the other) in a nod to Julia Roberts's iconic line in the film *Steel Magnolias*. The ingredient list for these cookies might seem long because it makes cookies as well as two different icings. Some components can be made in advance (see Make Ahead), and the icings come together fast.

INGREDIENT	VOLUME	WEIGHT
LIGHT AND PUFFY ALMOND COOKIES		
Unbleached all-purpose flour	1¾ cups plus 2 tablespoons	266 grams
Baking powder	1 teaspoon	
Salt	½ teaspoon	
Baking soda	¼ teaspoon	
Unsalted butter, at room temperature	8 tablespoons	113 grams
Granulated sugar	¾ cup plus 2 tablespoons	175 grams
Eggs, at room temperature	2 large	100 grams (weighed without shells)
Pure vanilla extract	1 teaspoon	
Almond extract	¼ teaspoon	
Buttermilk, preferably cultured buttermilk made from whole milk, at room temperature	½ cup plus 2 tablespoons	152 grams
RHUBARB ICING		
Rhubarb Reduction (recipe follows)	3 tablespoons	
Confectioners' sugar, preferably made with tapioca starch (see "Starch Madness," page 115)	1 cup	113 grams
Light corn syrup	1 teaspoon	
Salt	Pinch	
Water, for thinning	As needed	

(continued)

STRAWBERRY ICING

Strawberry Reduction (recipe follows)	3 tablespoons	
Confectioners' sugar, preferably made with tapioca starch (see "Starch Madness," page 115)	1 cup	113 grams
Light corn syrup	1 teaspoon	
Salt	Pinch	
Water, for thinning	As needed	

1. Make the Light and Puffy Almond Cookies: Position a rack in the center of the oven and preheat to 400°F. Line an 18-by-13-inch baking sheet with a silicone baking mat (see Note).

2. Whisk together the flour, baking powder, salt, and baking soda in a medium bowl; set aside.

3. Combine the butter and granulated sugar in a stand mixer fitted with a flat beater, and cream together until light and fluffy, about 3 minutes. Beat in the eggs, one at a time, waiting for the first egg to be fully incorporated before adding the second. Beat in the vanilla and almond extracts.

4. Reduce the mixer speed to low and mix in half of the flour mixture until it's almost combined. Stop mixing and scrape down the sides of the bowl and the beater with a silicone spatula. Beat in the buttermilk until incorporated, 20 to 30 seconds. Mix in the remaining flour mixture just until no dry flour is visible. Scrape the sides of the bowl and ensure that no rogue pieces of unincorporated butter or flour are hiding out in the bottom of the bowl. The dough will be very soft.

5. Portion 2 tablespoons (33 grams) of batter (a #30 scoop will help to ensure the roundest, most uniform cookies). When using a cookie scoop, release the batter as close to the baking sheet as you can get (½ inch is perfect). It helps keep the cookies rounder and more equally sized than dropping them from several inches above the pan. Place the scoops 2 inches apart on a prepared baking sheet (you can fit eight on a pan; see page 86). These cookies are best when they are baked one sheet at a time.

6. Bake until the domed tops spring back when gently pressed (if the cookies start to brown at the edges, they have baked too long), 8 to 10 minutes. Halfway through baking, rotate the pan from front to back. Remove from the oven and let cool for just 2 to 3 minutes on the baking sheets, until the cookies are set enough to transfer to a wire rack to cool completely. Repeat with the remaining batter once the baking sheet has completely cooled, or prepare additional baking sheets.

7. Make the Rhubarb Icing: Whisk together the Rhubarb Reduction, confectioners' sugar, corn syrup, and salt in a medium bowl. Add additional water, bit by bit, if needed, to make a glaze with the consistency of honey. If the icing is too thin, whisk in additional confectioners' sugar, one spoonful at a time, to thicken it up.

8. Flip the cookies over so the flat side is facing up. Use an offset spatula to lift and drag a thin drizzle of icing down the center of the cookie to mark two halves. Spread icing over one half in a thin layer (but not so thin that you can still see the light brown color of the cookie bottom).

9. Make the Strawberry Icing: Whisk together the Strawberry Reduction, confectioners' sugar, corn syrup, and salt in a medium bowl. Add more water, bit by bit, if needed, to make a glaze with the consistency of honey. If the icing is too thin, whisk in additional confectioners' sugar, one spoonful at a time, to thicken it up. Making the Strawberry Icing after glazing with the rhubarb helps to make the cookies easier to handle, as the glaze will have begun to set.

10. Glaze the icing-free half of each cookie with the strawberry mixture just as you did with the rhubarb mixture. For the cleanest seam, try to slightly overlap the drizzled line of icing over the edge of the rhubarb icing rather than right next to it.

11. Leave the cookies to dry completely; this might take several hours if your home is humid. The cookies can be loosely covered and stored at room temperature. Don't keep glazed cookies in an airtight container because the moisture in the cookies can soften the icing. For the softest cookies, enjoy within a day or two of baking.

NOTE: These cookies are one of the few that we prefer to bake on silicone baking mats. The cookies release more cleanly from the silicone and leave a smoother base for the icings. Don't sweat it: parchment paper will still work if that's all you've got.

Starch Madness

COOKIE BYTE

While trying to perfect the icings for these cookies, we kept running into the same problem: the icings tasted flavorless no matter how flavorful the rhubarb or strawberry reductions were. We wondered if the issue might be the confectioners' sugar. Powdered sugars are often "cut" with starch to reduce clumping, and the one most commonly used is cornstarch. We know from baking pies that cornstarch can mute the flavor of fresh fruits. A "Serious Eats" column written by Stella Parks—chef, author, and dessert doyenne—opined on the virtues of confectioners' sugar made with tapioca starch as an alternative to traditional cornstarch-based formulations. We conducted side-by-side taste tests to confirm, and she is right. Upgrading our confectioners' sugar to a tapioca starch–based product made all the difference in the world! The vibrant flavors of the rhubarb and strawberry came through marvelously. Several organic brands of confectioners' sugar are made with tapioca starch, but check the ingredients label to confirm. Because tapioca-based confectioners' sugar can be more expensive than those made with cornstarch, we reserve the pricier option for glazes where the taste really matters. We still use traditional cornstarch-based confectioners' sugar in cookie doughs and batters.

(continued)

Rhubarb Reduction

MAKES ½ CUP

INGREDIENT	VOLUME	WEIGHT
Rhubarb, fresh or thawed from frozen, diced into ¼-inch pieces	1⅔ cups	227 grams
Water	¼ cup	59 grams
Sugar	¼ cup	50 grams
Lemon juice, freshly squeezed	¼ teaspoon	
Salt	⅛ teaspoon	

1.   Bring the rhubarb and any accumulated juice, water, sugar, lemon juice, and salt to a boil in a medium saucepan over medium heat.

2.   Lower the heat to a gentle boil and continue to cook, stirring frequently, until the rhubarb pieces have broken down and the mixture is like a thick applesauce, about 15 minutes. You'll know the consistency is correct when you try to pile the reduction onto one side of the saucepan, and it stays instead of slouching out of place. Press the mixture through a fine-mesh sieve to remove any fibrous pulp; set aside to cool. Store in the refrigerator for up to 1 week. This recipe makes more than you'll need for one batch of Rhubarb Icing. Any leftover reduction can be frozen for later use.

MAKE AHEAD: The rhubarb and strawberry reductions will keep in the refrigerator for up to 1 week.

Strawberry Reduction

MAKES ⅔ CUP

INGREDIENT	VOLUME	WEIGHT
Strawberries, fresh or thawed from frozen, cut into ¼-inch slices	3¼ cups	454 grams (1 pound)
Water	½ cup	118 grams
Sugar	¼ cup	50 grams
Lemon juice, freshly squeezed	½ teaspoon	
Salt	¼ teaspoon	

1. Bring the strawberries and any accumulated juice, water, sugar, lemon juice, and salt to a boil in a medium saucepan over medium heat.

2. Lower the heat to a gentle boil and continue to cook, stirring frequently and pressing on the strawberries to break them down, until the mixture is like a thick applesauce, about 20 minutes. Press the mixture through a fine-mesh sieve to remove seeds and any fibrous pulp; set aside to cool. Store in the refrigerator for up to 1 week. This recipe makes more than you'll need for one batch of Strawberry Icing. Any leftover reduction can be frozen for later use.

Teatime Stamped Shortbread

MAKES 2 DOZEN (2-INCH) COOKIES

Buttery and delightfully crumbly, these shortbread cookies are made extra special with the addition of Earl Grey tea (see "Steep Learning Curve"). Earl Grey tea is tea made with oil from the skin of the bergamot orange. It's a distinctive taste, and it pairs wonderfully with notes of vanilla. While optional, using a cookie stamp to emboss the shortbread adds an elegant touch to this refined teatime treat that's at home on both party trays and tea saucers.

INGREDIENT	VOLUME	WEIGHT
Earl Grey tea, either loose-leaf tea or removed from about 5 tea bags	2 tablespoons	10 grams
Bleached cake flour, plus additional flour for dusting	3 cups plus 2 tablespoons	354 grams
Unsalted European butter, cold, cut into 16 pieces (see Note)	16 tablespoons	227 grams
Confectioners' sugar	1 cup	113 grams
Salt	½ teaspoon	
Pure vanilla extract	1 teaspoon	

1. Position two racks to divide the oven into thirds and preheat to 275°F (see Note). Line two 18-by-13-inch baking sheets with parchment paper.

2. If using loose-leaf tea, grind the tea to a fine powder, using either a mortar and pestle, a spice grinder, or the small bowl of a food processor. (Most tea removed from tea bags is fine in texture and won't need this step, but if the tea is coarse, give it a quick grind.) Sift the tea through a mesh sieve to remove any large unground pieces that can create an unpleasant texture in the finished cookie.

3. Place the tea powder, flour, butter, confectioners' sugar, and salt in the regular-size bowl of a food processor. Process in 1-second pulses until the mixture is fine and sandy. (Alternatively, use a pastry blender to cut the butter into those dry ingredients.) Add the vanilla and continue to pulse (or stir with a spoon) just until the dough comes together.

4. Portion 1½ tablespoons (29 grams) of dough, using a #40 scoop, and roll into smooth balls. Place the balls 2 inches apart on the prepared baking sheets (you can fit 13 cookies on each baking sheet; see page 86). Using even pressure, press the dough into a 2-inch circle, using a decorative cookie stamp. If the dough sticks to the stamp, it can be gently peeled off and placed back on the pan. Dipping the stamp into a bit of flour after each press can help prevent sticking. (If you don't have a cookie stamp, simply press the cookies to a flat 2-inch circle with the bottom of a drinking glass or dry measuring cup.)

(continued)

5. Bake until the edges are set and just beginning to show the merest hint of brown, 55 to 60 minutes. Halfway through baking, rotate the pans from front to back and top to bottom. Remove from the oven and let the cookies cool on the baking sheets for 5 minutes before using a thin spatula to transfer them to wire racks to cool completely. After cooling, the cookies can be stored in an airtight container at room temperature for several days.

NOTE: It is worth splurging a bit on the fancy higher-fat European-style butter in these cookies. The richer flavor and superior texture that the additional butterfat provides will be your reward. The baking temperature of 275°F is not a typo. The low-and-slow approach results in a marvelous texture that's not too crisp or too sandy.

Steep Learning Curve

Tea is a very versatile ingredient but one that is often overlooked in baking. As we do for wine, we recommend baking with only tea that you like to drink. While we're partial to Earl Grey, nearly any black tea could work in this cookie, from a traditional orange pekoe to a hearty Irish break-fast blend. For this recipe, shy away from herbal and green teas—their delicate flavors often can't withstand the heat of the oven.

COOKIE BYTE

Cookie Stamps

A cookie stamp can add a very sophisticated look to a cookie with little effort. They are designed to be pushed into a portion of dough to create a design or impression. Stamps work best with doughs that don't spread while baking. In addition to these shortbread cookies, the recipes in the Rolled Cookies chapter are designed to spread very little, and they are also ideal for stamping. Instead of rolling flat, portion the dough into 1½-tablespoon balls, using a #40 scoop, roll into smooth balls, and stamp as directed. Cookie stamps can be made from a variety of materials, from metal to plastic to silicone. The highest-quality stamps are not only beautiful but also feature designs with a lot of depth that create wonderful textures once the cookies are stamped and baked.

Variation: Best Vanilla Bean Shortbread

To convert this cookie into the best-tasting vanilla shortbread, simply omit the tea and increase the vanilla to 1 tablespoon. For a bolder vanilla flavor, you can replace the vanilla extract with vanilla paste.

A Puff Piece

COOKIE BYTE

You probably already understand more about chemistry and physics than you might realize. When a cookie rises (or puffs) in the oven, that is physics and chemistry at work! Cookies rise from three different types of leavening gases: air, steam, and carbon dioxide.

Air is beaten into uncooked doughs and batters while they are being mixed; mostly when butter and sugar crystals are creamed together, forming millions of tiny pockets in the dough. Whereas cakes are very dependent on a proper creaming with lots of air beaten in, cookies are less exacting. We don't often want a cakelike cookie that's fluffy and light, so we cream the butter and sugar for less time and, as a result, beat less air into the dough. When exposed to the heat of the oven, the air in these pockets expands and causes a cookie to rise. These air pockets are also important for the other leavening gases of steam and carbon dioxide.

Steam is exactly what you know it to be: the result of heating water. Water can be added to cookie doughs directly through the addition of liquid, such as milk or cream, but is also present in butter, eggs, brown sugar, and honey. When the water in these ingredients heats up, the resulting steam fills up and expands the air pockets that were beaten into the dough. These air pockets swell and cause the cookie to puff and rise. As the dough dries out, browns, and crisps, the air and steam escape and the walls of those little balloons form the internal structure of the baked cookie. Changing the moisture content of the dough can affect how much a cookie rises. For example, adding additional moisture can make a cookie cakier because it produces more steam. Reducing the amount of liquid can make a cookie drier and chewier because there is less steam to contribute to a cookie's rise.

Carbon dioxide is formed by chemical leavening agents, such as baking soda or baking powder (see page 20). All leavening agents, when added in different amounts or combinations, are used to vary the size, density, and other structural qualities of cookies.

Pumpkin Snickercrinkles

MAKES ABOUT 36 (2¼-INCH)
COOKIES

snickercrinklification (snik·er·krink·li·fi·kay·shun) *noun* **1.** the process by which a yummy cookie is made with traits of both a snickerdoodle and crinkle cookie

Traditional crinkle cookies are made by coating portions of chocolate dough in confectioners' sugar just before baking. As the cookies puff in the oven, dark chocolate fissures emerge in the sugary white surface to create a texture not unlike a crinkled volcanic landscape. For these treats, we combined the warm cinnamon-sugar flavors of a classic snickerdoodle with the puffed cracked surface of a chocolate crinkle. Swapping out the chocolate for pumpkin and nutty brown butter makes a cookie that is the definition of pure snickercrinklification!

INGREDIENT	VOLUME	WEIGHT
Unbleached all-purpose flour	2¼ cups	319 grams
Baking soda	1¼ teaspoons	
Salt	½ teaspoon	
Unsalted butter	6 tablespoons	85 grams
Dark brown sugar	Packed 1½ cups	300 grams
Ground cinnamon	1 tablespoon	
Canned pumpkin puree (not pie filling)	⅔ cup	163 grams
Egg yolks, at room temperature	3 large	45 grams
Pure vanilla extract	¾ teaspoon	
Confectioners' sugar	½ cup	57 grams

1. Position two racks to divide the oven into thirds and preheat to 350°F. Line two 18-by-13-inch baking sheets with parchment paper or silicone baking mats.

2. Whisk together 2 cups (283 grams) of the flour, the baking soda, and salt in a medium bowl; set aside

3. To make brown butter (see "Better Baking with Brown Butter," page 19), melt the butter in a small saucepan with a light-colored bottom (so you will be able to see the butter browning) over medium heat. Continue to cook and it will start to bubble noisily as the water boils off. Once the bubbling begins to quiet down, swirl the pan constantly for about 1 minute, or until the milk solids at the bottom of the pan have turned golden brown and the butter has a nutty aroma. Remove the pan from the heat and add the

(continued)

brown sugar and 2 teaspoons of the cinnamon. Stir with a whisk or silicone spatula, making sure to scrape all of those luscious, browned bits off the bottom of the pan. Transfer the mixture to the bowl of a stand mixer.

4. Stir together the remaining ¼ cup (36 grams) of flour and the pumpkin puree in a small, microwave-safe bowl. Microwave this mixture on high (100%) power, stirring every 30 seconds, until the mixture has thickened into a paste, about 2 minutes (see "The Tangzhong Technique," page 125). If you don't have a microwave, cook the mixture in a small nonstick pan over medium heat for about 2 minutes, stirring constantly with a silicone spatula. Transfer the pumpkin paste to the brown sugar mixture. Fit the stand mixer with a flat beater and beat the mixtures together on medium speed to break up the pumpkin paste and incorporate the sugar. Allow this mixture to cool completely before proceeding, 10 to 15 minutes.

5. Once cool, mix the egg yolks and the vanilla into the batter on medium speed. Reduce the mixer speed to low and mix in the flour mixture. Use a silicone spatula to scrape the sides of the bowl and the beater to make sure all the dry ingredients have been incorporated.

6. Whisk together the remaining 1 teaspoon of cinnamon and the confectioners' sugar in a shallow bowl. Portion 1½ tablespoons (22 grams) of dough, using a #40 scoop, and drop them directly into the bowl of cinnamon-sugar. (The dough is a little too soft to roll in your hands.) Gently roll them around to get them completely coated and place them 2 inches apart on the prepared baking sheets (you can fit 13 on each sheet; see page 86).

7. Bake until the cookies have puffed, cracked, and the edges are set, 11 to 15 minutes. Halfway through baking, rotate the pans from front to back and top to bottom. Remove from the oven and let cool for 10 minutes on the baking sheets before transferring to a wire rack to cool completely. Repeat with the remaining dough once the baking sheets have completely cooled, or prepare additional baking sheets. After cooling, the cookies can be stored in an airtight container at room temperature for several days.

The Tangzhong Technique

We first learned about the Japanese technique called *tangzhong* from the folks at America's Test Kitchen when making their recipe for Japanese Milk Bread (delicious, by the way). The technique involves heating a portion of the flour and the liquid together to form a paste. Once cooled, this paste can be incorporated into the rest of the dough.

As they explained, flour can absorb more water when it is hot. This allows bakers to create a dough with higher hydration (in other words, more water in the dough) that was not as sticky to work with because that water was already hidden in the paste. Neat concept! Further research from King Arthur Baking Company provided some additional details. The extra liquid that is trapped in the gelatinized starch is not contributing to gluten formation in the kneading process; can be released as steam when the dough gets hot enough; and most interestingly, helps to delay the staling process. It occurred to us that all of these tangzhong properties that were so useful in breadmaking might also be useful in cookies.

There are many very flavorful ingredients that are hard to get into a cookie recipe because they are just too wet, most notably fresh fruits. Simply adding a mashed banana to a sugar cookie recipe introduces great authentic banana flavor. However, because bananas are almost 80 percent water, the cookie becomes soft and cakey. Sometimes that is fine, but not if the goal is a crisp banana cookie. By incorporating the tangzhong method, we were able to create a crisp banana cookie, the Banana Pick-a-Chips (page 165), without a hint of cakiness. Comparing the straight banana cookie (where banana is simply added as an extra ingredient) to one modified with the tangzhong method was striking. The tangzhong cookie tastes like a real banana but was thin, crisp, and held its shape. We use this technique throughout the book for recipes that require moisture-laden ingredients, such as bananas, lemons, pumpkin, and liquids like grenadine, but where we don't want a cakey texture.

Curiously, it's also possible to do the exact opposite with tangzhong. The technique can also be used to transform a crisp cookie into a softer, cakier cookie. Simply adding more liquid to a crisp cookie dough would make it too wet and sticky to scoop properly. By introducing the extra moisture in the tangzhong, the qualities of the dough remain unchanged, but the steam released during baking is enough to make a cakier texture. For people who prefer more tender, cake-style cookies (we've met some, so we know they exist), this could be a useful way to adapt your recipes.

Golden Bites

This small chewy cookie is a prime example of cookie alchemy—turning simple ingredients into delicious gold. (Actually, a golden-brown cookie. Not actual gold, of course. We're not sorcerers.) These small cookies shine with the mild earthiness of turbinado sugar and the zip of tart lemon melded together with just a smidge of nuttiness from almonds. Instead of any one flavor dominating, they synergize into harmonious little golden bites.

INGREDIENT	VOLUME	WEIGHT
Unbleached all-purpose flour	2¼ cups	319 grams
Salt	1 teaspoon	
Baking soda	¾ teaspoon	
Lemon	1 medium	
Turbinado sugar	⅔ cup	133 grams
Unsalted butter, at room temperature	12 tablespoons	170 grams
Golden syrup (see page 18)	½ cup	168 grams
Egg yolk, at room temperature	1 large	15 grams
Almond extract	¼ teaspoon	
Almond flour (see Note)	¼ cup	28 grams

1. Position two racks to divide the oven into thirds and preheat to 350°F. Line two 18-by-13-inch baking sheets with parchment paper or silicone baking mats.

2. Whisk together the flour, salt, and baking soda in a medium bowl; set aside.

3. Remove the peel of the entire lemon, including the yellow zest and just a bit of the underlying pith, using a vegetable peeler or paring knife. Place the peel and the turbinado sugar in the small bowl of a food processor. Process the mixture until it is finely ground, about 1 minute. Transfer the mixture to the bowl of a stand mixer fitted with a flat beater. The remainder of the lemon can be saved for another use.

4. Add the butter to the lemon mixture and beat on medium speed until smooth and creamy, 1 to 2 minutes. Beat in the golden syrup, egg yolk, and almond extract until the mixture is smooth and uniform.

5. Reduce the mixer speed to low and mix in the flour mixture until no dry flour is visible. Scrape the sides of the bowl and the beater with a silicone spatula to make sure all of the dry ingredients are incorporated.

6. Place the almond flour in a shallow bowl. Portion 2 teaspoons (11 grams) of dough, using a #100 cookie scoop, and drop them directly onto the almond flour. Roll the dough to ensure an even coat of almond flour and place the dough balls on the baking sheet (you

can fit 18 cookies on each sheet; see page 86). Gently flatten each dough ball to half of its original height by pressing on the top with your fingers or the bottom of a drinking glass lightly sprayed with nonstick cooking spray.

7. Bake until the edges of the cookies are golden and set, 8 to 12 minutes. Halfway through baking, rotate the pans from front to back and top to bottom. Remove from the oven and let cool for 10 minutes on the baking sheets before transferring to a wire rack to cool completely. Repeat with the remaining dough once the baking sheets have completely cooled, or prepare additional baking sheets. After cooling, the cookies can be stored in an airtight container at room temperature for several days.

NOTE: If you don't have almond flour available, you can substitute ¼ cup of finely ground almonds.

Peanut Satay Cruncers

MAKES 44 (2¼-INCH) COOKIES

While several parts of the world feature peanuts regularly in savory foods, many Americans are only familiar with peanuts and peanut butter in desserts or sweeter foods, such as PB&J sandwiches. Satay—skewered and grilled meat—enjoyed in Indonesia, Thailand, and other parts of Southeast Asia, is regularly served with an enchanting spiced peanut sauce that inspires this modern take on the classic peanut butter cookie. This cookie's subtle orange blush hints at its complex (but not overwhelming) spice provided by a hit of fiery red curry paste. The warm spice is bolstered by the crunch of roasted peanuts and subtle notes of coconut.

INGREDIENT	VOLUME	WEIGHT
Unbleached all-purpose flour	1 cup plus 2 tablespoons	159 grams
Baking powder	½ teaspoon	
Baking soda	½ teaspoon	
Salt	¼ teaspoon	
Unsalted butter, at room temperature	8 tablespoons	113 grams
Granulated sugar	½ cup	100 grams
Light brown sugar	Packed ½ cup	100 grams
Creamy peanut butter	½ cup	135 grams
Egg, at room temperature	1 large	50 grams (weighted without shell)
Red curry paste (see Note)	4 teaspoons	
Roasted salted peanuts, coarsely chopped	⅔ cup	85 grams
Unsweetened coconut flakes	½ cup	28 grams

1. Position two racks to divide the oven into thirds and preheat to 350°F. Line two 18-by-13-inch baking sheets with parchment paper or silicone baking mats.

2. Whisk together the flour, baking powder, baking soda, and salt in a medium bowl; set aside.

3. Combine the butter, granulated sugar, brown sugar, and peanut butter in a stand mixer fitted with a flat beater, and beat together on medium speed until smooth and creamy, 1 to 2 minutes. Beat in the egg and curry paste until combined.

4. Reduce the mixer to its lowest speed, then stir in the flour mixture followed by the peanuts and coconut. Scrape down the sides of the bowl and the beater with a silicone spatula to be sure that no unincorporated bits of flour or butter are hiding out.

5. Portion 1 tablespoon (18 grams) of dough, using a #60 scoop, roll into balls, and evenly arrange 13 portions on the prepared baking sheets (see page 86).

6. Bake until the edges of the cookies are set and just beginning to turn a light golden-brown, 12 to 15 minutes. Halfway through baking, rotate the pans from front to back and top to bottom. Remove from the oven and let cool for 5 minutes on the baking sheets before transferring to a wire rack using a thin metal spatula. Repeat with the remaining dough once the baking sheets have completely cooled, or prepare additional baking sheets. After cooling completely, the cookies can be stored in a sealed container at room temperature for several days.

NOTE: We tested this recipe using commercially made (rather than homemade) red curry paste. Thai Kitchen brand red curry paste is accessible in many supermarkets, and its spice level works well in these cookies.

Raspberry Lemonades

MAKES 2½ DOZEN (3-INCH) COOKIES

These cookies are made with one of the most unusual—but most flavorful—ingredients we've ever used: a whole boiled lemon. The idea for boiling a whole lemon came from Mary Ann Esposito, host of *Ciao Italia*, the longest running cooking show on TV (and one of our personal favorites). Mary Ann was making a traditional Sicilian lemon cake that included a whole lemon that was boiled and pureed. We don't mean blanching a lemon by tossing it in hot water for a few minutes—the lemon is actually boiled for 45 minutes! We tried it ourselves, and boiling a lemon is a very efficient way to remove some of the lemon's bitter flavors (especially those found in the pith) while retaining its striking citrus zing. Pairing the lemon with flavorful freeze-dried raspberries, these soft and chewy cookies are bursting with remarkable flavor.

INGREDIENT	VOLUME	WEIGHT
Lemon (see Note)	1 large	
Unbleached all-purpose flour	2¼ cups	319 grams
Sugar	1¾ cups	350 grams
Freeze-dried raspberries (see "Freeze-Dried Fruits," page 133)	1¾ cups	28 grams
Baking powder	1 teaspoon	
Baking soda	½ teaspoon	
Salt	½ teaspoon	
Unsalted butter, at room temperature	8 tablespoons	113 grams
Sour cream (full fat), cold from the refrigerator	¼ cup plus 1 tablespoon	75 grams
Vegetable oil	¼ cup	50 grams
Egg, cold from the refrigerator	1 large	50 grams (weighed without shell)
Pure vanilla extract	1 tablespoon	

1. Place the whole lemon in a tall saucepan. Add 2 inches of water to the pan to allow the lemon to float. Bring the water to a boil over medium heat. Cover the pan, lower the heat to low, and simmer the lemon for 45 minutes. The lemon will balloon as it cooks—this is completely normal. Remove the lemon with a slotted spoon and place it on a cutting board to cool.

2. When the lemon is cool enough to handle, chop it into several large chunks. Remove and discard all of the seeds. Finely mince the whole lemon—pulp, peel, and pith—and scrape it into a small, microwave-safe bowl (see "Puttin' on the Blitz"). Stir in 2 tablespoons (18 grams) of the flour. Microwave the lemon mixture

(continued)

on high (100%) power, stirring every 20 seconds, until it has thickened into a paste, about 1 minute (see "The Tangzhong Technique," page 125). If you don't have a microwave, cook the mixture in a small nonstick pan over medium heat for about 2 minutes, stirring constantly with a silicone spatula. Transfer the lemon paste to the bowl of your stand mixer and fit the mixer with a flat beater. Add 1½ cups (300 grams) of the sugar and beat on medium speed to break up the lemon paste and incorporate the sugar. Allow this mixture to cool completely before proceeding, 10 to 15 minutes.

3. While the lemon mixture is cooling, pour the freeze-dried raspberries into the bowl of a food processor. Finely grind the raspberries into a powder. Using a silicone spatula, scrape the powder out of the food processor into a fine-mesh sieve placed over a medium bowl. Strain out and discard the raspberry seeds. (It's okay if some of the smaller seeds make it through the holes of your sieve, but too many dried seeds add an unpleasant texture to the cookies.)

4. Add the remaining 2 cups plus 2 tablespoons (301 grams) of the flour, the baking powder, baking soda, and salt to the raspberry powder. Whisk them all together and set aside.

5. Add the butter to the cooled lemon mixture and continue to mix until smooth and creamy, 1 to 2 minutes more. Depending on how finely chopped the lemon is, you will likely still see the lemon pieces. Beat in the sour cream, vegetable oil, egg, and vanilla until the mixture is uniform.

6. Reduce the mixer speed to low, and stir in the flour mixture until no dry flour is visible. Scrape the sides of the bowl and the beater with a silicone spatula, incorporating any stray ingredients. Allow the dough to rest for 15 minutes before scooping while the oven preheats.

7. Position two racks to divide the oven into thirds and preheat to 350°F. Line two 18-by-13-inch baking sheets with parchment paper or silicone baking mats.

8. Place the remaining ¼ cup (50 grams) of the sugar in a small shallow bowl. Portion 2 tablespoons (31 grams) of dough, using a #30 scoop. Roll the dough portions between the palms of your hands to form a ball. Roll the ball in the sugar and then place it on the baking sheet (you can fit eight cookies per sheet; see page 86).

9. Bake until the cookies are set at the edges but not yet beginning to brown, 12 to 14 minutes. Halfway through baking, rotate the pans from front to back and top to bottom. Remove from the oven and let

Puttin' on the Blitz

Instead of mincing the lemon by hand, you can also blitz it in a food chopper or a small food processor. If using the food processor, make sure the bowl that you use to grind the freeze-dried raspberries is clean and completely dry; otherwise, the berries will form clumps.

cool for 10 minutes on the sheet before transferring to a wire rack to cool completely. Repeat with the remaining dough once the baking sheets have completely cooled, or prepare additional baking sheets. After cooling, the cookies can be stored in an airtight container at room temperature for several days.

NOTE: If you can't find a large lemon (about 5 ounces or 140 grams), just use the largest of the lemons that are available to you. Don't use two small lemons. That would make the dough too wet.

COOKIE BYTE

Freeze-Dried Fruits

In the past decade, there has been a revolution in the freeze-dried fruit industry. We first started noticing it in the cereal aisle in the grocery store. Almost every variety of boring old healthy adult cereal started releasing new and improved versions featuring real strawberries, peaches, or blueberries. Freeze-drying technology has been around forever, but improvements in efficiency and product quality have resulted in a real boom. How does it work? They start by taking fresh fruits that are at their peak and freezing them superfast. Fast freezing makes smaller ice crystals that don't damage the fruit so much. Through the use of vacuums and a process called sublimation, the ice (which is all of the moisture in the fruit) is then removed from the fruit, resulting in the completely dried crispy piece of fruit. Because this process involves no heating step, colors remain vibrant and the flavor compounds are mostly intact. Because

they still taste a lot like fresh fruits but without added moisture, freeze-dried fruits have become popular both in industry and in baking. Many bakers, including us, have been experimenting with these fruits in pies, cakes, and cookies.

Usually, the freeze-dried fruits are ground into powders and added directly to a dough in an attempt to introduce potent fruit flavors and colors without resorting to artificial ingredients and the added water that comes along with fresh fruits. It doesn't always work. Blueberries, while delicious, can create an off-putting gray cookie when added to a dough that uses egg yolks. Additionally, because baking involves intense heat, some fruit flavor compounds can bake off and end up completely lost. We find this to be especially true of freeze-dried strawberries and peaches. Raspberry is one of the few freeze-dried fruits that seems to retain strong flavor when baked into a cookie.

CHAPTER THREE
rolled cookies

Rolled cookies, also known as roll-outs or cookie-cutter cookies, are probably the kind that we make most often. Cookie decorating is one of Chris's artistic passions, and after thousands of cookies and years of experience, we are so happy to share the tips and techniques that we use to make these cookies. Although the cookie is simply rolled flat, the infinite number of shapes and varied methods of decoration make rolled cookies the most promising for artistic adornment.

Helpful Tools

- **Parchment paper.** Optional, but helps roll out dough without adding additional flour that can dry out the dough.
- **Rolling pins.** Roll out soft cookie dough to thin, even layers.
- **Rolling pin spacers.** Ensure layers of rolled dough have an even thickness.
- **Cookie cutters.** Cut out shapes from rolled dough, using metal or plastic forms.
- **Piping bags.** Hold glazes and icings for piping onto a cookie (see "Plastic Alternatives," page 216).
- **Piping tips.** Help when you are looking to pipe a filling with a unique pattern or design. These are not required, but they do add an extra-special touch.

Tips and Techniques

Lessen the leavening. When we make the cookies for decorating, we usually do not use the optional baking powder. Baking powder can cause the tops of cookies to lightly puff, resulting in a slightly domed top that is not ideal when using icing to decorate, because the icing will run. We like the tops of the cookies as flat as possible. Baking powder can also cause a little bit of spread, making the cookies larger than their cookie cutter shape. When making very detailed cookies with intricate shapes, it's important to minimize spread to help the cookies keep their shape as they bake. We give the option in our recipes to use baking

Rolling Pin   *Piping Bag and Tips*

powder. The little bit of puff can create a softer texture that you might prefer.

Double up. For larger projects, we will often make a double batch of cookie dough. We simply double the ingredients (by weight) in the recipe, mix as directed, and divide the dough into three pieces before rolling. Note that smaller stand mixers might not have the capacity to properly mix the 6 cups of flour needed for a double batch.

Roll fresh. Many traditional recipes for rolled cookies call for making the dough, wrapping the dough, chilling the dough, and then rolling out the dough once it's cold and hard. It's certainly doable, but we find it so much easier to roll the dough right after we are finished mixing it. The soft dough is easy to roll. To help with rolling, we roll portions of dough between two sheets of waxed or parchment paper. When rolling between paper, no additional flour is necessary to prevent the dough from sticking to the counter. After rolling, the sheets of dough are stacked on top of each other on a baking sheet and chilled in the refrigerator until they are ready to be cut.

Roll even. Because an evenly rolled dough is a must, we use rolling pin rings, guides, or spacers to make sure that the sheets of dough have an even thickness from edge to edge. Rolling pin rings slip around the ends of your rolling pin and lift the pin off the counter at a specified height. This prevents the pin from rolling the dough too thin. Guides and spacers, which are long pieces of wood, metal, or plastic work the same way. The guides are laid on either side of your rolling surface and allow the rolling pin to stay a specified thickness above the dough. You don't need anything fancy—a ¼-inch dowel from the hardware store does the job just fine.

Roll thick (or not). We prefer to roll our cookies to ¼-inch thickness, but some people prefer thicker or thinner cookies. You can experiment and roll cookie dough to any thickness as long as the dough is rolled evenly. If you roll your dough thicker or thinner than what we recommend, your cookies might require changes in baking time. Cookies that are very thick (approaching ½ inch) might not only require increased time in the oven but also a reduced baking temperature to prevent excess browning on the edges before the center is fully baked.

Cut cold. We prefer to cut out shapes from the dough once it is rolled and then chilled and firm. When cold dough is cut with a cookie cutter, it will often stay inside the cutter as it's lifted from the dough sheet.

This makes it very easy to position the cut dough on the baking sheet and gently press it off the cutter with your fingertips. Because the dough is cold, you don't have to worry about making dents in the dough when you touch it. In contrast, room-temperature dough can flop and stretch out of shape as it's moved. When cold and firm, the dough keeps its shape as it's moved from the counter to the baking pan. Cold dough also keeps its shape and spreads the least when baked.

Know your cutters. Not all cookie cutters are made equal! In general, cookie cutters are either made of metal (often aluminum, copper, or stainless steel) or plastic. Each substance has its pros and cons, and the only bad cookie cutter is one that doesn't cut well. Metal cutters are sturdy and can even cut through frozen sheets of cookie dough, but some can rust or tarnish and can be easily misshaped. Plastic cutters can cut through refrigerated doughs but not frozen ones. Some plastic cutters, particularly those made using a 3-D printer, cannot handle very hot water for washing and can be brittle if not handled with care.

Mat finish. We prefer to bake our rolled cookies on perforated silicone baking mats. The perforations in the mat allow the cookie to bake flat on the bottom without forming air bubbles. This is especially helpful when using rerolled dough that might have some air bubbles worked into it.

Group work. Because we are often making cookies of multiple shapes and sizes, we usually have three baking sheets nearby as we are cutting out our cookies:

one sheet each for small, medium, and large shapes. We bake cookies of similar sizes together so all the cookies on the sheet bake for the same amount of time. Mixing cookies of different sizes will result in overbaked small cookies or underbaked large ones. Because the cookies spread very little while baking, you can arrange shapes as close as 1 inch apart on the baking sheet without worry. When cutting from a sheet of dough, begin by cutting out the largest shapes first and then cutting the small shapes from the areas of dough that remain.

Eye for details. When we arrange the cut-out shapes on the pans, we try to arrange small shapes or details in the middle of the baking sheet. Very small parts, such as the tips of flower petals, can brown too quickly if they are near the rimmed edge of the metal baking sheet.

Bake cold. After the cookies are cut and arranged on the baking sheets, we will often stack the pans in the freezer. Baking the cookies directly from the freezer ensures that cookie edges set fast and result in very, very little spread. Parking the dough in the freezer also gives us the ability to cut the cookies one day and bake the next. It's a great way to allow us to plan our time, especially for large projects. Not everyone has a freezer than can hold a stack of baking sheets, though, and baking rolled cookies directly from the freezer is not crucial. Frozen cookie dough will need to bake for 5 to 15 minutes more than what is listed in each recipe (depending on the size of the cookie).

Reroll. Because no additional flour is used when rolling out the dough, rerolling dough scraps is easy because the dough hasn't been dried out with additional flour. Be gentle, though—cookies can become tough if they are overworked. We will reroll dough three or four times without worry.

Poke (when necessary). When we rotate the pans halfway through baking, if there are any bubbles on the surface of the cookies, we prick them with a metal cake tester or the tip of a toothpick and carefully press on the bubble to flatten it.

Cool down. After we bake the cookies, we let them cool completely on the baking sheets. If you need to use the baking sheets, wait for the cookies to cool for at least 5 minutes before transferring them to a wire rack. Large shapes (over 4 inches) might need a few minutes longer to cool and are especially fragile when moved. Once completely cool, the cookies can be decorated (or eaten) right away or stored in an airtight container at room temperature before decorating.

Royal occasion. More than 90 percent of the cookies that we decorate are decorated with Royal Icing (page 334) made with meringue powder and usually flavored with pure vanilla or lemon extract. We also decorate cookies with glaze, but royal icing is the medium we use most often. We do occasionally decorate a whole cookie with rolled fondant, but most often use fondant to create small accent pieces that are applied after the royal icing has completely dried.

Dry time. After decorating, we leave our cookies to dry, uncovered, overnight. The royal icing acts as a wonderful seal to keep the cookies fresh. Royal icing needs air circulation to properly dry. If you cover cookies before the icing has completely dried, the icing might not fully dry or might wrinkle and mar the beautifully smooth surface you created.

Yield. When using cookie cutters of different sizes and shapes, it can be difficult to tell exactly how many cookies you will be able to get from one batch of dough. An easy way is to cut out one shape and weigh the raw cookie on a scale (preferably in grams—the cookie will not be heavy). Divide the total weight of the dough by the weight for the unbaked shape to determine how many cookies you can get from one recipe of dough. Remember that different recipes will give different weights for the same shape, so don't assume that the one recipe will give the same yield as another.

COOKIE BYTE

Cookiefficiency

Tessellating is the process of creating patterns of repeating interlocking shapes with no space between them. You see it mostly in tile floors or M. C. Escher drawings. However, it is also useful for making cutter cookies and trying to calculate an expected yield for a cutter cookie recipe. Depending on the size and shape of the cutters and the skill of the baker, a single sheet of cookie dough can yield different numbers of cookies and different amounts of leftover dough. Granted, cookie dough can usually be mashed back together and rerolled, but it is always preferable to get as many cookies as possible out of a single round. Tessellating-shaped cutters allow you to cut a cookie right up against the space where the previous one was removed, resulting in no wasted dough scraps. Rolling the dough into a perfect square and using a small square cookie cutter would give you near-perfect cookiefficiency and use up all of the dough with no waste or rerolling. But where is the joy in that? We all want to be able to use our fun cookie cutter shapes (most of which are not tessellating) for holidays, parties, or just the pure enjoyment of cookie decorating.

Very Vanilla Cookie Artists' Best Butter Cookies

MAKES ABOUT 30 (3-INCH)
ROUND COOKIES

This is our ever-faithful, never-fail decorator's butter cookie. This butter cookie is the base for so many of the cookies that we have decorated over the years. It's a perfect blank canvas that works flawlessly with a variety of decorations, including royal icing, glaze, buttercream, and rolled fondant. Because it holds its shape marvelously without spreading or puffing, even intricately cut cookies will bake up looking just like the cookie cutter. While they are of our secret weapons for making beautiful cookies, their tender, buttery goodness makes them delicious enough to enjoy naked (the cookies, not you). In addition to the Orange Harvest Spice variation, this cookie base can be adapted into an almost endless variety of flavors (see "Endless Possibilities").

INGREDIENT	VOLUME	WEIGHT
Unbleached all-purpose flour	2¾ cups plus 1 tablespoon	400 grams
Salt	½ teaspoon	
Baking powder (optional; see "Staying in Shape," page 142)	¼ to ½ teaspoon	
Unsalted butter, at room temperature	16 tablespoons	227 grams
Sugar	1 cup	200 grams
Egg, at room temperature	1 large	50 grams (weighed without shell)
Vanilla bean paste or pure vanilla extract	1 tablespoon	

1. Whisk together the flour, salt, and baking powder (if using) in a medium bowl; set aside.

2. Combine the butter and sugar in a stand mixer fitted with a flat beater, and cream together on medium speed until smooth and creamy, 1 to 2 minutes. Beat in the egg and vanilla just until the mixture is uniform. Scrape down the sides of the bowl with a silicone spatula.

3. Reduce the mixer speed to low and mix in half of the flour mixture until just combined. Stop mixing and scrape down the sides of the bowl and the beater with a silicone spatula. Mix in the remaining flour mixture just until no dry flour is visible. Scrape the sides of the bowl.

4. Divide the dough in half. Roll each half of the dough to a ¼-inch thickness between two sheets of parchment or waxed paper. Stack the paper-covered sheets of dough on an 18-by-13-inch baking sheet, and refrigerate until cold and firm throughout, at least 2 hours or up to 3 days.

5. Position two racks to divide the oven into thirds and preheat to 350°F. Line two 18-by-13-inch baking sheets with parchment paper or silicone baking mats.

(continued)

6. Release the dough from one sheet of parchment paper by peeling the paper from the top of one layer of chilled dough. Lay the paper back onto the dough and flip the whole dough sheet over so that loosened sheet of paper is now underneath it. Peel off the top layer of parchment paper. Cut your desired shapes from the dough and transfer them to the prepared baking sheets, leaving about 1 inch of space between cookies.

7. Bake until the edges are just starting to lightly brown, 10 to 20 minutes, depending on the size of the cookie. Halfway through baking, rotate the pans from front to back and top to bottom. Remove from the oven and let cool completely on the baking sheets to allow the cookies to properly bake through. If you have to transfer the cookies to a wire rack, keep in mind that large (over 4 inches) and delicate shapes will be particularly fragile while still warm. Repeat with the remaining dough, rerolling the scraps of dough, if necessary, once the baking sheets have completely cooled, or prepare additional baking sheets. The cookies will keep their shape best during baking if put into the oven while still cold. After cooling, the cookies can be stored in an airtight container at room temperature for 2 weeks.

COOKIE BYTE

Staying in Shape

Cookies made without baking powder are best when using cookie cutters with small details or intricate shapes, because the cookies will keep their shape and won't spread. Even without baking powder, these cookies have a soft and tender texture but are firm enough to hold up to handling while being decorated.

Variation: Orange Harvest Spice

Spices, such as cinnamon, nutmeg, and cloves, pair perfectly with orange to make wonderful autumn-inspired cookies for back-to-school, Halloween, and Thanksgiving.

To the flour and salt, whisk in 2 teaspoons of ground cinnamon, ½ teaspoon of ground nutmeg, ¼ teaspoon of ground allspice, and ¼ teaspoon of ground cloves. Place the sugar and the freshly grated zest of 1 medium orange in a separate bowl. For the most orange flavor, rub the sugar and the zest between your thumbs and fingertips until the sugar is fragrant, light orange in color, and has a texture like wet sand (see "Live Your Zest Life," page 25). Cream the butter and orange-infused sugar together. Follow the recipe and bake as directed.

Endless Possibilities

This cookie can be modified in a variety of ways to create nearly endless possibilities for different flavors and textures. Some ideas:

- 1 cup of finely chopped nuts, dried fruits, or chocolate stirred into the dough after the flour is incorporated (make sure the pieces are small or the cookie edges will get mangled when you cut out shapes from the dough).
- Freshly grated citrus zest from 1 medium orange, lemon, or lime, beaten into the butter mixture.
- Swap out the vanilla for 1 teaspoon of lemon, almond, or peppermint extract.
- Whisk 1 tablespoon of a spice mixture of your choice into the flour mixture. Apple pie spice and pumpkin pie spice are great starts.

Deep Chocolate Fantasy Rolled Cookies

Toss the spices and make your gingerbread guys and gals from this at your next holiday party! A hit of chocolaty goodness from Dutch-processed cocoa powder with a little boost from espresso powder provides these rolled cookies with a deep chocolate flavor as well as a velvety dark brown color.

MAKES ABOUT 30 (3-INCH) ROUND COOKIES

INGREDIENT	VOLUME	WEIGHT
Unbleached all-purpose flour	2 cups plus 2 tablespoons	301 grams
Dutch-processed cocoa powder	⅔ cup	57 grams
Instant espresso powder	1 teaspoon	
Salt	½ teaspoon	
Baking powder (optional; see "Staying in Shape," page 142)	¼ to ½ teaspoon	
Unsalted butter, at room temperature	16 tablespoons	227 grams
Light brown sugar	Packed 1 cup	200 grams
Egg, at room temperature	1 large	50 grams (weighed without shell)
Pure vanilla extract	1 tablespoon	

1. Whisk together the flour, cocoa powder, espresso powder, salt, and baking powder (if using) in a medium bowl; set aside.

2. Combine the butter and brown sugar in a stand mixer fitted with a flat beater, and cream together on medium speed until smooth and creamy, 1 to 2 minutes. Beat in the egg and vanilla just until the mixture is uniform.

3. Reduce the mixer speed to low and mix in half of the flour mixture until just combined. Scrape down the sides of the bowl and the beater with a silicone spatula. Mix in the remaining flour mixture just until no dry flour is visible.

4. Divide the dough in half. Roll each half of the dough to a ¼-inch thickness between two sheets of parchment or waxed paper. Stack the paper-covered sheets of dough on an 18-by-13-inch baking sheet, and refrigerate until cold and firm throughout, at least 2 hours or up to 3 days.

5. Position two racks to divide the oven into thirds and preheat to 350°F. Line two 18-by-13-inch baking sheets with parchment paper or silicone baking mats.

(continued)

6. Release the dough from one sheet of parchment paper by peeling the paper from the top of one layer of chilled dough. Lay the paper back onto the dough and flip the whole dough sheet over so that loosened sheet of paper is now underneath it. Peel off the top layer of parchment paper.

7. Cut your desired shapes from the dough and transfer them to the prepared baking sheets, leaving about 1 inch of space between cookies.

8. Bake until the cookies are fragrant, the edges are set, and the centers are beginning to firm but are not squishy when gently pressed, 10 to 20 minutes, depending on the size of the cookie. Halfway through baking, rotate the pans from front to back and top to bottom. Remove from the oven and let cool completely on the baking sheets to allow the cookies to properly bake through. If you have to transfer the cookies to a wire rack, keep in mind that large (over 4 inches) and delicate shapes will be particularly fragile while still warm. Repeat with the remaining dough, rerolling the scraps of dough, if necessary, once the baking sheets have completely cooled, or prepare additional baking sheets. The cookies will keep their shape best during baking if put into the oven while still cold. After cooling, the cookies can be stored in an airtight container at room temperature for 2 weeks.

Bronze Butter Pecan Cut-Outs

MAKES ABOUT 30 (3-INCH) ROUND COOKIES

Every good fireworks show is always capped by a spectacular finale during which layer after layer of sparkle, boom, and flash are combined into one gigantic sensory overload. Not to oversell it, but this simple-looking, brown-speckled cut-out is a fireworks finale in cookie form. We start this cookie by toasting the pecans, filling the house with warm nuttiness. The next layer is not just brown butter. We pull out the turbocharged bronze butter (see "Bronze Butter," page 89) to combine with rich brown sugar for an intensely toffee-flavored cookie base. A satisfying splash of bourbon is the final layer that launches this cookie heavenward.

INGREDIENT	VOLUME	WEIGHT
Unsalted butter, cut into chunks	16 tablespoons	227 grams
Nonfat dry milk powder, sifted through a fine-mesh sieve to remove lumps	½ cup	46 grams
Light brown sugar	Packed ¾ cup plus 2 tablespoons	175 grams
Pecan pieces, toasted and cooled (see page 24)	¾ cup	85 grams
Unbleached all-purpose flour	2½ cups	354 grams
Salt	½ teaspoon	
Baking powder (optional; see "Staying in Shape," page 142)	¼ teaspoon	
Egg, at room temperature	1 large	50 grams (weighed without shell)
Bourbon or pure vanilla extract	1 tablespoon	
Water	1 tablespoon	

1. To make bronze butter, melt the butter in a small saucepan with a light-colored bottom (so you will be able to see the butter browning) over medium-low heat. Whisk the milk powder into the melted butter. The milk powder will clump and float on the surface of the butter. Bring to a boil, whisking occasionally. Once the mixture starts to boil, begin whisking constantly until the bubbling has slowed, the mixture smells nutty, and all of the solids have become chestnut brown, about 5 minutes.

2. Remove the saucepan from the heat, and immediately whisk in the brown sugar, being sure to scrape up all the flavorful bits of bronzed butter on the bottom of the pan. Transfer the mixture to the bowl of your stand mixer and cool until the mixture is barely

(continued)

warm, about 30 minutes. (The mixture will appear separated because there is no liquid left in the butter to dissolve the sugar. It might also start to appear hard and crystalline—no need to worry. This will change once the egg is mixed in.)

3. Place the pecans in the bowl of a food processor, and grind as finely as possible. (Large pieces of nut will make rolling the dough difficult and can cause problems when cutting the dough, especially if you are using a plastic cookie cutter that cannot cut through nuts.) Add the flour, salt, and baking powder (if using) to the pecans. Process the mixture with a few 1-second pulses to combine all the ingredients; set aside.

4. Once the butter mixture has cooled to room temperature, fit the mixer with a flat beater, and beat together the bronze butter mixture, egg, bourbon, and water on medium speed until smooth and uniform, 1 to 2 minutes. Stop mixing and scrape down the sides of the bowl and the beater with a silicone spatula.

5. Reduce the mixer speed to low and mix in half of the flour mixture until just combined. Stop mixing and scrape down the sides of the bowl and the beater with a silicone spatula. Mix in the remaining flour mixture just until no dry flour is visible.

6. Divide the dough in half. Roll each half of the dough to a ¼-inch thickness between two sheets of parchment or waxed paper. Stack the paper-covered sheets of dough on an 18-by-13-inch baking sheet, and refrigerate until cold and firm throughout, at least 2 hours or up to 3 days.

7. Position two racks to divide the oven into thirds and preheat to 350°F. Line two 18-by-13-inch baking sheets with parchment paper or silicone baking mats.

8. Release the dough from one sheet of parchment paper by peeling the paper from the top of one layer of chilled dough. Lay the paper back onto the dough and flip the whole dough sheet over so that loosened sheet of paper is now underneath it. Peel off the top layer of parchment paper. Cut your desired shapes from the dough and transfer them to the prepared baking sheets, leaving about 1 inch of space between cookies.

9. Bake until the edges are just starting to lightly brown, 10 to 20 minutes, depending on the size of the cookie. Halfway through baking, rotate the pans from front to back and top to bottom. Remove from the oven and let cool completely on the baking sheets to allow the cookies to properly bake through. If you have to transfer the cookies to a wire rack, keep in mind that large (over 4 inches) and delicate shapes will be particularly fragile when still warm. Repeat with the remaining dough, rerolling the scraps of dough, if necessary, once the baking sheets have completely cooled, or prepare additional baking sheets. The cookies will keep their shape best during baking if put into the oven while still cold. After cooling, the cookies can be stored in an airtight container at room temperature for 2 weeks.

Peanut Butter Cup Cut-Out Cookies

MAKES ABOUT 30 (3-INCH) ROUND COOKIES

Those two great tastes (that taste great together) are together again in this roll-out cookie. While playing around with peanut butter cookies in the bakery, we had the idea to add just a bit of cocoa to the recipe—not enough to make it a really chocolaty cookie—just enough to change the color and make it a bit more interesting. It shouldn't have been so surprising, but the first bite of the cookie evoked the flavor of a Reese's peanut butter cup; mostly peanut butter with just the right amount of milk chocolate goodness.

INGREDIENT	VOLUME	WEIGHT
Unbleached all-purpose flour	2½ cups	354 grams
Salt	½ teaspoon	
Creamy peanut butter	⅔ cup	180 grams
Unsalted butter, at room temperature	8 tablespoons	113 grams
Sugar	1 cup	200 grams
Dutch-processed cocoa powder	3 tablespoons	16 grams
Egg, at room temperature	1 large	50 grams (weighed without shell)
Pure vanilla extract	2 teaspoons	

1. Whisk together the flour and salt in a medium bowl; set aside.

2. Combine the butter and peanut butter in a stand mixer fitted with a flat beater, and cream together on medium speed until smooth and uniform, about 2 minutes. Add the sugar and cocoa powder and continue to beat until the sugar is incorporated and the mixture is uniform, about 1 minute. Scrape down the sides of the bowl and the beater with a silicone spatula.

3. Beat in the egg and vanilla just until the mixture is uniform. Once again, scrape down the sides of the bowl and the beater with a silicone spatula.

4. Reduce the mixer speed to low and mix in half of the flour mixture until just combined. Scrape down the sides of the bowl and the beater with a silicone spatula. Mix in the remaining flour mixture just until no dry flour is visible. The mixture will be crumbly, but when pressed together it will form a dough.

5. Divide the dough in half. Roll each half of the dough to a ¼-inch thickness between two sheets of parchment or waxed paper. Stack the paper-covered sheets of dough on an 18-by-13-inch baking sheet, and refrigerate until cold and firm throughout, at least 2 hours or up to 3 days.

6. Position two racks to divide the oven into thirds and preheat to 350°F. Line two 18-by-13-inch baking sheets with parchment paper or silicone baking mats.

7. Release the dough from one sheet of parchment paper by peeling the paper from the top of one layer of chilled dough. Lay the paper back onto the dough and flip the whole dough sheet over so that loosened sheet of paper is now underneath it. Peel off the top layer of parchment paper.

8. Leave the dough at room temperature for about 5 minutes before cutting (see Note). Cut your desired shapes from the dough and transfer them to the prepared baking sheets, leaving about 1 inch of space between cookies.

9. Bake until the cookies are fragrant, the edges are set and beginning to lightly brown, and the centers are beginning to firm but are not squishy when gently pressed, 10 to 20 minutes, depending on the size of the cookie. Halfway through baking, rotate the pans from front to back and top to bottom. Remove from the oven and let cool completely on the baking sheets to allow the cookies to properly bake through. If you have to transfer the cookies to a wire rack, keep in mind that large (over 4 inches) and delicate shapes will be particularly fragile while still warm. Repeat with the remaining dough, rerolling the scraps of dough, if necessary, once the baking sheets have completely cooled, or prepare additional baking sheets. The cookies will keep their shape best during baking if put into the oven while still cold. After cooling, the cookies can be stored in an airtight container at room temperature for 2 weeks.

NOTE: Because the dough is made with peanut butter, it is very firm directly out of the refrigerator. Using a cookie cutter when the dough is very cold can cause cracks in the dough. Allowing the dough to warm up for a few minutes will eliminate the risk of cracking but still leaves the dough cold enough to easily work with and keep its shape in the oven. If the dough cracks after waiting 5 minutes, wait 2 minutes before cutting the dough again. Dough will keep its shape and spread the least when baked cold. If desired, stash the baking sheets with the unbaked cookies in the refrigerator or freezer for 10 minutes before baking to help the cookies keep their shape.

The Cookier Community

Many may see cookie decorating as simply an annual tradition, with a couple bottles of store-bought icing and a plateful of gingerbread men set out for the kids or grandkids to have at. For many others who use cookie decorating as an expressive outlet of artistry, a part-time hobby, or a family-owned business, the commitment to cookie decorating is a passion. Regardless of the motive, the community of cookie decorators (or cookiers, as we call ourselves) is driven by the zeal for creating edible art as a form of love.

In recent years, the cookier community has grown by leaps and bounds. There are now countless social media groups, online video classes, blog tutorials, and in-person workshops with valuable information for all skill levels, from the enthusiastic newbie to the seasoned pro. We have learned so much and made so many friends in the cookier community. Hardworking cookiers invest their time (and heart) into developing new techniques, teaching students new skills, or even inventing new tools to make decorating more satisfying or just more fun.

In the last decade, the cookier community has been able to come together in a new way—at CookieCon, a cookie art convention and show. CookieCon, held regularly and attended by hundreds of eager cookiers, is a priceless opportunity to be inspired by fellow cookie artists' work, make new friends, shop for new and exciting cookie decorating products, and learn through both innovative classes as well as hands-on workshops that allow attendees to practice what they've learned. We have attended and taught at several CookieCons, and it never fails to be one of the highlights of our year, not only because of how much we learn and how many friends we get to see but also because of the many new ones we never fail to make. We are honored to be a part of such a wonderful, caring community of like-minded men and women who support one another and continue to work to make cookie decorating an inspiring form of art.

Dessert Dream Roll-Out Cookies

These cream cheese–based rolled cookies bake up as nicely as our Very Vanilla Cookie Artists' Best Butter Cookies, but the addition of cream cheese makes them a bit softer while still having enough body to hold up to rounds of decorating. These four variations are inspired by some of our favorite (noncookie) desserts: lemon cheesecake, cherry chip ice cream, coconut cream pie, and cinnamon rolls.

Lemon Cheesecake Roll-Outs

MAKES ABOUT 3 DOZEN (3-INCH) ROUND COOKIES

These lemon cheesecake cookies are wonderful when decorated with a lemon-flavored Royal Icing (page 334) and are a great neutral base if you're looking for something with a little more oomph than vanilla that will please everyone. The other dessert-themed variations for this recipe are equally delicious and provide some great new flavor ideas to step up this year's holiday cookies!

INGREDIENT	VOLUME	WEIGHT
Sugar	1 cup	200 grams
Lemon zest, freshly grated	2 medium lemons	
Cream cheese (full fat), at room temperature	One 8–ounce package	227 grams
Unsalted butter, at room temperature	16 tablespoons	227 grams
Salt	¾ teaspoon	
Egg	1 large	50 grams (weighed without shell)
Lemon extract	2 teaspoons	
Unbleached all-purpose flour	3⅔ cups	520 grams

1. Combine the sugar and lemon zest in a medium bowl, and rub the sugar and zest between your thumbs and fingertips until the sugar is fragrant, very light yellow in color, and has a texture like wet sand (see "Live Your Zest Life," page 25). Set aside. (This can be done the day before and kept in a covered bowl at room temperature.)

2. Place the cream cheese in a stand mixer fitted with a flat beater, and beat on medium speed until creamy and smooth, about 2 minutes. Add the butter and salt, and beat until well combined and creamy. Scrape the sides of the bowl and the beater with a silicone spatula.

3. Add the lemon-infused sugar and cream together with cream cheese mixture on medium speed until smooth, 1 to 2 minutes. Beat in the egg and lemon

(continued)

extract just until the mixture is uniform. Once again, scrape the sides of the bowl and the beater with a silicone spatula.

4. Reduce the mixer speed to low and mix in the flour just until it is incorporated and a soft dough has formed. Scrape the sides of the bowl with a silicone spatula to ensure that no clumps of flour remain.

5. Divide the dough in half. Roll each half to a ¼-inch thickness between two sheets of parchment or waxed paper. Stack the paper-covered sheets of dough on an 18-by-13-inch baking sheet, and refrigerate until cold and firm throughout, at least 2 hours or up to 3 days.

6. Position two racks to divide the oven into thirds and preheat to 350°F. Line two 18-by-13-inch baking sheets with parchment paper or silicone baking mats.

7. Release the dough from one sheet of parchment paper by peeling the paper from the top of one layer of chilled dough. Lay the paper back onto the dough and flip the whole dough sheet over so that loosened sheet of paper is now underneath it. Peel off the top layer of parchment paper. Cut your desired shapes from the dough and transfer them to the prepared baking sheets, leaving at least 1 inch of space between cookies. These cookies keep their shape well, so you can crowd the pan a little more than with cookies that spread more during baking.

8. Bake until the edges are just starting to lightly brown, 10 to 20 minutes, depending on the size of the cookie. Halfway through baking, rotate the pans from front to back and top to bottom. Remove from the oven and let cool completely on the baking sheets to allow the cookies to properly bake through. If you have to transfer the cookies to a wire rack, keep in mind that large (over 4 inches) and delicate shapes will be particularly fragile while still warm. Repeat with the remaining dough, rerolling the scraps of dough, if necessary, once the baking sheets have completely cooled, or prepare additional baking sheets. The cookies will keep their shape best during baking if put into the oven while still cold. After cooling, the cookies can be stored in an airtight container at room temperature for 2 weeks.

Variation: Cherry Chip Ice Cream Roll-Outs

These cookies remind us of the old-school ice cream flavor of vanilla dotted with maraschino cherry chunks sometimes marketed as White House (or Whitehouse) Cherry. Our addition of white chocolate and almond extract to the cream cheese base is an unexpected variation on the traditional cookie cutter cookie.

Weigh out 170 grams (about 50 cherries or 1 cup) of drained maraschino cherries. Finely chop the cherries and blot well with a double layer of paper towels to absorb any excess liquid. Make the dough as directed for the Lemon Cheesecake Roll-Outs, omitting the lemon zest and replacing the lemon extract with 1 teaspoon of pure vanilla extract and ½ teaspoon of almond extract. After the flour is incorporated, slowly beat in the chopped cherries and ⅔ cup (113 grams) of mini white chocolate chips or finely chopped white chocolate. Roll out, cut, and bake as directed.

Variation: Coconut Cream Pie Roll-Outs

These cookies aren't creamy, but the flavor of toasty coconut accented with a bit of coconut extract is the closest that a cutout cookie can get to this classic diner dessert.

Make the dough as directed for the Lemon Cheesecake Roll-Outs, omitting the lemon zest and replacing the lemon extract with 1½ teaspoons of coconut extract. After the flour is incorporated, slowly beat in 1⅓ cups (113 grams) finely ground sweetened coconut flakes that have been toasted to a crunchy golden brown (see page 22). It's important that the coconut is finely ground (we use a food processor) because larger pieces are difficult to cut through with cookie cutters. Roll out, cut, and bake as directed.

Variation: Cinnamon Roll Swirl Roll-Outs

These cookies are marvelously inviting, with their subtle swirling and warm cinnamon aroma incorporated into the cream cheese–based dough. Perfect for the winter holidays, the cinnamony swirl is made with a cinnamon dough that is frozen, chopped, and mixed into the dough after the flour just until it's starting to incorporate.

(continued)

INGREDIENT	VOLUME	WEIGHT
Unsalted butter, melted and cooled but still pourable	4 tablespoons	57 grams
Dark or light brown sugar	Packed ¼ cup	50 grams
Granulated sugar	2 tablespoons	25 grams
Ground cinnamon	2½ teaspoons	
Milk (whole, reduced-fat, or nonfat)	2 teaspoons	
Salt	¼ teaspoon	
Pure vanilla extract	2 teaspoons	
Unbleached all-purpose flour	½ cup plus 2 tablespoons	89 grams

1. Before making the cookie dough, prepare the cinnamon swirl dough: Stir together the melted butter, brown sugar, granulated sugar, 1 teaspoon of cinnamon, milk, salt, and ½ teaspoon of vanilla in a medium bowl until combined. Stir in the flour to make a very soft dough. Roll the dough to ⅛-inch thickness between two layers of parchment or waxed paper. Transfer to a small baking sheet and freeze for about 15 minutes.

2. Make the cookie dough as directed for the Lemon Cheesecake Roll-Outs, omitting the lemon zest, replacing the lemon extract with 1½ teaspoons of pure vanilla extract, and adding 1½ teaspoons of ground cinnamon with the flour. Mix as directed but do not remove from the mixer.

3. After the flour is just incorporated, remove the frozen cinnamon dough from the freezer. Discard the parchment paper and chop the frozen dough into ½-inch squares. Add the dough pieces to the dough still in the mixing bowl and mix on low speed just until most of the squares seem to disappear but before they are completely beat into the dough.

4. Roll out, cut, and bake as directed. Because this dough is swirled, any rerolled dough will not be as swirled as the original, but the flavor will still be awesome

Coffee Bean Crunchers

MAKES ABOUT 4 DOZEN (2-INCH) COOKIES.

Throughout the book, we talk about layering flavors together, sometimes to provide subtle nuance. Not in this cookie. This cookie is COFFEE. Straightforward joe. No milk foam, caramel, or frappiness to be found. We even made it look like a coffee bean. There is coffee flavor in the dough and chunks of actual coffee bean in the coffee bean–shaped cookie for that added crunch and burst of coffee flavor.

INGREDIENT	VOLUME	WEIGHT
Unbleached all-purpose flour	3 cups	425 grams
Salt	½ teaspoon	
Unsalted butter, at room temperature	16 tablespoons	227 grams
Granulated sugar	½ cup	100 grams
Light brown sugar	Packed ½ cup	100 grams
Egg, at room temperature	1 large	50 grams (weighed without shell)
Instant espresso powder	2 teaspoons	
Pure vanilla extract	1 teaspoon	
Whole roasted coffee beans (see Note)	½ cup	35 grams

1. Whisk together the flour and salt in a medium bowl; set aside.

2. Combine the butter, granulated sugar, and brown sugar in a stand mixer fitted with a flat beater, and cream together on medium speed until smooth and creamy, 1 to 2 minutes. Beat in the egg, espresso powder, and vanilla until the mixture is uniform.

3. Reduce the mixer to low speed, and mix in the flour mixture until combined and no dry flour is visible. Scrape the sides of the bowl and the beater with a silicone spatula to make sure all ingredients have been incorporated.

4. Place the coffee beans in a bag, such as a 1-quart resealable storage bag. Crush the beans coarsely, using a heavy object, such as a rolling pin or the bottom of a small pan. The goal is to still have crunchy bits of coffee bean that are smaller than ¼-inch chunks but not a fine powder. Stir the crushed beans into the cookie dough, using a silicone spatula.

5. Divide the dough in half. Roll each half of the dough to a ¼-inch thickness between two sheets of parchment or waxed paper. Stack the paper-covered sheets of dough on an 18-by-13-inch baking sheet, and refrigerate until cold and firm throughout, at least 2 hours or up to 3 days.

(continued)

6. Position two racks to divide the oven into thirds and preheat to 350°F. Line two 18-by-13-inch baking sheets with parchment paper or silicone baking mats.

7. Cut your desired shapes from the dough and transfer them to the prepared baking sheets, leaving about 2 inches of space between cookies. If you don't have a coffee bean–shaped cutter, find an oval or ellipse that seems reasonably close. Drag the back of a butter knife through the center of the cookie to draw that central coffee bean line. (Be sure to use the back of the knife— you just want to draw a line, not cut through it.) These cookies keep their shape well, so you can crowd the pan a little more than with cookies that spread more during baking. But keep them about 1 inch apart for proper heat circulation.

8. Bake until the edges are just starting to brown, 10 to 20 minutes. Halfway through baking, rotate the pans from front to back and top to bottom. Remove from the oven and let cool for 5 minutes on the sheet before transferring to a wire rack to cool completely. Large (over 4 inches) or delicate shapes should be allowed to cool completely on the sheets to prevent breaking. Repeat with the remaining dough, rerolling the scraps of dough, if necessary, once the baking sheets have completely cooled, or prepare additional baking sheets. After cooling, the cookies can be stored in an airtight container at room temperature for several days.

NOTE: Even though it would take a couple of these cookies to equal the caffeine content of a cup of coffee, decaffeinated coffee beans can be used, if you prefer.

Mustachios

I honestly can't remember which way it went. Either we were working on a pistachio cookie and Chris came up with the name "mustachio." Or we wanted to make mustache-shaped cookies and Chris came up with the rhyming ingredient. You have to believe me that both scenarios are equally possible in our house. Regardless of how it happened, once the idea of a pistachio cookie named mustachio came into existence, we knew we had to make it happen. Decorating the cookies with the complementary flavor of chocolate was just the icing on the cookie. —P.A.

INGREDIENT	VOLUME	WEIGHT
Unbleached all-purpose flour	3 cups	425 grams
Salt	½ teaspoon	
Unsalted butter, at room temperature	16 tablespoons	227 grams
Sugar	1 cup	200 grams
Egg, at room temperature	1 large	50 grams (weighed without shell)
Pure vanilla extract	1 teaspoon	
Almond extract	¼ teaspoon	
Unsalted pistachios, shelled and roasted	1 cup	128 grams
Bittersweet, semisweet, or milk chocolate, finely chopped, or chocolate chips (optional; see Note)	2 cups	340 grams (12 ounces)

1. Whisk together the flour and salt in a medium bowl; set aside.

2. Combine the butter and ¾ cup (150 grams) of the sugar in a stand mixer fitted with a flat beater, and cream together on medium speed until smooth and creamy, 1 to 2 minutes. Scrape the sides of the bowl and the beater with a silicone spatula. Return the mixer to medium speed and beat in the egg, vanilla, and almond extract until the mixture is uniform.

3. Finely grind the pistachios in a food processor (or finely chop by hand). Add the remaining ¼ cup (50 grams) of sugar and pulse the food processor a few more times to mix in the sugar and grind the pistachios a bit more. Pour the ground pistachio mixture into the butter mixture and beat on medium speed until incorporated.

4. Reduce the mixer to low speed and mix in the flour mixture just until combined and no dry flour is visible. Scrape the sides of the bowl with a silicone spatula to make sure all ingredients have been incorporated.

(continued)

5. Divide the dough in half. Roll each half of the dough to a ¼-inch thickness between two sheets of parchment or waxed paper. Stack the paper-covered sheets of dough on an 18-by-13-inch baking sheet, and refrigerate until cold and firm throughout, at least 2 hours or up to 3 days.

6. Position two racks to divide the oven into thirds and preheat to 350°F. Line two 18-by-13-inch baking sheets with parchment paper or silicone baking mats.

7. Cut mustache shapes from the dough and transfer them to the prepared baking sheets, leaving about 2 inches of space between cookies. These cookies keep their shape well, so you can crowd the pan a little more than with cookies that spread more during baking.

8. Bake until the edges are just starting to brown, 10 to 20 minutes. Halfway through baking, rotate the pans from front to back and top to bottom. Remove from the oven and let cool for 5 minutes on the sheet before transferring to a wire rack to cool completely. Large (over 4 inches) or delicate shapes should be allowed to cool completely on the sheets to prevent breaking. Repeat with the remaining dough, rerolling the scraps of dough, if necessary, once the baking sheets have completely cooled, or prepare additional baking sheets.

9. If using, place the finely chopped chocolate in a large, microwave-safe bowl. Melt the chocolate at high (100%) power, stopping to stir every 30 seconds, until about 80 percent of the chocolate is melted. Continue to stir the chocolate to allow the residual heat of the chocolate and bowl to melt any remaining pieces.

10. Arrange several sheets of parchment or waxed paper on a flat surface. Dip the tops of the cookie into the melted chocolate and allow any excess to drop back into the bowl. Place the dipped cookies, chocolate side up, on the sheets of parchment or waxed paper and allow the chocolate to set, 10 to 15 minutes.

11. Transfer the remaining chocolate to a piping bag. Use scissors to snip a small (⅛-inch) opening in the bag. Drizzle the melted chocolate over the dipped cookies to create some hairlike texture. Let the chocolate set completely before stacking the cookies.

12. The cookies can be stored in an airtight container at room temperature for several days. If you live in a particularly warm environment where the chocolate never quite sets, you can store these in the refrigerator in a closed container.

NOTE: You don't actually have to cut these into mustache shapes or cover them in chocolate. This is a yummy cookie on its own that can be shaped based on whatever cookie cutters happen to be in your possession.

Banana Pick-a-Chips

MAKES ABOUT 4 DOZEN (2-INCH) COOKIES

We've struggled with banana cookies. Bananas contain so much water and fiber that their addition to a cookie dough usually results in a soft, cakey cookie. Our goal was to get a crisp cookie packed with natural banana flavor. Precooking the banana with a bit of the flour did the trick. You can skip the chips altogether and enjoy these as pure banana cookies or as the base for decorated cookies. However, the addition of different types of mini chips works really well with the bananas. We used semisweet chocolate, but banana also pairs well with peanut butter, cinnamon, caramel, or white chocolate. Feel free to mix and match! For standard-size chips, chop the chips into small (⅛-inch or so) pieces so that the dough will roll out flat and even.

INGREDIENT	VOLUME	WEIGHT
Unbleached all-purpose flour	2¾ cups plus 2 tablespoons	408 grams
Salt	½ teaspoon	
Ground cloves	Pinch	
Banana	1 medium	100 grams (weighed without peel)
Light brown sugar	Packed 1 cup	200 grams
Unsalted butter, at room temperature	16 tablespoons	227 grams
Egg, cold from the refrigerator	1 large	50 grams (weighed without shell)
Pure vanilla extract	1 teaspoon	
Miniature semisweet chocolate chips	½ cup	85 grams

1. Whisk together 2¾ cups (390 grams) of the flour, the salt, and cloves in a medium bowl; set aside.

2. Use a fork to mash the banana in a small, microwave-safe bowl. Stir in the remaining 2 tablespoons (18 grams) of flour. Microwave the banana mixture on high (100%) power, stirring every 30 seconds, until the mixture has thickened to a paste, about 2 minutes (see "The Tangzhong Technique," page 125). If you don't have a microwave, cook the mixture in a small nonstick pan over medium heat for about 2 minutes, stirring constantly with a silicone spatula. Transfer the banana paste to the bowl of a stand mixer.

3. Combine the banana paste and brown sugar in a stand mixer fitted with a flat beater, and beat together on medium speed to break up the banana paste and incorporate the sugar. Allow this mixture to cool completely before proceeding, 10 to 15 minutes.

(continued)

4. Once cool, add the butter and resume mixing until the mixture is smooth and creamy, 1 to 2 minutes. Beat in the egg and vanilla until the mixture is uniform.

5. Reduce the mixer speed to low and mix in the flour mixture until combined and no dry flour is visible. Scrape the sides of the bowl with a silicone spatula and stir in the chocolate chips.

6. Divide the dough in half. Roll each half of the dough to a ¼-inch thickness between two sheets of parchment or waxed paper. Stack the paper-covered sheets of dough on an 18-by-13-inch baking sheet, and refrigerate until cold and firm throughout, at least 2 hours or up to 3 days.

7. Position two racks to divide the oven into thirds and preheat to 350°F. Line two 18-by-13-inch baking sheets with parchment paper or silicone baking mats.

8. Cut desired shapes from the dough (use your banana-shaped cutter, if you have one) and transfer them to the prepared baking sheets, leaving about 1 inch of space between cookies. These cookies keep their shape well, so you can crowd the pan a little more than with cookies that spread more during baking.

9. Bake until the edges are just starting to brown, 18 to 22 minutes. Halfway through baking, rotate the pans from front to back and top to bottom. Remove from the oven and let cool for 5 minutes on the sheet before transferring to a wire rack to cool completely. Large (over 4 inches) or delicate shapes should cool completely on the sheets to prevent breaking. Repeat with the remaining dough, rerolling the scraps of dough, if necessary, once the baking sheets have completely cooled, or prepare additional baking sheets. After cooling, the cookies can be stored in an airtight container at room temperature for several days.

Stonewalls

MAKES ABOUT 30 (3-INCH) HEART-SHAPED COOKIES

"Happy Pride, everyone!"

It's a wonderful greeting called out by rainbow-festooned parade-goers each year. It's a reminder to not just accept each other but also be proud of who you are. Most Pride parades are held in June to commemorate the origins of the Pride movement, which began at The Stonewall Inn in New York City. There are many ways to celebrate Pride, including with cookies! We've built our Stonewalls out of pebbles—specifically rainbow-colored Fruity Pebbles cereal. Bake some heart-shaped Stonewalls for someone you love and celebrate pride in yourself. No one is better at being you than you.

INGREDIENT	VOLUME	WEIGHT
Fruity Pebbles cereal	2 cups	85 grams
Unbleached all-purpose flour	2½ cups	354 grams
Baking powder	1 teaspoon	
Salt	1 teaspoon	
Unsalted butter, at room temperature	16 tablespoons	227 grams
Confectioners' sugar	1½ cups	170 grams
Lemon zest, freshly grated	Half of 1 medium lemon	
Lime zest, freshly grated	1 medium lime	
Orange zest, freshly grated	Half of 1 medium orange	
Egg	1 large	50 grams (weighted without shell)
Pure vanilla extract	1 teaspoon	

1. Crush 1 cup of Fruity Pebbles cereal and place in a medium bowl. Whisk together the crushed cereal, flour, baking powder, and salt; set aside.

2. Combine the butter, confectioners' sugar, lemon zest, lime zest, and orange zest in a stand mixer fitted with a flat beater, and cream together on medium speed until smooth and creamy, 1 to 2 minutes. Stop mixing and scrape down the sides of the bowl and the beater with a silicone spatula. Beat in the egg and vanilla just until the mixture is uniform.

3. Reduce the mixer speed to low and mix in half of the flour mixture until just combined. Stop mixing and scrape down the sides of the bowl and beater with a silicone spatula. Return the mixer to low speed and mix in the remaining flour mixture just until no dry flour is visible.

(continued)

4. Divide the dough in half. Roll one half of the dough to a ¼-inch thickness between two sheets of parchment or waxed paper. Peel off the top layer of paper and sprinkle ½ cup of the remaining Fruity Pebbles over the top of the dough. Replace the parchment paper and roll over the dough until the cereal pieces are pressed into the soft dough and the top is smooth and flat. Repeat with the second half of dough and the remaining ½ cup of Fruity Pebbles. Stack the paper-covered sheets of dough on an 18-by-13-inch baking sheet, and refrigerate until cold and firm throughout, at least 2 hours or up to 3 days.

5. Position two racks to divide the oven into thirds and preheat to 350°F. Line two 18-by-13-inch baking sheets with parchment paper or silicone baking mats.

6. Release the dough from one sheet of parchment paper by peeling the paper from the top of one layer of chilled dough. Lay the paper back onto the dough and flip the whole dough sheet over so that loosened sheet of paper is now underneath it. Peel off the top layer of parchment paper. Cut your heart or other desired shapes from the dough and transfer them to the prepared baking sheets, leaving about 2 inches of space between cookies.

7. Bake until the edges are just starting to lightly brown, 10 to 20 minutes, depending on the size of the cookie. Halfway through baking, rotate the pans from front to back and top to bottom. Remove from the oven and let cool for 5 minutes on the sheet before transferring to a wire rack to cool completely. Large (over 4 inches) or delicate shapes should be allowed to cool completely on the sheets to prevent breaking. Repeat with the remaining dough once the baking sheets have completely cooled, or prepare additional baking sheets. The dough can be rerolled, but the appearance of those rerolled cookies won't be the same because the larger cereal pieces will be incorporated throughout the dough instead of just the top. The cookies will keep their shape best during baking if put into the oven while still cold. After cooling, the cookies can be stored in an airtight container at room temperature for 2 weeks.

NOTE: These cookies are colorful on their own without an additional decoration. However, if you would like to decorate these cookies, you certainly can. Because the cereal is pressed into the top of the cookies, the tops are more textured (slightly bumpy, actually). If you wish to decorate these cookies with fondant or royal icing, decorate the bottoms of the cookies because that surface will be smooth and flat. Decorating on the underside of the cookie will create a cookie with a mirror image of your cutter shape if your cookie cutter is not symmetrical.

I Shudder to Utter of My Cookie Cutters

While I was growing up, my family didn't bake very many cookie cutter cookies, so we didn't really need any cookie cutters. I'm sure we had a few lying around in the odd kitchen drawer or in a set-aside box of Christmas decorations, but no more than a handful (and certainly nothing close to the more than 250 that I own now). At some point while I was in graduate school more than 15 years ago, I stumbled upon a video segment about someone creating cookie cutters in the shape of someone's face. With that, I was absolutely hooked with the joy of decorating cookies.

Of course, acquiring more than 500 cookie cutters didn't happen overnight. Like any collection, it was a slow creep. In the beginning, I sought to assemble a basic collection of enough shapes to make and decorate anything that I could ever want. Before 2010 or so, most cookie cutters were either aluminum or the occasional copper along with mass-marketed collections of plastic cutters sold by the bucket at the craft store. Cookie cutters then were mostly the traditional shapes that most people have seen or had, like snowmen, gingerbread people, hearts, circles, letters, yada, yada, yada. I bought what I liked, and the collection started to grow. More cutters came as gifts from well-meaning friends looking to support my new hobby. Sometimes it grew inadvertently. There were plenty of times when cutters were sold as a set of five or so cutters, and while I really only wanted one of them, I had to buy the set instead.

In more recent years, 3-D printing technology has advanced, creating new types of cutters. These printers (about the size of a standard laser printer) can print cookie cutters (among other things) on demand in an hour or so, using a relatively inexpensive plastic. This allowed virtually any shape to be designed and printed with few resources in the way of manufacturing. With the 3-D printing came a new generation of cutters that were, really, artisanal. Most cutters made through 3-D printing are created with a specific design in mind, and this allows decorators who purchase the cutter to more easily envision the finished cookie. There are so many successful cookie cutter manufacturers now, both classic aluminum and copper cutters as well as those available from 3-D printing shops (see Sources, page 350). We are friends with owners of many of the shops, and knowing them so well makes it easy to support their businesses (though maybe a little too easy).

With 3-D printed cutters flooding the market, anything that exists in the world can be cut out of dough and decorated as a cookie. *Anything.* While the shapes themselves are limitless, the variations of a single shape are just as limitless. There is no longer one single heart or pumpkin shape. Hearts can be found as wide and curvy or tall and thin or even asymmetrical. Pumpkin shapes match the variety found in a pumpkin patch—short and squat, tall and wide, round, or pinched in the middle and nearly pearlike.

I'm always enamored when shops release new cutter designs, which is often seasonal to account for holiday trends. While I certainly have plenty of Christmas-,

(continued)

Easter-, and Halloween-themed cookie cutters, what I really relish are cutters with less conventional shapes, such as fruits and vegetables, clothing, or body parts. In fact, I would wager that a majority of our 1,000+ cutters are probably not what many people (outside of the world of die-hard cookie decorators) would consider a predictable shape for cookie decorating. Cookies that look like other foods are a particular passion of mine. Nothing more fun than cookies decorated like turkey drumsticks or avocados. Dozens of pie-themed cutters (for obvious reasons). I am also partial to cookies shaped like clothes (count me in for an edible ball gown or a sweet pair of argyle socks). Shoes, too. Lots of flowers. A smattering of cutters ostensibly medical themed, but many of which are unmistakably *adult* shapes that might not be the best choice for a bake sale. *Sooo* many hearts. Probably too many Easter rabbits.

With so many cutters, I finally broke down and created an electronic inventory. It wasn't so much to keep track of them, but to prevent me from buying duplicates. While more than 2,000 cutters seems like a lot, they all stay well organized in about two dozen plastic containers in a range of sizes, each sorted into (mostly consistent) categories. In all, the curated tubs contain what I sincerely hope is *not* the largest cookie cutter collection in the southeastern United States. But at more than 2,500 cutters, if it's not the biggest, it's probably close. *—C.T.*

A Collection, Unconventional

You may be feeling skeptical of this cutter-based confessional.
Is such a thing defensible? This collection reprehensible?
Should I seek health professionals for flaws in neurochemicals?
That I seek shapes of vegetables or animals with tentacles,
Or the random naughty genital (and others themed as medical)
For baking up incredible, delicious bite-size edibles?
Some shapes now seem regrettable but none incomprehensible,
Of shapes completely sensible or simply unforgettable.
Some may see as condemnable a thirst for shapes unquenchable.
But I see as commendable a collection so respectable,
Of something not collectible and yet still plainly plentiful.
And storage keeps it sensible (conditions quite exceptional),
This borderline obsessional: a collection, unconventional.

—C.T.

CHAPTER FOUR
slice-and-bake cookies

Also called refrigerator or icebox cookies, at their simplest, these cookies are rolled into a log, chilled, and sliced before baking. Many cookie doughs can be prepared using this technique. This method is particularly good for doughs with large pieces of fruit or nuts that would be difficult to roll flat but can be easily sliced through with a sharp knife. Because the dough freezes well, these cookies can be prepped days, weeks, or months in advance and baked a few cookies at a time for a small snack. A few basic tools and techniques can help turn you into a slice-and-bake rock star.

Helpful Tools

- **Ruler.** Create a tight, even log of dough and measure even slices for cutting.
- **Cardboard tubes.** Keep logs of dough nice and round while they firm up in the refrigerator.
- **Parchment or waxed paper.** Make a tight, even log of dough.
- **Plastic wrap.** Keep cookie dough fresh and nicely shaped while it chills.
- **Sharp knife.** Cut even slices of cookie dough.
- **Pastry brush.** Use to brush egg white over the outside of the dough if you want to add texture with edible decorations.
- **Molds.** Create sliceable dough logs in a variety of different shapes.

Tips and Techniques

Size matters. Dough logs for slice-and-bake cookies work best for cookies between 1 and 2½ inches wide. Dough logs larger than that can be difficult to slice properly.

Roll with it. For perfectly uniform cookies shaped by hand, it's important to roll the dough into an even cylinder. Start by rolling the dough into as smooth a log as you can and placing on a sheet of parchment paper. Fold the sheet of parchment paper over the log. Use one hand to press the edge of a ruler under the front edge of the parchment-covered dough. Gently pull the bottom layer of paper taut with your other hand while you apply pressure with the ruler. Keep the pres-

Cardboard Rolls and Dough Molds

sure even and the ruler straight. The pressure from the parchment will squeeze the dough into a smooth, even cylinder. Making sure that the side edges of the parchment stay aligned will help you keep the pressure even across the dough log.

Keep in shape. Store dough in cardboard poster tubes or empty paper towel rolls to prevent the round bottom of the dough from flattening. Cut a paper towel tube lengthwise to allow it to hold thicker logs of dough.

Shape up. In addition to round cookies, the doughs can be molded into other shapes before chilling:

- **For triangles, start with a round log of dough.** Gently pinch a ridge of dough down the center of the top. Roll the dough over gently and press it flat to create a second side between the edge of the bottom and the ridge on top. Repeat to create the third side. Keep turning and pressing the dough to make the sides smooth and flat.
- **For squares, start with a round log of dough.** Flatten the bottom of the dough log, then flip it over to flatten the top. Repeat to flatten the sides. Keep flipping and flopping the dough log and gently pressing until the sides are smooth and flat.

Turn to the pros. You can find a number of commercially manufactured cookie molds that make shaping slice-and-bake cookies very easy. Additionally, other kitchen tools not used for cookies also work great as molds for cookie dough. Nontraditional molds that we have used include pâté/terrine molds, sushi molds (especially a Spam musubi sushi rice press), loaf pans, poster tubes, and baguette loaf pans. For easier molding, lightly grease the mold and line it with plastic wrap. Press the dough into the plastic-lined mold, chill, and use the plastic wrap to help remove the dough from the mold.

Wrap it up. Wrap logs of dough with parchment paper or plastic. For cylinders, twist the ends of the paper or plastic to apply a bit of pressure, keep the paper taut, and prevent the dough from slumping as it chills. If using a mold, cover any exposed dough with plastic wrap. Keep the dough in the mold until it has completely firmed and chilled.

Shimmer and sparkle. After the dough is cold but before it's sliced, you can adorn the edges with edible decorations, such as sparkling sugar (colored or clear), finely chopped nuts, crushed coffee beans, or sprinkles, just to name a few. Brush the outside of the dough log with a thin layer of lightly beaten egg white. Spread 1/3 to 1/2 cup of your chosen edible decorations on a small baking sheet or other flat, rimmed pan. Roll the dough in the decorative material to coat the outside edge. We find it's best to do this just before slicing and baking. There's a good chance that rewrapping the dough in plastic again will knock off most of your coating.

First cut. A sharp, thin knife works best to cut chilled cookie dough into slices. Cookie dough cuts best when cold but not frozen. Most cookies in this book are cut into 1/4-inch slices, but a few are a bit thicker or thinner. If you're a stickler for perfection, use a ruler to make sure that your slices are equal. If you cut the dough thicker or thinner than the recipe calls for, be sure to adjust your baking time.

Spin class. To help keep the shape of your dough, spin the log either toward or away from you after each cut to prevent the bottom from flattening with the pressure from the knife.

Freeze for later. Logs of slice-and-bake cookie dough freeze well for months. To freeze, wrap the log in plastic wrap, then in aluminum foil. Store in a heavy-duty resealable freezer storage bag. To cut, allow the dough to thaw in the refrigerator overnight, then cut and bake as directed. The dough can be rewrapped and frozen again.

Stollen Glances

MAKES 4 DOZEN COOKIES

One of our favorite culinary cold weather traditions is baking a loaf of home-made stollen and enjoying several fresh slices as breakfast on a wintry morning. Stollen is a German fruitcake made as a yeasted bread dough, and we bake ours surrounding a decadent rope of rich marzipan. We transformed the flavors of stollen into the perfect wintertime cookie. Fragrant with citrus and warm spices, the fruit- and nut-studded dough pairs splendidly with a delicate swirl of almond paste. Be sure to chop the almonds and dried fruit finely. Pieces larger than ¼ inch will make the dough difficult to roll.

INGREDIENT	VOLUME	WEIGHT
Unbleached all-purpose flour	1¼ cups	177 grams
Salt	½ teaspoon	
Ground cinnamon	¼ teaspoon	
Ground cardamom	⅛ teaspoon	
Ground nutmeg	⅛ teaspoon	
Unsalted butter, at room temperature	12 tablespoons	170 grams
Confectioners' sugar	½ cup	57 grams
Lemon zest, freshly grated	1 medium lemon	
Orange zest, freshly grated	1 medium orange	
Pure vanilla extract	1 teaspoon	
Slivered almonds, toasted, cooled, and finely chopped (see page 24)	½ cup	57 grams
Dried apricots, finely chopped	⅓ cup	57 grams
Dried cherries, finely chopped	¼ cup	43 grams
Raisins, preferably golden raisins (a.k.a. sultanas)	¼ cup	35 grams
Almond paste, at room temperature (see Note)		227 grams (8 ounces)

1. Whisk together the flour, salt, cinnamon, cardamom, and nutmeg in a medium bowl; set aside.

2. Combine the butter, confectioners' sugar, lemon and orange zests, and vanilla in the bowl of a stand mixer. Fit the mixer with a flat beater, and cream together on medium speed until smooth and creamy, 1 to 2 minutes.

3. Reduce the mixer speed to low and mix in the flour mixture until combined. Stop mixing and scrape down the sides of the bowl and the beater with a silicone spatula.

4. Fold in the almonds, dried apricots, dried cherries, and raisins.

(continued)

5. Roll the dough to a 13-by-9-inch, ¼-inch-thick rectangle between two sheets of parchment or waxed paper. Using rolling pin guides can ensure that the dough is rolled evenly (see page 138). Transfer the parchment-covered dough to a baking sheet, and refrigerate until cold and firm throughout, at least 2 hours or overnight.

6. Fold a 16-by-12-inch sheet of parchment paper in half to create a 12-by-8-inch rectangle. Knead the almond paste for a few minutes until the heat of your hands has slightly softened the paste to make it easier to roll. Roll the almond paste to a 12-by-8-inch, 1/16-inch-thick rectangle between the folded sheet of parchment. Using rolling pin guides can ensure that the paste is rolled evenly (see page 138).

7. Remove the chilled dough from the refrigerator. Peel off the top layer of parchment, then lay the paper back on the dough. Turn the dough over, and completely remove and discard the second sheet of parchment.

8. Peel back the top layer of the parchment envelope around the almond paste. Flip the almond paste over (so the parchment is on top) and center it on the cookie dough. Gently press to adhere the paste to the dough and peel off the parchment from the paste. This will leave you with a thin layer of almond paste on a layer of cookie dough sitting on a sheet of parchment paper.

9. Starting from the longer side, roll the dough into a tight log. If the dough is too cold to roll without cracking, let the dough rest at room temperature for a few minutes until it has softened slightly. Press the dough to seal the spiral.

10. Tightly wrap the dough log in a sheet of plastic wrap and refrigerate until cold and firm throughout, at least 2 hours or overnight. Keeping the dough in a poster or paper towel tube (see page 177) will keep the bottom round while it chills.

11. Position a rack in the center of the oven and preheat to 300°F. Line two 18-by-13-inch baking sheets with parchment paper or silicone baking mats. We prefer to bake these cookies one baking sheet at a time. The second baking sheet can be used to prepare the dough once the foil is removed from the first batch, so the next batch can go into the oven immediately after the first sheet comes out.

12. Trim away about ½ inch of dough from each end of the log and discard. Cut the log into ¼-inch slices, and place 1 inch apart on one prepared baking sheet (you can fit 18 on each pan, see page 86). Because these cookies should be baked one pan a time, only cut off as many slices as will fit on one baking sheet. Return the dough to the refrigerator while the first batch bakes.

13. Cover the pan with aluminum foil (see "It's Not Just the Heat, It's the Humidity," page 183). Bake for 25 minutes, rotating the pan from front to back halfway through baking. Carefully remove the foil and bake until the cookies have firmed, the edges are just set, and have barely begun to turn light golden brown, about 5 more minutes.

14. Remove from the oven and let the cookies cool for 15 minutes on the baking sheet (this allows them to continue setting) before transferring to a wire rack to cool completely. Repeat with the remaining dough once the baking sheet has completely cooled, or prepare an additional baking sheet. The cookies can be stored in a sealed container at room temperature for several days.

(continued)

NOTE: Almond paste is most often sold in 7- or 8-ounce cans or tubes. For these cookies, we prefer to use 8 ounces of paste because it is easier to roll into the large rectangle needed for the filling. If you can only find almond paste in 7-ounce portions, you can make do with that. Roll the paste to the dimensions described. It may seem that there's not enough almond paste to roll to that size, but there is. It will be a very thin layer—so thin that it might be translucent in spots.

MAKE AHEAD:
These cookies don't require much effort, but they do need some time to chill between steps. As long as the dough is cold and firm, these cookies can be made in one day. However, the process can be stretched over three days. On day 1, make the dough and refrigerate it overnight. On day 2, roll the almond paste and cookie dough into a log and refrigerate overnight to bake on day 3, or freeze for up to 3 months.

It's Not Just the Heat, It's the Humidity

COOKIE BYTE

One of the essential steps for converting dough to an edible cookie is moisture loss. The hot and dry oven causes water in the dough to turn to steam and escape. For most cookies, a one-size-fits-all approach to water loss works fine for all of its components. We found that for some cookies, especially those with some dried fruits, we needed a bit more control over the process. Dried fruits, by their very nature are, well, *dry*. Grapes, for example, have already lost a fair amount of moisture during their journey to raisinhood. It makes sense that by the time some doughs have become fully baked cookies, their dried fruits have crossed the threshold from sweet flavor bombs to leathery flakes of bitterness. This is especially true for cookies that are crisper and have less moisture for dried fruits to hold on to during baking. For these cookies, we create a sealed environment by covering the baking sheet with aluminum foil for most of the baking time. While covered, the dough is still heating up and meeting all of its other baking benchmarks like pasteurization and leavening. Dried fruits, on the top surface of the dough especially, are protected from the direct radiant heat while the steam released from the dough is trapped inside the foil, slowing down further water loss from the fruits. Removing the foil during the last portion of the baking period allows that extra moisture to escape, and the dough can finish baking before the fruits have a chance to dry out.

Rum Puncharoos

MAKES ABOUT 30 (2½-INCH)
COOKIES

Ordering a "rum punch" almost anywhere close to the equator is almost the surest way to receive a different cocktail every time. It is also not uncommon to see signs posted in some of these establishments assuring patrons that they are indeed the home of the *original* rum punch. The word *punch* is thought to be derived from the Hindi word for "five" (pronounced paanch), meaning that it was an alcoholic beverage with five ingredients. So, it seems that as long as you hit that magic number, you can lay claim to having *an* original punch (if not *the* original punch). The rum punch of my hometown (and now of our cookies) seems to fit the bill, consisting of orange, pineapple, grenadine, nutmeg, and a healthy dose of Virgin Islands rum. —P.A.

INGREDIENT	VOLUME	WEIGHT
COOKIE DOUGH		
Granulated sugar	½ cup	100 grams
Orange zest, freshly grated	1 medium orange	
Unbleached all-purpose flour	1½ cups	213 grams
Baking soda	½ teaspoon	
Salt	½ teaspoon	
Ground nutmeg	½ teaspoon	
Cream of tartar	¼ teaspoon	
Canned crushed pineapple, packed in juice	One 8–ounce can	227 grams
Grenadine (see Note)	¼ cup	70 grams
Unsalted butter, melted and cooled but still pourable	8 tablespoons	113 grams
Egg yolk, at room temperature	1 large	15 grams
Rum extract	1 teaspoon	
GLAZE		
Confectioners' sugar, preferably made with tapioca starch (see "Starch Madness," page 115)	¾ cup	85 grams
Rum, dark or light	5 teaspoons	

1. Make the Cookie Dough: Combine the granulated sugar and orange zest in the bowl of your stand mixer. To extract the most orange flavor, rub the zest and sugar between your thumbs and fingertips until the sugar is fragrant, very light orange in color, and has a texture like wet sand (see "Live Your Zest Life," page 25).

2. Whisk together 1¼ cups plus 2 tablespoons (195 grams) of the flour along with the baking soda, salt, nutmeg, and cream of tartar in a bowl; set aside.

3. Drain and discard the juice from the canned pineapple, using a sieve. Press on the pineapple with a silicone spatula to remove as much juice as possible. Spread the pineapple on a microwave-safe plate and microwave it on high (100%) power for about 5 minutes, stopping to stir it every minute. Stop when the pineapple is mostly dry and has started to brown at the edges. Set it aside to cool.

4. Pour the grenadine into a small, microwave-safe bowl. Stir in the remaining 2 tablespoons (18 grams) of flour. Microwave the grenadine mixture on high (100%) power, stirring every 20 seconds, until the mixture has thickened into a paste, about 1 minute (see "The Tangzhong Technique," page 125). If you don't have a microwave, cook the mixture in a small nonstick pan over medium heat for 1 to 2 minutes, stirring constantly with a silicone spatula. Add the grenadine paste to the bowl of orange sugar.

5. Fit the stand mixer with a flat beater, and beat the grenadine paste mixture on medium speed to break up the grenadine paste and incorporate the orange sugar. Add the melted butter and continue to mix for an additional 1 to 2 minutes, until the mixture is again uniform. (Depending on the capacity of your stand mixer, this might be more convenient to mix using an electric hand mixer.) Allow this mixture to cool completely before proceeding, 10 to 15 minutes.

6. Once the mixture has cooled, beat in the egg yolk and the rum extract, followed by the cooled pineapple. Reduce the mixer speed to low and mix in the flour mixture until no dry flour is visible. Scrape the sides of the bowl with a silicone spatula. Roll the dough into a log 11 inches long (it will measure about 1¾ inches in diameter). Wrap the dough log in plastic wrap and refrigerate until cold and firm throughout, at least 2 hours or up to 3 days.

7. Position two racks to divide the oven into thirds and preheat to 350°F. Line two 18-by-13-inch baking sheets with parchment paper or silicone baking mats.

8. Cut the log into ⅓-inch (8 mm) slices using a sharp knife. You may need to use a gentle sawing motion to cut through the pineapple pieces. Place the cookies 2 inches apart on the prepared baking sheets (you can fit 13 on each pan; see page 86).

9. Bake until the cookies are just golden brown at the edges, 10 to 13 minutes. Halfway through baking, rotate the pans from front to back and top to bottom. Remove from the oven and transfer the cookies to a wire rack to cool completely. Repeat with the remaining dough once the baking sheets have completely cooled, or prepare an additional baking sheet.

10. Make the Glaze: Sift the confectioners' sugar into a small bowl. Add 4 teaspoons of the rum and whisk. Test the glaze by lifting the whisk and watching the glaze drip off. It should flow like honey. If too thick, add some or all of the remaining rum. Drizzle the glaze over the cookies, using a piping bag, squeeze bottle, or spoon. Once the glaze has dried and firmed up, the cookies can be stored in an airtight container at room temperature for several days.

NOTE: Grenadine is a pomegranate-flavored, nonalcoholic sweet syrup that is a common cocktail ingredient. You can find it at most liquor stores or in the mixers section of your grocery store.

Badam Milk Bites

MAKES ABOUT 4 DOZEN (2-INCH) ROUND COOKIES

Badam milk is a sweet drink from India with flavors of almond (*badam* is "almond" in Hindi), saffron, and cardamom. We particularly enjoy it with a sprinkle of chopped emerald green pistachios. The combination is heavenly, and we are wild for it in these cookies. Saffron provides a remarkable depth of flavor that pairs so well with the almond and cardamom. These cookies are tender and crisp, and the pistachios scattered throughout the dough—along with a coating of coarse sugar—offer a satisfying crunch.

INGREDIENT	VOLUME	WEIGHT
Unsalted butter, at room temperature	16 tablespoons	227 grams
Saffron threads	Pinch	
Unbleached all-purpose flour	1¾ cups	248 grams
Ground cardamom	1¼ teaspoons	
Salt	½ teaspoon	
Almond paste, broken into small clumps, at room temperature	⅓ cup	107 grams
Granulated sugar	¾ cup	150 grams
Egg yolks, at room temperature	2 large	30 grams
Pure vanilla extract	½ teaspoon	
Almond extract	¼ teaspoon	
Unsalted pistachios, shelled, roasted, and chopped	½ cup	60 grams
Coarse sanding sugar or turbinado sugar, for sprinkling	About ½ cup	about 100 grams

1. Melt 4 tablespoons (57 grams) of the butter. With your fingertips, crush the saffron threads, add them to the butter, and stir to combine. Set aside until the butter has completely cooled and the edges are beginning to turn opaque, about 30 minutes.

2. Whisk together the flour, cardamom, and salt in a medium bowl; set aside.

3. Combine the remaining 12 tablespoons (170 grams) of butter, saffron-infused butter, and almond paste in a stand mixer fitted with a flat beater, and cream together on medium speed until the mixture is smooth and the clumps of almond paste are mostly mixed throughout.

4. Add the granulated sugar and cream the mixture until it's light and fluffy, 2 to 3 minutes. Beat in the egg yolks, vanilla, and almond extract.

5. Beat in the flour mixture on low speed just until no dry flour is visible. Scrape the sides of the bowl and the beater with a silicone spatula and stir in the pistachios.

6. Divide the dough in half (about 400 grams each) and roll each piece into a 10-inch log (see page 177). Tightly wrap the dough logs in sheets of parchment or waxed paper and refrigerate until cold and firm throughout, at least 2 hours or up to 3 days, or freeze the dough for up to 3 months (see page 178). Keeping the dough in a poster or paper towel tube (see page 177) will keep the bottom round while it chills.

7. Position two racks to divide the oven into thirds and preheat to 375°F. Line two 18-by-13-inch baking sheets with parchment paper or silicone baking mats.

8. Spread the coarse sanding sugar on a small sheet pan or other flat, rimmed surface. Roll each log in the sugar, gently pressing to ensure that the sugar sticks.

9. Cut the logs into ⅓-inch (8 mm) slices, rotating the dough to keep the log round, and place slices 2 inches apart on the prepared baking sheets (you can fit 13 on each pan; see page 86). Return any dough to the refrigerator while the cookies bake.

10. Bake until the edges begin to lightly brown and the centers feel firm when gently pressed, 8 to 12 minutes. Halfway through baking, rotate the pans from front to back and top to bottom. Remove from the oven and let cool for 5 minutes on the baking sheets before transferring to a wire rack to cool completely. Repeat with the remaining dough once the baking sheets have completely cooled, or prepare additional baking sheets. After cooling, the cookies can be stored in an airtight container at room temperature for several days.

COOKIE BYTE

Saffron

Saffron is considered by many to be a savory spice, but it is featured in desserts across the world. The bright red threads are the stigmas (female organ) of an autumn-blooming crocus flower. Each crocus produces three threads, and these threads are each harvested by hand. This labor-intensive effort is why saffron is considered the world's most expensive spice. Thank-fully, because it is so flavorful, only a small amount is required to infuse an entire recipe with its distinctive flavor and yellow hue. We crush the threads (your fingers are fine for this) and bloom them in warm butter to allow the flavor to incorporate more evenly throughout the dough. You can purchase powdered saffron, but threads are considered to be of higher quality.

Tiger Tails

MAKES ABOUT 4 DOZEN (2¼-INCH) COOKIES

These cookies are our homage to the Canadian ice cream flavor that most Americans have never heard of. Tiger tail (or tiger-tiger) ice cream is an orange ice cream base churned with a black licorice ripple. When we learned of it, the contrast of the bright citrus with the herbaceous licorice was an intriguing blend—even for the two of us, who are decidedly *not* fans of black licorice candy. Instead of licorice extract (which is hard to find anyway), use freshly ground star anise for these elegant, two-tone marbled treats. Star anise's licorice-like flavor is mild but still potent enough to stand up to the zing of fresh orange zest in this delicate butter cookie inspired by America's neighbors to the north.

INGREDIENT	VOLUME	WEIGHT
Egg, at room temperature	1 large	50 grams (weighed without shell)
ORANGE DOUGH		
Unbleached all-purpose flour	1½ cups	213 grams
Baking powder	1 teaspoon	
Salt	½ teaspoon	
Unsalted butter, at room temperature	8 tablespoons	113 grams
Confectioners' sugar	¾ cup	85 grams
Orange zest, freshly grated	1 medium orange	
Pure vanilla extract	1 teaspoon	
BLACK ANISE DOUGH		
Unbleached all-purpose flour	1⅓ cups	189 grams
Black cocoa powder (see Note)	2 tablespoons	11 grams
Ground star anise (see Additional Note)	2 teaspoons	
Baking powder	1 teaspoon	
Salt	½ teaspoon	
Unsalted butter, at room temperature	8 tablespoons	113 grams
Confectioners' sugar	¾ cup	85 grams
Absinthe, Galliano, or other anise-flavored liqueur, or pure vanilla extract	1 teaspoon	

(continued)

1. Whisk the egg in a small bowl until it is completely uniform. Each dough will use half of the beaten egg, about 25 grams or 1½ tablespoons. Weighing (without the shell) will give you the most accurate way to split the egg.

2. Make the Orange Dough: Whisk together the flour, baking powder, and salt in a medium bowl; set aside.

3. Combine the butter, confectioners' sugar, and orange zest in a stand mixer fitted with a flat beater, and cream together on medium speed until smooth and creamy, 1 to 2 minutes. Beat in the vanilla and half of the beaten egg. The mixture might appear to separate, but keep mixing until it becomes smooth again. Stop mixing and scrape down the sides of the bowl and the beater with a silicone spatula.

4. Reduce the mixer speed to low and mix in the flour mixture until just combined. Set the dough aside as you make the other dough. (If you use the same bowl, there's no need to wash the bowl between batches.)

5. Make the Black Anise Dough: Whisk together the flour, cocoa powder, star anise, baking powder, and salt in a medium bowl; set aside.

6. Combine the butter and confectioners' sugar in the stand mixer fitted with a flat beater, and cream together on medium speed until smooth and creamy, 1 to 2 minutes. Beat in the absinthe and the remaining half of the beaten egg. As with the orange dough, the mixture might appear to separate, but keep mixing until it becomes smooth again. Stop mixing and scrape down the sides of the bowl and beater with a silicone spatula.

7. Reduce the mixer speed to low and mix in the cocoa mixture until just combined. Stop mixing and scrape down the sides of the bowl with a silicone spatula.

8. Divide each dough in half to make four separate portions (no need to be exact). Roll each portion of both the orange and black anise doughs into approximately 12-inch logs. (The logs should all be the same length.)

9. Lay one log of orange dough next to one log of black anise dough. Twist the two logs around each other three or four times and pinch the ends together. Bend the twisted logs in half to make a tight U shape with the ends of the dough touching. Press the dough together and use your hands to roll the marbled dough into a 12-inch log.

10. To finish marbling the dough, bend the dough in half again to create a U shape. Twist the two halves around each other just like before. Pinch the ends together and roll into a smooth 7-inch log (it will measure about 2 inches in diameter). Don't overwork the dough (see "Don't Lose Your Marble(s)" at right).

11. Press the dough into a mold (see page 178) or use parchment paper to smooth the dough into a log. Repeat with the two-step marbling technique with the two remaining dough logs.

12. Wrap and refrigerate the dough until it's cold and firm throughout before slicing, at least 2 hours or up to 3 days. The dough can be frozen at this point (see page 178).

13. Position two racks to divide the oven into thirds and preheat to 350°F. Line two 18-by-13-inch baking sheets with parchment paper or silicone baking mats.

14. Cut the logs into ¼-inch slices, and place 2 inches apart on the prepared baking sheets (you can fit 13 cookies on each pan; see page 86).

15. Bake until the edges of the dough have just begun to color, and the tops are firm when gently pressed, 13 to 16 minutes. Halfway through baking, rotate the pans from front to back and top to bottom. Remove from the oven and let cool for 5 minutes on the sheet before transferring to a wire rack to cool completely. Repeat with the remaining dough once the baking sheets have completely cooled, or prepare additional baking sheets. After cooling, the cookies can be stored in an airtight container at room temperature for several days.

NOTE: Two tablespoons of black cocoa powder, a form of Dutch-processed cocoa powder, give the dough a rich black color without adding much chocolate flavor. You can substitute traditional Dutch-processed cocoa powder or even natural cocoa powder, but the anise dough will be brown rather than black.

ADDITIONAL NOTE: You might be able to purchase ground star anise, but we grind our own because star anise can lose its flavor quickly when ground and stored for more than a few months. To grind, use a mortar and pestle or spice grinder and grind the whole star-shaped spice to a powder. Be sure that you use star anise—which has a very distinct star shape—and not anise seeds (a.k.a. aniseed). Both are licorice-like, but star anise provides a milder, more pleasing flavor in these cookies.

COOKIE BYTE

Don't Lose Your Marble(s)

Marbling the dough is an additional step, but the effect is well worth it.

It is important to not overwork the dough while you marble it. Remember: Less is more. If you keep massaging the dough, the colors will begin to blend into each other instead of having a marbled appearance. This is why we make these cookies as slice-and-bakes instead of rolled.

Fig and Maple Nut Slices

MAKES ABOUT 4 DOZEN (2-INCH) COOKIES

We admit to having some vices:
Kitchen tools, electronic devices.
But none of those toys
Can bring us the joys
Of these Fig and Maple Nut Slices!

The combo of maple and nut
It's a classic, no doubt there, but
The addition of fig
Is something you'll dig
If your cookie game's stuck in a rut.

INGREDIENT	VOLUME	WEIGHT
Unbleached all-purpose flour	2½ cups	354 grams
Salt	½ teaspoon	
Baking powder	¼ teaspoon	
Unsalted butter, at room temperature	16 tablespoons	227 grams
Maple sugar (see Note)	¾ cup	150 grams
Egg	1 large	50 grams (weighed without shell)
Pure maple syrup	⅓ cup	104 grams
Pure maple extract (optional; see Note)	¼ teaspoon	
Dried figs, stems removed and coarsely chopped into ½-inch pieces	¾ cup	113 grams
Walnut pieces, toasted and cooled (see page 24)	¾ cup	85 grams
Water	1 teaspoon	
Turbinado sugar	¼ cup	50 grams

1. Whisk together the flour, salt, and baking powder in a medium bowl; set aside.

2. Combine the butter and maple sugar in a stand mixer fitted with a flat beater, and cream together on medium speed until smooth and creamy, 1 to 2 minutes.

3. Separate the egg, refrigerating the egg white in a covered bowl. Beat the egg yolk, maple syrup, and maple extract (if using) into the butter mixture. Stop mixing and scrape down the sides of the bowl and beater with a silicone spatula.

(continued)

4. Reduce the mixer speed to low and mix in half of the flour mixture until incorporated. Stop mixing and scrape down the sides of the bowl with a silicone spatula. Mix in the remaining flour mixture just until no dry flour is visible. Scrape the sides of the bowl and stir in the figs and walnuts.

5. Divide the dough in half. Roll each half of the dough into 7-inch logs. Wrap each log in plastic wrap and refrigerate until cold and firm throughout, at least 2 hours or up to 3 days. The dough can be frozen at this point (see page 178).

6. Position two racks to divide the oven into thirds and preheat to 350°F. Line two 18-by-13-inch baking sheets with parchment paper or silicone baking mats. Remove the egg white from the refrigerator.

7. Cut the logs into ¼-inch slices, and place 2 inches apart on the prepared baking sheets (you can fit 13 on each pan; see page 86).

8. Whisk together the egg white and water in a small bowl. Brush a thin layer of the egg white mixture over each cookie. Sprinkle 1 tablespoon of the turbinado sugar over the cookies on each baking sheet.

9. Bake until the edges are set, and the tops are golden brown and firm when gently pressed, 15 to 18 minutes. Halfway through baking, rotate the pans from front to back and top to bottom. Remove from the oven and let cool for 5 minutes on the baking sheets before transferring to a wire rack to cool completely. Repeat with the remaining dough once the baking sheets have completely cooled, or prepare additional baking sheets. After cooling, the cookies can be stored in an airtight container at room temperature for several days.

NOTE: Maple sugar can be replaced with an equal amount of granulated sugar. To account for the lost maple flavor, increase the pure maple extract to ½ teaspoon. The maple extract gives a wonderful boost of maple flavor. If you are using maple sugar, the extract is optional, but we keep it in because the boosted hit of maple is absolutely divine.

Orange Rosemary Bites

MAKES 4 DOZEN (2-INCH) COOKIES

The previous owners of our current house had not lived here very long before selling it to us. As such, they had not had much opportunity (or perhaps inclination) to do a whole lot of landscaping. The ubiquitous azaleas and crepe myrtles were in place as seemingly required of all Atlanta houses, but there was still plenty of opportunity for us to augment and make it our own. We started with a stately pink Queen Elizabeth rose outside our dining room window and a yellow Julia Child rose to view from the kitchen. Julia apparently chose this variety of rose to bear her name because the blooms were the exact shade of butter. The next choice was more utilitarian. By the front door, we planted some rosemary that is still growing vigorously today, providing us a perennial supply for our kitchen. Every time you enter the house, you can run your fingers through the evergreen tendrils, releasing a potent cloud of herbal perfume into the air. This is the rosemary we used in an earlier version of this cookie that won a blue ribbon at the Georgia National Fair, and it is the same rosemary that we are still using today. Baked in the wells of muffin tins, these cylindrical cookie disks may look plain, but they taste deliciously complex. The sharp herbaceous notes are balanced by the orange zest and vanilla.

INGREDIENT	VOLUME	WEIGHT
Unbleached all-purpose flour	1¾ cups	248 grams
Salt	½ teaspoon	
Confectioners' sugar	1 cup	113 grams
Orange zest, freshly grated	1 medium orange	
Unsalted butter, at room temperature	16 tablespoons	227 grams
Fresh rosemary, finely chopped	1 tablespoon	
Pure vanilla extract	1 teaspoon	

1. Whisk together the flour and salt in a medium bowl; set aside.

2. Combine the confectioners' sugar and orange zest in the bowl of your stand mixer. Add the butter, fit the mixer with a flat beater, and cream together the butter and the orange sugar, initially on low speed and increasing to medium speed, 1 to 2 minutes. Add the rosemary and vanilla and beat until the mixture is uniform.

3. Reduce the mixer speed to low and mix in the flour mixture until combined. Scrape the sides of the bowl

(continued)

and the beater to make sure that all of the ingredients are incorporated and no dry flour is visible.

4. Divide the soft dough in half, spreading each portion on a piece of parchment paper or plastic wrap. Roll each portion into a 6-inch log (it will measure about 1¾ inches in diameter). Chill the wrapped dough in the refrigerator until cold and firm throughout, at least 2 hours or up to 3 days.

5. Position two racks to divide the oven into thirds and preheat to 350°F.

6. Cut the logs into ¼-inch slices and place each disk in the well of a standard muffin tin.

7. Bake for 12 to 15 minutes, until the cookies are golden brown at the edges. Halfway through baking, rotate the pans from front to back and top to bottom. Remove from the oven and let the cookies cool for 5 minutes in the muffin tin before unmolding. The cookies should slide out of the wells easily. Use an offset spatula or the tip of a butter knife if you need a bit of leverage to encourage their release. Let the cookies cool completely on a wire rack. Repeat with the remaining dough once the muffin tins have completely cooled. After cooling, the cookies can be stored in an airtight container at room temperature for several days.

Grapefruit and Pistachio Stained-Glass Slices

MAKES 3½ DOZEN (2-INCH) COOKIES

People have been making stained-glass cookies for decades. Most cookie compendiums will have a sugar or gingerbread cookie that has been cut out in the center and filled with crushed hard candies that melt into a pane of colored glass in the oven. We approached the idea of stained glass a bit differently to make a cookie that transilluminates beautifully with a first-rate flavor. Our stained glass is shards of candied grapefruit peel embedded in the dough, accented with slices of beautiful green pistachios. The added grapefruit zest in the cookie provides a zippy base for the bittersweet-tart slivers of pink-orange grapefruit alongside the creamy, sweet emerald pistachio slivers.

INGREDIENT	VOLUME	WEIGHT
Sugar	⅓ cup	67 grams
Pink grapefruit zest, freshly grated	1 medium grapefruit	
Unsalted butter, at room temperature	12 tablespoons	170 grams
Unbleached all-purpose flour	1¼ cups	177 grams
Salt	½ teaspoon	
Candied grapefruit peel (recipe follows), finely diced	½ cup	100 grams
Unsalted pistachios, shelled, roasted, and coarsely chopped	½ cup	64 grams

1. Combine the sugar and grapefruit zest to the bowl of your stand mixer. To extract the most grapefruit flavor, rub the zest and sugar between your thumbs and fingertips until the sugar is fragrant, very light orange in color, and has a texture like wet sand (see "Live Your Zest Life," page 25).

2. Add the butter, fit the mixer with a flat beater, and cream together on medium speed until smooth and creamy, 1 to 2 minutes. Stop mixing and scrape down the sides of the bowl and beater with a silicone spatula.

3. Reduce the mixer speed to low and mix in the flour and the salt until no dry flour is visible. Scrape the sides of the bowl with a silicone spatula and stir in the candied grapefruit and pistachios.

4. Roll the dough into a 10½-inch log (it will measure about 1¾ inches in diameter). If you prefer to use a mold instead, choose one with a 25-cubic-inch or 1¾-cup capacity. Wrap the log in plastic wrap and refrigerate until cold and firm throughout, at least 2 hours or up to 3 days. The dough can be frozen at this point (see page 178).

5. Position two racks to divide the oven into thirds and preheat to 350°F. Line two 18-by-13-inch baking sheets with parchment paper or silicone baking mats.

6. Cut the chilled dough into ¼-inch slices, and place 2 inches apart on the prepared baking sheets (you can fit 13 on each pan; see page 86).

(continued)

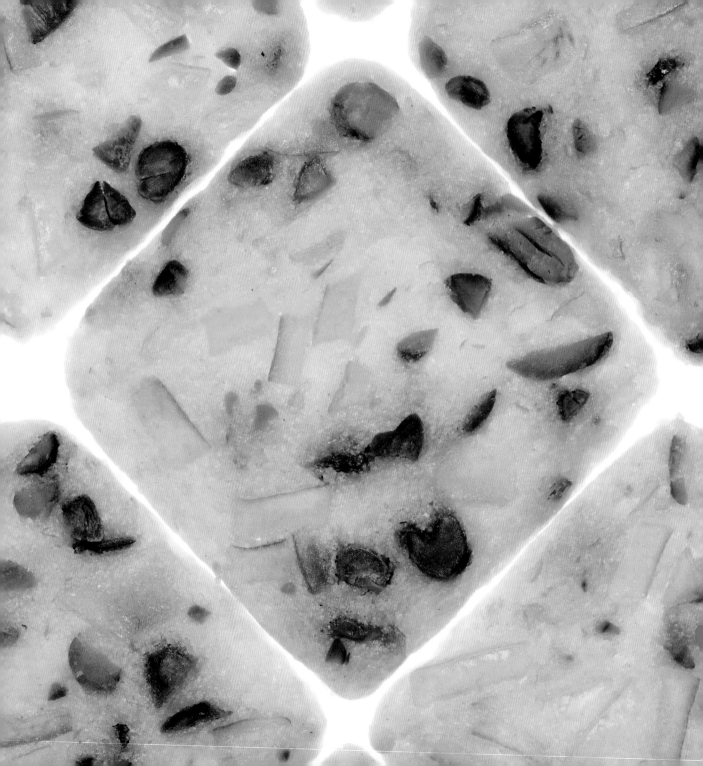

7. Bake until the edges are set, and the tops are golden brown and firm when gently pressed, 15 to 18 minutes. Halfway through baking, rotate the pans from front to back and top to bottom. Remove from the oven and let cool for 5 minutes on the sheet before transferring to a wire rack to cool completely. Repeat with the remaining dough once the baking sheets have completely cooled, or prepare additional baking sheets. After cooling, the cookies can be stored in an airtight container at room temperature for several days.

NOTE: These cookies can also be cut thinner for an even more spectacular stained-glass effect. If cut ⅛-inch thick, they will bake for 8 to 12 minutes. You'll need two grapefruits to make this recipe; one for the zest and the other for the candied peel.

(continued)

Candied Grapefruit Peel

MAKES ABOUT 100 GRAMS OF
CANDIED GRAPEFRUIT PEEL

This recipe makes enough candied grapefruit peel for one batch of Grapefruit and Pistachio Stained-Glass Slices. This recipe can be doubled or tripled if you want to make more. Do not be tempted to omit the corn syrup. It prevents crystallization and is an essential ingredient for the proper texture of the candied grapefruit.

INGREDIENT	VOLUME	WEIGHT
Pink grapefruit	1 medium	
Sugar	1¼ cups	250 grams
Light corn syrup	1 tablespoon	21 grams

1. Cut the grapefruit in half. Squeeze and reserve the juice, taking care not to damage the rind. Use a spoon to scrape out the segment skins and other pulp left behind after squeezing. Discard these. Slice the grapefruit rind (zest and white pith) into ¼-inch strips and place them in a small saucepan.

2. Add enough water to cover the strips and bring it to a boil over high heat. Lower the heat to medium-low and simmer the strips for 5 minutes. Drain and discard this water. Repeat this step two more times. This process softens the grapefruit rind and removes most of the unpleasantly bitter compounds from it.

3. Add ½ cup (120 grams) of the reserved grapefruit juice, 1 cup (200 grams) of the sugar, and the corn syrup to the saucepan. If your grapefruit yielded less juice than that, add just enough water to bring it up to ½ cup. Place the saucepan over medium heat and stir with a silicone spatula. The sugar will dissolve, and the liquid will come to a boil. Monitor the temperature periodically with an instant-read thermometer. When the temperature is consistently between 230° and 235°F (110° to 113°C), stir in the blanched grapefruit strips. Reduce the heat to low and cook the strips in the syrup for 15 minutes.

4. Remove the strips from the syrup with a slotted spoon, placing them on a wire rack to cool and dry for several hours. (The strips might drip a little, so feel free to position the rack over a sheet of parchment paper if you want to keep your counter clean.) Once dry, toss the strips with the remaining ¼ cup (50 grams) of sugar in a small bowl until the strips are well coated with sugar. Store the candied grapefruit peel in an airtight container in the refrigerator. It can last for several months.

Elderflower Dainties

MAKES ABOUT 4 DOZEN (1¾-INCH) COOKIES

Because these are made with low-protein cake flour and white rice flour, these are the most tender and delicate of all of our shortbread cookies. Made without eggs, the texture is divinely fragile with the merest hint of delicate floral elderflower liqueur. To boost the flavor (and add a bit of a kick), the tops are coated with a simple glaze of confectioners' sugar and additional liqueur. If elderflower's not your thing, this recipe works with nearly any liqueur—check out the Pick-Your-Potion variation.

INGREDIENT	VOLUME	WEIGHT
TENDER BUTTER COOKIES		
Bleached cake flour	1¾ cups	198 grams
Confectioners' sugar (see Note)	¾ cup	85 grams
White rice flour	½ cup	80 grams
Salt	¼ teaspoon	
Unsalted butter, cold, cut into 16 pieces	16 tablespoons	227 grams
Elderflower liqueur, preferably St-Germain	¼ cup	68 grams
LIQUEUR GLAZE		
Confectioners' sugar, preferably made with tapioca starch (see "Starch Madness," page 115)	1 to 1¼ cups	113 to 142 grams
Elderflower liqueur, preferably St-Germain	2 to 3 tablespoons	34 to 51 grams
Salt	Small pinch	

1. Make the Tender Butter Cookies: Combine the cake flour, confectioners' sugar, rice flour, and salt in the bowl of a food processor and pulse once or twice to blend the ingredients.

2. Add the cold butter pieces to the flour mixture and process the mixture until it looks like coarse cornmeal, about ten 1-second pulses. You don't want to see any large chunks of butter. Scrape the bottom of the food processor bowl to pick up any unincorporated dry flour.

3. Drizzle the liqueur into the mixture and process until the dough starts to come together and form a ball. Don't process too much, or the mixture will become too sticky and difficult to handle.

4. Remove the dough from the processor, and gently knead in any dusty flour bits (the dough might be a little sticky). Divide the dough in half and roll each half into a 6-inch log (see page 177). Wrap each log in plastic wrap and refrigerate until cold and firm throughout, at least 2 hours or up to 3 days.

(continued)

5. Position two racks to divide the oven into thirds and preheat to 350°F. Line two 18-by-13-inch baking sheets with parchment paper or silicone baking mats.

6. Cut the logs into ¼-inch slices, and place 2 inches apart on the prepared baking sheets (you can fit 18 on each pan; see page 86).

7. Bake until the edges of the cookies are set and light golden brown, 12 to 15 minutes. Halfway through baking, rotate the pans from front to back and top to bottom. Remove from the oven and let cool for 5 minutes on the baking sheets before transferring to a wire rack to cool completely before glazing. Repeat with the remaining dough once the baking sheets have completely cooled, or prepare additional baking sheets.

8. Make the Liqueur Glaze: Whisk together 1 cup (113 grams) of the confectioners' sugar, 2 tablespoons of elderflower liqueur, and salt in a small bowl. The glaze should be thickened but pourable, sort of like the consistency of honey; adjust the sugar or liqueur as needed. To glaze, grab each cookie confidently by the edges and dip the cookie into the glaze just to cover the top. Gently lay the cookie (glazed side facing up) on a wire rack to allow the glaze to set and any excess glaze to drip off. After the glaze has set (it takes an hour or two), the cookies can be stored in an airtight container at room temperature for several days.

NOTE: This recipe uses confectioners' sugar in both the cookie dough and the glaze. For the dough, feel free to use standard confectioners' sugar. For the glaze, we recommend confectioners' sugar made with tapioca starch, which is often labeled as organic (see page 115). Of course, you can use the more expensive tapioca-based sugar for the dough, but we save the pricier sugar for the glaze.

Variation: Pick-Your-Potion Glazed Butter Cookies

This recipe is endlessly adaptable! We haven't tried a liqueur (or cordial) yet that hasn't worked well. The substitution is easy: just replace equal amounts of elderflower liqueur in the base cookie dough and glaze recipe with another liqueur. Some of our favorite spirits swaps have included:

- Cream sherry (such as a Pedro Ximénez)
- Triple sec or Grand Marnier
- Literally any flavor schnapps (our favorites include banana, root beer, peppermint, and butterscotch)
- Midori melon liqueur (with the zest of one medium orange added to the dough with the cold butter)
- Fuzzy navel cocktail (peach schnapps with the zest of one medium orange added to the dough with the cold butter)

Rice Flour Power

COOKIE BYTE

Rice flour is uncooked grains of rice that have been pulverized to a fine powder. White rice flour is made from white rice; brown rice flour, from brown rice. Rice flour is essential in this recipe because it gives the cookie a great crunchy texture in two ways. First, rice flour has a low protein content and absorbs little water. This means that the moisture in the cookie that isn't absorbed by the wheat flour can bake out in the oven, resulting in a drier texture and crunchier cookie. Second, because rice flour is gluten-free, substituting it for some of the wheat flour traditionally in a recipe can make for a crisper texture because the amount of gluten (which contributes to a chewy texture) is reduced.

Whereas white rice is generally inexpensive, rice flour (per pound) is more costly. It might be tempting to make your own. Which you can do—*maybe*. Using our high-speed Vitamix blender, we are able to get rice ground to a very fine grain the texture of a fine salt, but not quite to a powder. These coarser pieces of uncooked rice flour can create an off-putting, grainy texture in your cookies. To get powder-fine rice flour at home, you would need to use a grain mill that is designed to grind hard wheat berries to a fine flour. A blender or food processor just won't get the rice to the texture that you need it for baking. Unless you have a grain mill, stick to using commercially made rice flour.

Because it is gluten-free, you might not find rice flour in your supermarket's baking aisle. Check for it in the gluten-free or other specialty foods sections. A little goes a long way, and you might be able to buy it in small amounts from a bulk bin at a natural foods store.

Booze in Baking

Bourbon, rum, and elderflower liqueur are just a few of the boozy beverages featured in cookie recipes throughout this book. While you're probably familiar with the intoxicating properties of ethanol (the type of alcohol in liquor and spirits), it is ethanol's other physical functions that make it a valuable tool in baking. Chemically, ethanol is both a great solvent that can dissolve some oils and also highly miscible, meaning that it blends seamlessly with water. So, if you were to soak a highly flavored substance in alcohol, those flavor compounds will leach out and become captured and concentrated in the ethanol mixture. A classic example of this is vanilla extract. Vanilla beans are jam-packed with vanilla flavor in a slightly inconvenient natural container. By soaking vanilla beans in ethanol, those wonderful vanilla flavors and aromatic compounds are extracted from the leathery pod into the liquid alcohol and easily dispensed one teaspoon at a time.

But what about the intoxicating effects of alcohol? Will alcohol-containing cookies get people drunk? Probably not—and let's discuss why. The Elderflower Dainties (page 201) contain a total of about 6 tablespoons of liqueur in the cookie and the glaze. In common bar parlance, that is equivalent to three shots of elderflower liqueur (an order for which a bartender will give you some serious side-eye). Now, three shots seems like a substantial portion of alcohol. However, those three shots (6 tablespoons) are divided over four dozen cookies! That's only ⅛ teaspoon of liqueur per cookie. Not a particularly potent potable, elderflower liqueur is 40 proof, or 20 percent ethanol. This means there are only, at most, about eight *drops* of actual ethanol in each cookie. Finally, we also need to consider one of the other neat properties of ethanol: its low boiling point. Ethanol boils at 173°F. This means that, while the cookies are baking in the dry 350°F oven, some (but not all) of that ethanol will evaporate to further reduce the final alcohol concentration. For most people, the residual alcohol content in the baked cookie will not even be noticed and any boozy notes will be the alcohol included in the glaze. Of course, if you are someone who cannot be around alcohol safely, you should skip the boozy cookies. Bake (and drink) responsibly.

Birthday Cake Rugelach Slices

MAKES 56 COOKIES

Neither of us grew up with someone to teach us how to master the filled, flaky wonders that are rugelach. Fortunately, the world of cookbooks has brought us the knowledge of two exceptionally talented authors through whose books we have ably learned the fundamentals: including authors Rose Levy Beranbaum and Cathy Barrow. While many recipes for rugelach dough are similar proportions of butter, cream cheese, and flour, Rose Levy Beranbaum's recipe includes a little bit of sugar, which we think adds a welcomed sweetness. Additionally, Rose's cake crumb kugelhopf "schmear" from her book, *The Bread Bible*, is the foundation for both fillings. Cathy Barrow's innovative rugelach flavors, such as Nutella and brown butter, or her "Naughty" Rugelach with salted peanuts and bacon jam, motivated us to create our own novel fillings of Birthday Cake and Caramel-Pretzel.

INGREDIENT	VOLUME	WEIGHT
Confectioners' sugar	⅓ cup	38 grams
Unbleached all-purpose flour	1⅔ cups	236 grams
Salt	¼ teaspoon	
Unsalted butter, at room temperature	16 tablespoons	227 grams
Cream cheese (full fat), at room temperature	One 8-ounce package	227 grams
Birthday Cake Filling (recipe follows)	1 recipe	
Egg	1 large	50 grams (weighed without shell)
Water	1 teaspoon	

1. To make the parchment packets (see "Pushing the Envelopes," page 211), fold in one long side of a 16-by-12-inch sheet of parchment paper to create a 3-inch flap; unfold the flap. Fold the other long side to meet that crease and fold to create a 4½-inch-wide flap. Without unfolding, refold the first flap. Fold each of the 4½-inch-wide ends over 1 inch to create a 14-by-4½-inch packet. Repeat with three other sheets of parchment to create four packets.

2. Sift the confectioners' sugar into a medium bowl. Add the flour and salt and whisk together.

3. Combine the butter and cream cheese in a stand mixer fitted with a flat beater, and cream together on medium speed until smooth and creamy, 1 to 2 minutes. Scrape the sides of the bowl and the beater. Set the mixer speed to low and gradually mix in half of the flour mixture just until it is incorporated.

(continued)

4. Stop mixing and scrape down the sides of the bowl with a silicone spatula. Mix in the remaining flour mixture just until a soft, shaggy dough forms. Scrape the sides of the bowl to incorporate any remaining bits of flour.

5. Open one parchment packet so it lies flat. Use a small offset or silicone spatula to spread one-quarter of the dough (175 grams) over the middle 14-inch rectangle outlined by the folds of the paper (some gaps are fine at this point). Refold the paper to close the packet and press the dough down with the paper to flatten it. Flip the packet over so the flaps are underneath the dough. Use a rolling pin to press the dough so that it fills the packet and is an even thickness throughout. (Be sure that the end flaps remain closed while you roll, or the dough will squish out!) Repeat with the three remaining packets and dough portions. Refrigerate the dough on a baking sheet or other flat surface for at least 2 hours or overnight. (Well wrapped in foil, the dough can be frozen for 3 months. Thaw the dough in the refrigerator overnight before unwrapping and filling.)

6. After the dough has chilled and you are ready to assemble the rugelach, prepare the Birthday Cake Filling (recipe follows).

7. Transfer the dough to a lightly floured counter or silicone rolling mat. Open the dough packet and lightly flour the top of the dough. Flip the dough upside down onto the counter and peel off the parchment paper. (Be sure that the dough can move so you'll know that it won't be stuck once the time comes to roll it up. Add more flour if necessary.) Position the rectangle with the long side of the dough facing you.

8. Use a small offset spatula to spread ½ cup of the Birthday Cake Filling (or ⅔ cup of the Caramel-Pretzel Filling) over the dough rectangle, leaving a ½-inch border along the top edge. Starting from the side closest to you, roll the dough into a tight spiral and leave the seam side down. Repeat with the remaining portions of dough to create four logs. Transfer the rolls to a parchment-lined baking sheet and refrigerate for at least 30 minutes or overnight.

9. Position two racks to divide the oven into thirds and preheat to 350°F. Line two 18-by-13-inch baking sheets with parchment paper or silicone baking mats.

10. Whisk the egg and water together in a small bowl. Use a pastry brush to brush the egg mixture all over the top and sides of the chilled dough log. (Sprinkle ¼ teaspoon of pretzel salt over each log for the Caramel-Pretzel Rugelach.)

11. Trim away the uneven ends of the log to leave a 14-inch log. Slice the chilled log into 1-inch pieces. Place evenly on a parchment-lined baking sheet, leaving 2 inches between each cookie (you can fit all 14 cookies on one pan by using the 13-cookie configuration (page 86) and adding an additional cookie to one of the rows).

12. Bake until the tops are golden brown, the bottoms have browned, and the cookies do not feel squishy when gently pressed, 23 to 28 minutes. Halfway through baking, rotate the pans from front to back and top to bottom. Remove from the oven and immediately transfer the cookies to a wire rack to cool completely. Repeat with the remaining dough once the baking sheets have completely cooled, or prepare additional baking sheets. Rugelach will last for several days at room temperature, but they are really best within a day of baking.

(continued)

Birthday Cake Filling

MAKES ABOUT 2 CUPS, ENOUGH FOR 1 RECIPE OF RUGELACH DOUGH

Nothing says "Happy birthday to you!" like a slice of birthday cake flecked with rainbow sprinkles. Using repurposed cake crumbs augmented with vanilla, almond, and white chocolate, this filling provides the full birthday cake sensory experience in Technicolor.

INGREDIENT	VOLUME	WEIGHT
Unfrosted cake, crumbled into small pieces (see Note)	About 2½ cups	227 grams
Unsalted butter, cut into 4 pieces, at room temperature	4 tablespoons	57 grams
Almond paste, broken into small clumps, at room temperature	2 tablespoons	40 grams
Egg, at room temperature	1 large	50 grams (weighted without shell)
Light corn syrup	1 tablespoon	21 grams
Pure vanilla extract	½ teaspoon	
White chocolate, melted and cooled but still pourable		85 grams (3 ounces)
Rainbow sprinkles (preferably jimmies)	2 tablespoons	

1. Place the crumbled cake in the bowl of a food processor and process until it is finely ground. Add the butter, almond paste, egg, corn syrup, and vanilla to the cake crumbs and process, using 1-second pulses, until the mixture is well combined. Add the cooled melted white chocolate and pulse again until everything is uniform. Transfer the mixture to a bowl, and fold in the sprinkles with a silicone spatula.

NOTE: This recipe works with yellow, white, or pound cake (yes, store-bought is fine, but you just need the cake, not the frosting). This filling is easiest to make in a food processor. If you don't have a food processor, crumble the cake into fine crumbs by hand and beat the ingredients together using an electric hand mixer.

(continued)

Variation: Caramel-Pretzel Filling
MAKES 2⅔ CUPS, ENOUGH FOR 1 RECIPE OF RUGELACH DOUGH

This pretzel-packed filling is matched with creamy dulce de leche caramel for a perfect sweet and salty bite.

INGREDIENT	VOLUME	WEIGHT
Thin pretzel sticks or twists, broken into pieces	212 pretzel sticks	227 grams (8 ounces)
Unsalted butter, at room temperature, cut into 10 pieces	10 tablespoons	142 grams
Eggs, at room temperature	2 large	100 grams (weighed without shells)
Dulce de leche	¼ cup	78 grams
White chocolate, melted and cooled but still pourable		170 grams (6 ounces)
Pretzel salt or other large, flaky salt, for sprinkling	1 teaspoon	

1. Place the pretzel pieces in the bowl of a food processor and process until they are finely ground (see Note). Add the butter, eggs, and dulce de leche to the pretzel crumbs and process, using 1-second pulses, until the mixture is well combined. Add the cooled melted white chocolate and pulse again until everything is uniform. Transfer the mixture to a bowl for easier portioning.

2. Spread ⅔ cup of the filling over each dough rectangle following the directions in the main recipe. Sprinkle ¼ teaspoon of the pretzel salt over each chilled egg-washed dough log before it's sliced.

NOTE: This filling is easiest to make in a food processor. If you don't have a food processor, finely crush the pretzels by hand and beat the ingredients together using an electric hand mixer.

COOKIE BYTE

Pushing the Envelopes

Several cookies in this book involve rolling dough into rectangles of specified dimensions to produce attractive, equal-size cookies. Traditionally, this would involve flouring your rolling surface, rolling pin, and dough, and sometimes a bit of trial and error, only to end up with rectangles that are probably close enough but usually not exact. We like using envelopes of folded parchment paper to roll the dough in before it's chilled.

- All you need are sheets of parchment paper, a ruler, and a flat surface.
- Each recipe tells you how to make the four folds of specific lengths that are required to make the correctly sized envelope.
- Place the specified amount of dough inside the envelope and fold the flaps to close it.
- Roll the dough up to all of the edges and into the corners of the envelope until it is full. These recipes specify just the right amount of dough to fill the envelope to the proper thickness.
- Run your fingers over the envelope to make sure it feels pretty flat. If not, go over it once or twice with your rolling pin.

You will now have a perfect rectangle of dough that did not require adding a bunch of extra flour that can sometimes make the cookies dry and crumbly. It may seem like a bit of a hassle, but it works extremely well. If you really don't want to use the parchment paper envelopes, refrigerate the dough after it is mixed until cold and firm throughout before attempting to roll and shape the dough. Stop and check your progress frequently with your ruler to make sure you hit your marks.

CHAPTER FIVE

filled, stuffed, and sandwiched cookies

While cookies themselves are delightful, filling a cookie with a spoonful of jam or sandwiching two around a dollop of buttercream makes for an extra-special treat. With filled cookies, the world of cookies becomes even more infinite because many of the fillings can be swapped to match your personal preferences. Don't want to use raspberry jam? Swap it out for another fruit. Not in the mood for chocolate buttercream? Use vanilla instead.

The bases for many of these filled or sandwiched cookies use techniques from other chapters. Check out the introductory section referenced in each recipe for tips and tricks for making the cookie bases. The techniques outlined on page 215 will help guide you as you fill or sandwich your cookies.

Helpful Tools

- **Scoops.** Portion fillings accurately to prevent overfilled cookies. Also known as portion scoops or dishers. We prefer scoops that dispense dough with a "trigger" operated by pressing on a lever with your thumb or by squeezing the handle with your palm.
- **Piping bags.** Plastic bags hold fillings so portions can be piped through a tip onto a cookie.
- **Piping tips.** These help when you are looking to pipe a filling with a unique pattern or design. These are not required, but they do add an extra-special touch.
- **Offset spatula.** A small 4-inch offset spatula is great for smoothing filling into flat, even layers.
- **Ball Tool.** A pencil-size tool with marble-size balls at both ends is the perfect tool for creating wells in thumbprint cookies. This is certainly an optional tool but one that we turn to time and time again.

General Tips and Techniques

Don't overfill. This is the Golden Rule of filled cookies! We provide measurements for what we recommend as the right amount of filling for each cookie. If you choose to add more, you can create some avoidable problems.

- Using too much filling can make a cookie that's too difficult to eat. While the filling is delicious, having all the filling blast out of the back and sides of the cookie on the first bite can make a real mess!
- Using too much filling might mean that you don't have enough filling for all of your cookies. While the filling recipes do have some wiggle room, if you stuff your cookies with twice as much filling as we recommend, you'll only be able to fill half of your cookies (unless you make more).
- Using too much filling upsets the flavor and texture of the finished cookie. Generally, the filling in the cookie is sweeter than the cookie itself. Too much filling can make a cookie that is sweeter than you expect, and the flavor of the filling might overpower the flavor of the cookie.

Piping versus scooping. Smooth and creamy fillings and jams without fruit bits can be easily piped because they don't have any chunks that could block the piping tip. Fillings with bits of fruit, such as marmalade, are often better when scooped or spooned onto the cookie.

Double denting. During baking, cookies often puff. For thumbprint-style cookies, this puffing will shrink the size of the well (thumbprint) in the cookie and decrease the amount of delicious filling that it can hold. To counter this, we like to re-imprint the well of the cookie halfway through baking. For both the first (prebaking) and second (midbaking) impressions, we prefer something other than our own fingers. Other tools are better shaped, and, for the second impression, the cookies are fresh from the oven and quite hot. We like to use a ball tool, with a ¾- to 1-inch sphere (see Sources, page 350), to create the indentations for our thumbprint-style cookies. Without one, feel free to use a round measuring spoon or some other similarly shaped tool.

Piping dreams. Plastic piping bags are often the most convenient way to fill cookies (see "Plastic Alternatives" at right). If you use plastic bags, any type of plastic is fine, but we often use bags described as "tipless" because the thinner plastic is easy to handle. You can use smaller ones, but a good supply of 12-inch bags should be just fine for every recipe in this book. If you don't have piping bags, a quart-size resealable plastic storage bag works, too. Just cut off one of the bottom corners and pipe the filling as directed. Don't cut the tip of the bag too wide, or too much filling can be squeezed out and lead to overfilling.

Fill 'er up. To easily fill a piping bag, fold over the opening of the bag by about 3 inches to create a cuff. Insert a pastry tip and cut off just enough plastic at the tip of the bag to allow about half of the piping tip to sit snuggly outside the bag. Fill the bag about halfway full, unfold the cuff, and twist the top of the bag to keep the contents inside while you pipe. Not every filling needs to be filled with a decorative piping tip. To use a bag without a tip, simply fill the bag and then use scissors to snip away just enough of the bag at the tip to create a large enough hole to pipe through. If it is too difficult to pipe, the bag begins to bulge from pressure, or the hole becomes clogged, snip away a little more plastic to create a slightly larger hole.

Plastic Alternatives

If you don't want to use plastic, we understand. For some cookies, a spoon or scoop can be effectively used for depositing fillings into the cookies. Cones made from parchment paper are another alternative to plastic (check the Internet for videos on how to make them). If you don't use pastry bags that often, reusable cloth pastry bags are a good option. They are reusable but can be hard to clean completely. We avoid reusable pastry bags because we do a lot of cookie decorating with royal icing, and any residual fats left on the lining of the bag can break down the icing.

OMGs (Our Marvelous Gobs)

MAKES 2 DOZEN (2-INCH) COOKIE SANDWICHES

Although most of the United States knows these soft, cakey treats as whoopie pies, Chris grew up knowing them as gobs—a linguistic quirk particular mostly to western Pennsylvania in areas around Pittsburgh. We took the traditional recipe of palm-size chocolate cookies sandwiched around a shortening-based buttercream and modernized them for our tastes. First, we made them a little smaller so one batch can feed a whole crowd. Next, we boosted the chocolate flavor with Dutch-processed cocoa powder, espresso powder, and mini chocolate chips. We used cake flour for a softer, lighter bite and filled them with a creamy mascarpone filling that is rich but isn't heavy like traditional butter- or shortening-based frostings. You can make these with any filling, but pairing these chocolate sandwiches with the chocolate variation makes a particularly divine triple-chocolate treat. Refer to page 83 for tips and techniques on preparing drop cookies.

INGREDIENT	VOLUME	WEIGHT
Bleached cake flour	2½ cups	284 grams
Dutch-processed cocoa powder	½ cup plus 1 tablespoon	48 grams
Baking soda	1 teaspoon	
Salt	¾ teaspoon	
Unsalted butter, at room temperature	6 tablespoons	85 grams
Light brown sugar	Packed ¾ cup	150 grams
Granulated sugar	¼ cup	50 grams
Egg, at room temperature	1 large	50 grams (weighed without shell)
Instant espresso powder	½ teaspoon	
Pure vanilla extract	1½ teaspoons	
Sour cream (full fat), at room temperature	¾ cup	182 grams
Miniature semisweet chocolate chips	⅔ cup	113 grams
Creamy Mascarpone Filling, any flavor (page 339)	1 recipe (about 2 cups)	

(continued)

1. Position a rack in the center of the oven and preheat to 350°F. Line two 18-by-13-inch baking sheets with silicone baking mats. (We prefer silicone baking mats for this recipe because the cakey cookies tend to stick to parchment paper.)

2. Sift the flour, cocoa powder, baking soda, and salt in a medium bowl, using a fine-mesh sieve. Whisk together to combine and set aside.

3. Place the butter in a stand mixer fitted with a flat beater, and beat on medium speed until it's smooth and creamy, 1 to 2 minutes. While still beating, slowly add the brown sugar, followed by the granulated sugar, and beat until the mixture is light and fluffy, 2 to 3 minutes more.

4. Beat in the egg, espresso powder, and vanilla until the egg is incorporated and the mixture is smooth.

5. Reduce the mixer speed to low and mix in half of the flour mixture until almost combined. Stop mixing and scrape down the sides of the bowl and beater with a silicone spatula. Return the mixer to low speed and mix in the sour cream until incorporated, 20 to 30 seconds. Mix in the remaining flour mixture just until no dry flour is visible. Scrape the sides of the bowl to make sure that no butter or flour clumps are still hiding. Stir in the chocolate chips.

6. Portion 1 tablespoon of dough (the batter is soft, so a #60 scoop is recommended here) and place at least 2 inches apart on one of the prepared baking sheets (you can fit 13 on each pan; see page 86). When using a cookie scoop, release the batter as close to the baking sheet as you can get (½ inch is perfect). It helps keep the cookies rounder and more equal in size than dropping them from several inches above the pan.

7. Bake one sheet at a time until the edges have set and the centers of the cookies spring back when lightly pressed, 10 to 12 minutes. Halfway through baking, rotate the pan from front to back. Remove from the oven and let cool for 2 minutes on the baking sheet before transferring to a wire rack to cool completely. Repeat with the remaining dough once the baking sheet has completely cooled, or prepare additional baking sheets.

8. After cooling, the cookies can be filled. Match up cookies of the same size to make the most attractive cookie sandwiches. Use a spoon or scoop to portion 1 tablespoon of filling onto half of the cookies. Top with the second cookie, pressing the filling out to the edges, if needed. (Alternatively, you can pipe the filling using a pastry bag fitted with a star-shaped tip for a fancier look.)

9. After they are filled, store them in an airtight container in the refrigerator. They will keep in the refrigerator for about 1 week. Kept in an airtight container or individually wrapped and sealed in a heavy-duty resealable freezer storage bag, they can also be frozen for at least 3 months. Thaw for several hours (or overnight) in the refrigerator. They can be enjoyed cold or at room temperature.

Moonstrucks

MAKES 2 DOZEN (2-INCH) COOKIE SANDWICHES

Named for *Moonstruck*, one of our favorite date-night movies, these tender sandwich cookies are our ode to the Italian dessert tiramisu. Espresso, rum, mascarpone, and a dusting of cocoa powder are fantastic when served off the dessert cart at your neighborhood Italian restaurant, after a night at the opera, or sitting around listening to that damn Vikki Carr record. The next time you are sitting around craving a forkful or that rich plated dessert, snap out of it! We pack all of tiramisu's familiar flavor into a portable filled cookie—no forks necessary! Refer to page 83 for tips and techniques on preparing drop cookies.

INGREDIENT	VOLUME	WEIGHT
ESPRESSO COOKIES		
Bleached cake flour	2¾ cups	312 grams
Baking soda	¾ teaspoon	
Salt	½ teaspoon	
Baking powder	¼ teaspoon	
Unsalted butter, at room temperature	6 tablespoons	85 grams
Light brown sugar	Packed ½ cup	100 grams
Granulated sugar	½ cup	100 grams
Egg, at room temperature	1 large	50 grams (weighed without shell)
Instant espresso powder	4 teaspoons	
Dark rum	1 tablespoon	
Pure vanilla extract	1 teaspoon	
Sour cream (full fat), at room temperature	¾ cup	182 grams
COFFEE-RUM SOAKING SYRUP		
Strongly brewed coffee	½ cup	113 grams
Granulated sugar	½ cup plus 1 tablespoon	113 grams
Dark rum	1 tablespoon	
FOR ASSEMBLY		
Espresso Mascarpone Filling (page 339)	1 recipe (about 2 cups)	
Dutch-processed cocoa powder (for dusting)	About 2 tablespoons	

(continued)

1. Position a rack in the center of the oven and preheat to 350°F. Line two 18-by-13-inch baking sheets with silicone baking mats. (We prefer silicone baking mats for this recipe because the cakey cookies tend to stick to parchment paper.)

2. Make the Espresso Cookies: Sift the flour, baking soda, salt, and baking powder into a medium bowl; set aside.

3. Combine the butter, brown sugar, and granulated sugar in a stand mixer fitted with a flat beater, and cream together on medium speed until light and fluffy, about 3 minutes.

4. Beat in the egg, espresso powder, rum, and vanilla until the egg is incorporated and the mixture is smooth. Scrape down the sides of the bowl and beater with a silicone spatula.

5. Beat in half of the flour mixture on low speed until almost combined. Beat in the sour cream until incorporated, 20 to 30 seconds. Mix in the remaining flour mixture just until no dry flour is visible. Scrape the sides of the bowl to make sure that no butter or flour clumps are still hiding.

6. Portion 1 tablespoon of dough (the batter is soft, so a #60 scoop is recommended here) and place at least 2 inches apart on one of the prepared baking sheets (you can fit 13 on each pan; see page 86). When using a cookie scoop, release the batter as close to the baking sheet as you can get (½ inch is perfect). It helps keep the cookies rounder and more equal in size than dropping them from several inches above the pan.

7. Bake one sheet at a time until the edges have set and the centers of the cookies spring back when lightly pressed, 10 to 12 minutes. Halfway through baking, rotate the pan from front to back. Remove from the oven and let cool for 2 minutes on the baking sheet before transferring to a wire rack to cool completely. Repeat with the remaining dough once the baking sheet has completely cooled, or prepare additional baking sheets.

8. Make the Coffee-Rum Soaking Syrup: While the cookies are cooling, bring the coffee and sugar to a boil in a small saucepan, stirring until the sugar dissolves. Remove from the heat and stir in the rum. Set the mixture aside to cool completely. (This syrup can be made several days before using and stored in the refrigerator.)

9. After the cookies have cooled, brush the flat sides with the cooled soaking syrup. Match up cookies of the same size to make the most attractive cookie sandwiches. Use a spoon or scoop to portion 1 tablespoon of filling onto half of the cookies. Top with the second cookie, pressing the filling out to the edges, if needed. (Alternatively, you can pipe the filling using a pastry bag fitted with a star-shaped tip for a fancier look.)

10. After they are filled, lightly dust the cocoa powder over the tops of the cookies, using a fine-mesh sieve. Store the cookies in an airtight container in the refrigerator. They will keep in the refrigerator for about 1 week. Kept in an airtight container or individually wrapped and sealed in a heavy-duty resealable freezer storage bag, they can also be frozen for at least 3 months. Thaw for several hours (or overnight) in the refrigerator. They can be enjoyed cold or at room temperature.

Old Fashioned Ice Cream Sandwiches

MAKES 18 (1½-BY-3-INCH)
ICE CREAM SANDWICHES

When we spent time with my grandparents while growing up, my brothers and I would often be treated with a trip to Arctic Al's ice cream shop. Al's was a drive-up stand where orders were placed at walk-up windows with casements that slid open to briefly allow a chilled breeze to waft outside while cones and cash were exchanged across the counter. There was no indoor seating, and treats were enjoyed at picnic tables or standing around the car. Some families enjoyed their desserts inside their car, but Nana and Pap-Pap knew better than to let their rowdy grandsons knock around with drippy cones in the backseat of their Buick. Although Arctic Al's is now closed, I can still recall the sun-faded posters on its windows displaying all types of ice-cream sundaes, shakes, and slushies. If I wasn't getting a cone of soft-serve ice cream with sprinkles (my personal favorite), I would opt for an ice cream sandwich, one of Al's many ice cream novelties. Call me old-fashioned, but I think serving ice cream smashed between two cookies is still a really good idea. But being 30 years older, my tastes have changed, and this ice cream sandwich is no kiddie-style sweet. The no-churn vanilla ice cream is inspired by the classic old fashioned cocktail and laced with a healthy dose of bourbon, fresh orange peel, and sweet red cherries. Sandwiched between two ultrathin layers of fudgy brownie, it's my favorite new-fashioned old fashioned summertime treat. Refer to page 39 for tips and techniques on preparing bar cookies. —C.T.

INGREDIENT	VOLUME	WEIGHT
ICE CREAM		
Heavy cream	2 cups	464 grams
Piping gel (see "Piping Gel Intel," page 225)	2 tablespoons	38 grams
Sweetened condensed milk	One 14-ounce can	397 grams
Bourbon	2 tablespoons	25 grams
Pure vanilla extract	1 teaspoon	
Orange zest, freshly grated	1 medium orange	
Maraschino cherries, well drained, patted dry, and coarsely chopped	12 cherries	About 42 grams
COOKIE		
Midnight in Seville brownie batter (page 48; see Note)	1 batch	640 grams

(continued)

1. Line a 9-inch square baking pan with plastic wrap.

2. Place the cream in a stand mixer fitted with a whisk attachment, and whip on medium-high speed until it holds soft peaks when the whisk is removed. Add the piping gel and continue to whip until it reaches stiff peaks.

3. Whisk together the sweetened condensed milk, bourbon, vanilla, and orange zest in a separate bowl.

4. Use the whisk to scoop up a dollop of the whipped cream and stir it into the condensed milk mixture to lighten it. Now, pour this lightened mixture into the rest of the whipped cream. Use the whisk to gently fold the mixture together until it is all smooth and combined.

5. Use a silicone spatula to fold the cherries into the cream. Scrape the mixture into the prepared pan and smooth the top with a silicone or offset spatula. Place the pan in the freezer and let the mixture freeze solid overnight. Once frozen, use the plastic wrap to lift the frozen ice cream from the pan so that you can use it for baking one of the cookie layers. Return the ice cream to the freezer.

6. Position a rack in the center of the oven and preheat to 350°F. Line the bottom and sides of two 9-inch square baking pans with aluminum foil. Lightly spray the foil with baking spray.

7. Prepare the brownie batter as directed. Pour half (about 320 grams) of the brownie batter into each prepared pan. Use an offset spatula to spread the batter in a thin even layer over the entire bottom surface of the pan; smooth the top.

8. Bake until a toothpick inserted into the middle comes out clean, 10 to 15 minutes. (These brownies

---

Store-Bought is Fine

Two pints of softened ice cream can be substituted for the ice cream made in the recipe. Spread in the plastic-lined pan and freeze as directed.

---

are thin, so you should not bake these brownies in a water bath as for the Infinity Brownies.) Remove from the oven and place on a wire rack to cool completely. Use the foil edges to lift the cooled layers out of their pans.

9. Place the frozen ice cream block on your work surface. Place one cookie layer directly on top of the ice cream. Flip them over together, so that the first cookie layer is now on the bottom, and peel the plastic wrap off of the ice cream. Place the second cookie layer on top of the ice cream and gently press the sandwich together. Place the sandwich back in the freezer to make sure it is solidly frozen before cutting.

10. Cut the ice cream sandwich into eighteen 1½-by-3-inch bars. Return the sandwiches to the freezer until just before serving. Ice cream sandwiches can be individually wrapped and stored in a container frozen for several weeks.

NOTE: The Infinity Brownie makes a delicious cookie for these ice cream sandwiches. We prefer the Midnight in Seville variation with this ice cream, but the plain version without the orange will work just fine. For this recipe, the brownies are baked in 9-inch square pans and without a water bath.

COOKIE BYTE

Piping Gel Intel

Piping gel is a colorless, flavorless, jelly-like product made from corn syrup and cornstarch whose intended purpose is for cake decorating, such as writing "Happy Birthday" in shiny script on cakes. You can buy it at most craft or cake decorating stores. We know that adding a bit of it to whipped cream is a great way to stabilize it, allowing it to stay in shape longer without adversely affecting the texture, so we're using it in the ice cream recipe for a similar reason. The bourbon predisposes this ice cream to freeze a bit softer and melt a bit quicker because alcohol lowers the freezing point. The added piping gel helps the ice cream maintain its shape long enough to be enjoyed inside the sandwich layers. If omitted, you may want to consider serving the ice cream in a bowl with the cookies on the side.

Fruity Newties

MAKES 2 DOZEN COOKIES

While these pudgy slices are inspired by the familiar chewy/cakey Fig Newton, we reworked both the outer shell and fruit filling to deliver a cookie with a sultry dark side. We transformed the cookie's customary cover into a chocolate swaddle boosted by brown sugar and Dutch-processed cocoa powder that complements a sticky-sweet fig filling amped up with bright orange and crunchy toasted almonds. The variations for both tart cranberry-pomegranate and snappy ginger-apricot fillings are worlds apart from their packaged and peddled forebear. Refer to page 177 for tips and techniques on preparing slice-and-bake cookies.

INGREDIENT	VOLUME	WEIGHT
CHOCOLATE DOUGH		
Unbleached all-purpose flour	1 cup	142 grams
Dutch-processed cocoa powder	¼ cup	21 grams
Baking powder	¼ teaspoon	
Salt	⅛ teaspoon	
Unsalted butter, at room temperature	4 tablespoons	57 grams
Light brown sugar	3 tablespoons	38 grams
Egg, at room temperature	1 large	50 grams (weighed without shell)
Pure vanilla extract	½ teaspoon	
FILLING		
Filling (recipes follow)	1 recipe	

1.   Make parchment paper packets: Fold a 16-by-12-inch sheet of parchment paper lengthwise into thirds to create a 16-by-4-inch rectangle. Fold over each end by 3 inches to create a 10-by-4-inch rectangle. Repeat with a second sheet of parchment paper; set aside. (See "Pushing the Envelopes," page 211).

2.   Make the Chocolate Dough: In a small bowl, whisk together the flour, cocoa powder, baking powder, and salt until the cocoa is distributed evenly throughout.

3.   Depending on the capacity of your stand mixer, this might be more convenient to mix using an electric hand mixer. Combine the butter and brown sugar in a medium bowl, and use an electric hand mixer to beat together until well blended and creamy, 1 to 2 minutes, scraping the sides with a silicone spatula as needed.

4.   Add the egg and vanilla and continue to beat until the mixture is smooth. It might seem just a bit curdled; that's okay. Reduce the mixer speed to low and slowly

beat in the flour mixture until no flour is visible and the dough begins clumping. Using your hands or a stiff scraper, press the dough into a ball, gently kneading it to pick up any stray dough pieces left in the bowl. Divide the dough in half (each portion will weigh about 130 grams).

5. Unfold one parchment paper packet and roughly pat half of the dough across the bottom of the 10-by-4-inch center rectangle. Refold the parchment paper over the dough and use a rolling pin to roll the dough evenly through the parchment paper packet, being sure that the dough fills all four corners of the packet. Once the corners are filled and the dough has an even thickness throughout, place the packet on a baking sheet. Repeat with the second half of dough and the second parchment paper packet. Refrigerate both dough packets until cold and firm, at least 2 hours or up to 2 days.

6. Make the filling of your choice: If you are baking the cookies the same day, leave the filling to cool to room temperature before assembling the cookies. If you are baking the cookies in a day or two, refrigerate the filling in a sealed container. Bring the filling to room temperature before assembling and baking the cookies.

7. When the filling mixture has reached room temperature, position a rack in the center of the oven and preheat to 375°F. Line one baking sheet with parchment paper or a silicone baking mat.

8. Remove the dough packets from the refrigerator. Unwrap the packets and peel the parchment paper off both doughs. Position the dough on a cutting board or other knife-safe surface. The dough should be cold and not sticky. If the dough feels sticky, lightly dust the cutting board with a very small amount of flour. Add a few teaspoons of cold water to a small bowl; set aside.

9. Use a small offset spatula to spread half of the filling evenly down the center of each strip of dough. The strip of filling should be 10 inches long and about one-third of the width of the dough strip (no wider than 1½ inches).

10. Position the dough strip with the long side facing you. Fold the back third of dough up and over to cover about half of the filling. (If the dough is still too cold to roll without cracking, set the dough aside for about 5 minutes to warm up a bit.) Use a pastry brush to gently brush a ½-inch-wide strip of water over the flap of dough immediately facing you. Fold that dough flap up and over to cover the remaining half of the filling plus about ¼ inch of the chocolate dough to fully seal the filling. Turn the dough over so the seam is on the bottom. (This can be tricky if your strip of filling is not even. A small gap between the edges of the dough is okay, but if your coverage is way off, remove or redistribute some of the filling so that the dough will seal.)

11. Trim off the ends of the dough with a sharp knife. Cut the remaining log into ¾-inch pieces (you will get 12 pieces from each trimmed log). Position all 24 pieces on the prepared baking sheet (see page 86).

12. Bake the cookies until the dough is firm and set but not hard, 10 to 13 minutes, rotating the pan after 6 minutes. Remove from the oven and let the cookies cool on the baking sheet for 5 minutes before transferring them to a wire rack to cool completely. Sealed in an airtight container at room temperature, these cookies are at their best when eaten within a day or two.

(continued)

Fig-Orange-Almond Filling

**MAKES ENOUGH FOR 1 RECIPE OF
CHOCOLATE DOUGH**

If your family is Italian (or you have the great fortune to live near an Italian bakery), this filling might remind you of *cuccidati*, Sicilian fig cookies that were mostly likely the ancestors of what is today's Fig Newton. While recipes for cuccidati vary, including some with more fruits and spices than we use here, we love the combo of figs with the simple addition of orange and the crunch of toasted almonds. Wrapped in the chocolate dough, these are a mighty fine update to the everyday fig cookie.

INGREDIENT	VOLUME	WEIGHT
Dried figs, stemmed and coarsely chopped into ½-inch pieces	About 11 dried figs	198 grams (7 ounces)
Water	1 cup	237 grams
Grand Marnier or other orange liqueur, or freshly squeezed orange juice	2 tablespoons	28 grams
Light brown sugar	2 tablespoons	25 grams
Salt	⅛ teaspoon	
Orange zest, freshly grated	1 medium orange	
Slivered almonds, toasted, cooled, and chopped (see page 24)	¼ cup	30 grams

1. Combine the figs, water, Grand Marnier, brown sugar, and salt in a medium saucepan. Over medium heat, bring the mixture to a boil, stirring occasionally. Once the mixture boils, lower the heat to a simmer and continue to cook, stirring frequently, until the mixture is thick and jammy, 8 to 12 minutes. Even a slightly stiff mixture is okay here—if the mixture is too loose, it will ooze out of the cookies while baking.

2. Transfer the filling to the bowl of a food processor or some other small electric chopping device. Add the orange zest and process the mixture until it is mostly smooth (it doesn't have to be baby food). Transfer the mixture to a small bowl. Stir in the chopped almonds and set aside until the mixture reaches room temperature, about 30 minutes, or refrigerate for up to 2 days. (If refrigerated, bring to room temperature before assembling the cookies.)

MAKE AHEAD: Both the chocolate dough and filling can be made 2 days before assembling and baking the cookies.

Cranberry-Pomegranate Filling

MAKES ENOUGH FOR 1 RECIPE OF CHOCOLATE DOUGH

Cooking dried cranberries in pomegranate juice makes a tart filling that is bursting with bright red fruitiness. Wrapped in the sweet chocolate dough, this is a perfect snack for those who like their cookies decidedly less sweet. There is no need to add additional sugar because there is sugar in the pomegranate juice.

INGREDIENT	VOLUME	WEIGHT
Dried cranberries	1½ cups	198 grams (7 ounces)
Bottled pomegranate juice, such as POM Wonderful	1 cup	250 grams
Salt	⅛ teaspoon	
Pure vanilla extract	1 teaspoon	

1. Combine the cranberries, pomegranate juice, and salt in a medium saucepan. Over medium heat, bring the mixture to a boil, stirring occasionally. Once the mixture boils, lower the heat to a simmer and continue to cook, stirring frequently, until the mixture is thick and jammy and little moisture remains in the pan, 8 to 12 minutes. Even a slightly stiff mixture is okay here—if the mixture is too loose, it will ooze out of the cookies while baking.

2. Remove from the heat and stir in the vanilla. Transfer the filling to the bowl of a food processor or some other small electric chopping device. Process the mixture until it is mostly smooth. Transfer the mixture to a small bowl and set aside until the mixture reaches room temperature, about 30 minutes, or refrigerate for up to 2 days. (If refrigerated, bring to room temperature before assembling the cookies.)

(continued)

Ginger-Apricot Filling

MAKES ENOUGH FOR 1 RECIPE OF CHOCOLATE DOUGH

Chocolate and ginger are an exciting combination. By itself, the candied ginger can sometimes be a bit too fiery and aggressive for some palates. The addition of the sweet apricot helps round out the sharp edges and makes this variation truly sing!

INGREDIENT	VOLUME	WEIGHT
Dried apricots, diced into ¼-inch pieces	1 cup	160 grams (6 ounces)
Water	1 cup	237 grams
Light brown sugar	2 tablespoons	25 grams
Salt	⅛ teaspoon	
Pure vanilla extract	1 teaspoon	
Crystallized ginger, chopped into ¼-inch pieces	⅓ cup	57 grams

1. Combine the apricots, water, brown sugar, and salt in a medium saucepan. Over medium heat, bring the mixture to a boil, stirring occasionally. Once the mixture boils, lower the heat to a simmer and continue to cook, stirring frequently, until the mixture is thick and jammy, 8 to 12 minutes. Even a slightly stiff mixture is okay here—if the mixture is too loose, it will ooze out of the cookies while baking.

2. Remove from the heat and stir in the vanilla. Transfer the filling to the bowl of a food processor or some other small electric chopping device. Process the mixture until it is mostly smooth. Transfer the mixture to a small bowl. Stir in the chopped ginger and set aside until the mixture reaches room temperature, about 30 minutes, or refrigerate for up to 2 days. (If refrigerated, bring to room temperature before assembling the cookies.)

Goldilocks

MAKES 56 COOKIES

These crisp tubes of pastry dough filled with smooth buttercream might not be a cookie that many have seen or tasted before. Their inspiration, the lady lock cookie, was a staple of many cookie trays during Chris's childhood in western Pennsylvania. To many, the lady lock is the grande dame of the Allegheny Mountains wedding cookie table and the snowed-in Christmas cookie tray. To make these distinctly shaped cookies, strips of tender pastry dough are wrapped around cylindrical molds and baked. Traditionally, lady locks are soft and tender and filled with an American-style buttercream of butter or shortening and confectioners' sugar. We prefer to bake our flaky dough until it's golden brown and crisp like a well-baked piecrust. Our preferred fillings are made with mascarpone cream, which can be made in an endless variety of flavors. These are a labor of love, but the work can be stretched over 2 days, and the baked and unfilled shells freeze wonderfully for months!

INGREDIENT	VOLUME	WEIGHT
Unsalted butter, at room temperature	16 tablespoons	227 grams
Sour cream (full fat), cold	1 cup	242 grams
Sugar	2 tablespoons	25 grams
Salt	¾ teaspoon	
Unbleached all-purpose flour	2¼ cups	319 grams
Creamy Mascarpone Filling, any flavor (page 339)	1 recipe (about 2 cups)	

1. Make parchment paper packets: Fold in one short end of a 16-by-12-inch sheet of parchment paper by 4 inches to create a 12-inch square. Fold the opposite end up by 4½ inches, creating a 12-by-7½-inch rectangle. Fold each end over by ¾ inch to complete the shape, a 10½-by-7½-inch rectangle. Repeat with three more sheets of parchment paper for a total of four envelopes; set aside (see "Pushing the Envelopes," page 211).

2. Place the butter in a stand mixer fitted with a flat beater, and beat on medium speed until it is smooth, about 1 minute. Add the sour cream and beat for an additional minute, or until the mixture is creamy. Lower the mixer speed to low, and beat in the sugar and salt until the mixture is uniform. Add the flour and continue to mix on low speed until combined and no dry flour is visible. Scrape the sides of the bowl and the beater with a silicone spatula.

3. Divide the dough into four portions of about 200 grams each. Place the first portion of dough in the center of one of the opened packets. Close the packet and roll the dough flat to a thickness of about ⅛ inch, making sure the dough fills in the entire packet,

(continued)

including the corners. Repeat with the remaining three portions of dough. Refrigerate the flat dough packets overnight until firm.

4. Position a rack in the center of the oven and preheat to 325°F. Line two 18-by-13-inch baking sheets with parchment paper or silicone baking mats.

5. Remove one packet of dough from the refrigerator and carefully peel back the parchment paper. Flip the exposed dough surface onto a lightly floured silicone rolling mat or smooth countertop and peel the parchment paper off the back. Working quickly while the dough is still cold, slice the dough into fourteen 7½-by-¾-inch strips, using a sharp knife or pizza wheel.

6. Starting at one end of the mold (see Equipment Note), wrap the dough strip around in a lightly overlapping spiral. Place the wrapped molds about 2 inches apart on the baking sheet. Repeat with the remaining strips, placing all 14 on a single baking sheet. Until you get into a rhythm, you may need to pop the dough back into the refrigerator for a few minutes if it starts getting too warm and soft. Repeat with the next packet of dough while the first sheet is baking. For the remaining two dough packets, make sure that the baking sheets have completely cooled, or prepare additional baking sheets.

7. Bake until the edges are just starting to brown, 23 to 27 minutes. Halfway through baking, rotate the pans from front to back. Using form-fitting oven gloves, if you have them, or a kitchen towel to protect your fingertips, immediately slide each cookie off its mold while it is still hot from the oven. If they are tapered molds, slide the cookie toward the smaller end. Let the cookies cool completely on wire racks before filling them with the mascarpone filling.

8. Fill a piping bag fitted with a ¼-inch Bismarck tip (used for filling éclairs) or a standard round or star-shaped piping tip. Gently insert the tip into one end of an unfilled Goldilock. Fill the cookie opening halfway with the filling. Remove the tip and insert it into the other end to fill completely. Repeat with the other cookies and remaining filling.

EQUIPMENT NOTE: These cookies do require metal baking molds. We use molds made specifically for lady lock cookies (see Sources, page 350). They are hollow metal forms with a slightly tapered end that allow for easy removal of the hot cookie from the mold. Mini cannoli molds work well, too, but they are not tapered, so the dough is just a little more taxing to remove. Both molds are about 4 inches long and about ½ inch in diameter. Our Goldilocks dough is nice and buttery, so there's no need to grease metal molds. In a pinch, you can also cover wooden clothespins with aluminum foil. Because foil-wrapped all-wooden clothespins are an easy and inexpensive substitute for metal molds, these are sometimes called clothespin cookies. Be sure to use the dowel-shaped clothespins that are made entirely of untreated wood. Do not use clothespins with metal springs or ones that have been  treated with any stains, varnish, paints, or other potentially toxic coating. Lightly spray the foil-covered pins with nonstick cooking spray before wrapping the dough around them.

(continued)

Variation: Chocolocks

Because the traditional Goldilocks were not enough, we developed a chocolate version of the dough to further expand the flavor combination possibilities.

Add ½ cup (43 grams) of unsweetened (natural) cocoa powder and ½ teaspoon of instant espresso powder along with the sugar and salt in step 1. Increase the sugar to ⅓ cup plus 1 tablespoon (79 grams) and decrease the flour to 2 cups (283 grams). Each of the four dough portions should weigh about 215 grams. Bake the Chocolocks for 28 to 32 minutes. It can be difficult to tell when the Chocolocks are properly done because they are darker in color. The cookies should feel set enough and starting to firm. If the cookies crumble or easily break when removed from the mold, return them to the oven and let them bake for a couple more minutes.

The Grand Tradition of the Cookie Table

Depending on your upbringing, weddings often have many of the same events in one form or another: a large family get-together, a (hopefully) better-than-average dinner, dessert, and maybe music or dancing in some form. You might have danced the hora or the Chicken Dance before watching the bride chuck a flower bouquet at her unmarried friends, but American weddings are often mostly predictable affairs (though *affairs* may not be the right word for this context). In western Pennsylvania in the areas in and around Pittsburgh where I grew up, a lesser-known wedding tradition continues: the Cookie Table.

Going back several generations, the Cookie Table is basically a lavishly arranged cookie buffet placed steps away from both the dance floor and the open bar. When done right, it features a generous to overwhelming assortment of cookies of various provenance; the selections can be store-bought (*quelle horreur!*) or homemade. Most often, it is the mothers and aunts of the bride or groom who labor in the weeks before the wedding to prepare scores of cookies for inclusion at the Table. The exact timing of the Cookie Table might vary, but I am most familiar with its reveal almost immediately after all of the guests have arrived at the reception. Generally, the formal reception does not begin immediately because the wedding party is usually occupied with the photographer. The Cookie Table is an ingenious way to fill the time waiting for the newlyweds and their attendants to arrive and, more important, to stave off hunger (especially in younger school-aged guests).

As a predinner dessert might seem sacrilegious to some, not everyone takes advantage of the predinner nosh. Some (more than you might like to believe) will also load up deli containers and resealable storage bags shamelessly produced from purses solely for the purpose of smuggling away a late-night snack. Dinner will inevitably follow, as will the traditional wedding cake, but just a few bites of cookies to soften the stressful edge of the day works wonders.

As bakers, it's also a delightful opportunity for us to mingle and chat with the women who were not involved with the day's cookie creations. Although seemingly sweet, we have found that grandmas and aunts are always eager to dish to us on the shortcomings of *these* cookies when compared to their own. Accusations of dryness and lesser-quality ingredients are sometimes suggested, but everyone always gets seconds, and even those who begrudgingly concede that the cookies were "perfectly fine" head to their car crinkling with the sounds of snack bags filled to their brim.

Mai Tai Cremes

MAKES 4 DOZEN (2-INCH) SANDWICH COOKIES

If it is served in a hollowed-out pineapple, garnished with an orchid, or adorned with some gaudy fruit kebab, then that is the cocktail Chris will order. Rum, fruit juice, and a little bit of tiki bar panache are his kryptonite, so we had to include a cookie inspired by the iconic mai tai. The classic cocktail's flavors of almond, orange, lime, and rum are well represented here with a crisp almond and orange cookie sandwiched around a lime-almond filling. Although the cookie is booze-free, there is nothing stopping you from enjoying them with an adult beverage served with a paper umbrella. Refer to page 177 for tips and techniques on preparing slice-and-bake cookies.

INGREDIENT	VOLUME	WEIGHT
COOKIE		
Granulated sugar	¾ cup	150 grams
Orange zest, freshly grated	1 medium orange	
Unsalted butter, at room temperature	10 tablespoons	142 grams
Almond paste, broken into small clumps, at room temperature	6 tablespoons	120 grams
Egg yolk, at room temperature	1 large	15 grams
Rum extract	1½ teaspoons	
Salt	⅜ teaspoon	
Unbleached all-purpose flour	1¾ cups	248 grams
FILLING		
Unsalted butter, at room temperature	8 tablespoons	113 grams
Almond paste, broken into small clumps, at room temperature	4 tablespoons	80 grams
Lime zest, freshly grated	1 medium lime	
Maraschino cherry "juice" (see Note)	4 teaspoons	
Rum extract	1 teaspoon	
Salt	Pinch	
Confectioners' sugar	3 cups	340 grams

(continued)

1. Make the cookie: Combine the granulated sugar and orange zest in the bowl of your stand mixer. To extract the most orange flavor, rub the zest and sugar between your thumbs and fingertips until the sugar is fragrant, very light orange in color, and has a texture like wet sand (see "Live Your Zest Life," page 25).

2. Add the butter and the almond paste to the orange-sugar, fit the mixer with a flat beater, and cream together on medium speed until smooth and creamy, 1 to 2 minutes. Add the egg yolk, rum extract, and salt and continue to mix until they have been incorporated into the butter mixture. Stop the mixer and scrape the sides of the bowl and the beater with a silicone spatula.

3. Slowly mix in the flour on low speed. Scrape the sides of the bowl to make sure that all of the ingredients are incorporated and no dry flour is visible.

4. Divide the dough in half. Roll each half of the dough into 6½-inch logs (it will measure about 1¾ inches in diameter). Wrap each log in plastic wrap and refrigerate until cold and firm throughout, at least 2 hours or up to 3 days. The dough can be frozen at this point (see page 178).

5. Position two racks to divide the oven into thirds and preheat to 350°F. Line two 18-by-13-inch baking sheets with parchment paper or silicone baking mats.

6. Cut the logs into ⅛-inch slices, and place 2 inches apart on the prepared baking sheets (you can fit 13 on each pan; see page 86).

7. Bake until the cookies are just light brown at the edges, 8 to 12 minutes. Halfway through baking, rotate the pans from front to back and top to bottom. Remove from the oven and let cool for 5 minutes on the baking sheets before transferring to a wire rack to cool completely. Repeat with the remaining dough once the baking sheets have completely cooled, or prepare additional baking sheets.

8. Make the Filling: Combine the butter and almond paste in a stand mixer fitted with a flat beater, and cream together on medium speed until smooth.

9. Add the lime zest, cherry juice, rum extract, and salt, and beat until the mixture is uniformly smooth and creamy. Add the confectioners' sugar and start mixing on low speed to avoid creating a cloud of sugar in your kitchen. As the mixture starts to come together, increase the speed until the sugar has been incorporated into the filling. Using a cookie scoop or piping bag, portion about 2 teaspoons of filling onto the bottom surface of half of the cookies. Place a second cookie on top of the filling, forming the sandwich. The cookies can be stored in an airtight container at room temperature for several days.

NOTE: The bright red liquid that jarred maraschino cherries are floating in is not technically a juice. (We know this because there are no fruits on earth that garishly red.) It is actually an almond-flavored syrup that imparts the familiar flavor of that classic cocktail garnish to the cookie filling along with a pretty pink hue. If you don't already happen to have an open jar of them in your refrigerator, you can substitute 4 teaspoons of milk (full-, reduced-, or nonfat) plus ⅛ teaspoon of almond extract and a drop of red food coloring.

Buckeye Snaps

MAKES 2 DOZEN (2-INCH) COOKIE SANDWICHES

Buckeyes are a midwestern candy made by dipping a ball of peanut butter fudge into melted chocolate. They were named for their resemblance to the nut of the buckeye tree and serve as the flavor inspiration for these cookies. The base is a thin and crispy chocolate shortbread that is sandwiched around a fudgy peanut butter filling. Allergic to peanuts? Skip the filling—these cookies are also extraordinary by themselves—or fill with the Salted Caramel Ganache (page 337) to achieve true chocolate bliss. Refer to page 177 for tips and techniques on preparing slice-and-bake cookies.

INGREDIENT	VOLUME	WEIGHT
THIN CHOCOLATE COOKIE		
Bleached cake flour	1½ cups	170 grams
Dutch-processed or black cocoa powder (see Note)	¼ cup	20 grams
Unsalted butter, at room temperature	8 tablespoons	113 grams
Confectioners' sugar	½ cup	57 grams
Pure vanilla extract	1 teaspoon	
Salt	¾ teaspoon	
Instant espresso powder	½ teaspoon	
FILLING		
Peanut Butter Filling (page 338)	1 recipe (about 1 cup)	

1. Make the Thin Chocolate Cookie: Sift the flour and cocoa together into a small bowl; set aside.

2. Combine the butter and confectioners' sugar in a stand mixer fitted with a flat beater, and cream together. To avoid getting confectioners' sugar on the ceiling, start the mixer on low speed and gradually increase to medium. Beat until the mixture is smooth and creamy, 1 to 2 minutes. Add the vanilla, salt, and espresso powder and continue to mix until they have been incorporated into the mixture. Stop mixing and scrape the sides of the bowl and the beater with a silicone spatula.

3. Mix in the flour mixture on low speed until no dry flour is visible. Increase the mixer speed to medium and beat until the seemingly dry crumbles start to clump into a cookie dough, usually no more than 30 seconds or so.

4. Roll the dough into a 6¼-inch log (it will measure about 1¾ inches in diameter). Wrap the log in plastic wrap and refrigerate until cold and firm throughout, at

(continued)

least 2 hours or up to 3 days. The dough can be frozen at this point (see page 178).

5. Position two racks to divide the oven into thirds and preheat to 275°F. Line two 18-by-13-inch baking sheets with parchment paper or silicone baking mats.

6. Cut the logs into ⅛-inch slices, and place ½ inch apart on the prepared baking sheets (you can fit 24 on each pan; see page 86).

7. Bake until the cookies are set at the edges, 38 to 42 minutes. Halfway through baking, rotate the pans from front to back and top to bottom. Remove from the oven and immediately transfer the cookies to a wire rack to cool completely.

8. Fill the cookies: Using a cookie scoop or piping bag, portion about 1 teaspoon of filling onto the bottom surface of half of the cookies. Place a second cookie on top of the filling and gently press the cookies together to form a sandwich. The cookies can be stored in an airtight container at room temperature for several days.

NOTE: You have a choice to make. You can use all Dutch-processed cocoa or all black cocoa. We think the best version is a 50–50 mix.

How to Keep a Cookie

COOKIE BYTE

Like most food, cookies don't get better with time. Every day after baking, cookies get a little bit worse compared to the day before. Proper storage is important if you want to keep your scrummy cookies as fresh as possible for as long as possible. You will notice in our recipes that we don't say exactly how many days a cookie will last once baked. So many factors depend on how long a cookie will keep, including how well they've been baked, the temperature and humidity in your house, how well they are stored, and what your threshold for cookie quality is.

Staling is the biggest enemy of cookies stored at room temperature. Although stale cookies, like stale bread, might seem drier, it is not due to moisture loss. In fact, cookies can stale in a completely sealed environment. Staling is a chemical process that involves changes in starches over time in a process known as retrogradation. Proper storage is needed to prevent cookies from drying out, but even well-stored cookies will become stale when kept at room temperature.

We recommend that many cookies be stored in airtight containers. We use plastic storage containers with tight-fitting lids that seal out air. Some cookies that are very moist, such as the glazed Blush and Bashfuls (page 113), will weep and become soggy in an airtight container. For these cookies, we keep them in a container with a loose-fitting lid to prevent moisture loss as much as possible. We accept that these softer, cakier cookies do not keep well after more than two or three days. Similarly, cookies that are filled with jam or buttercream might soften over time because their firmer cookie texture will begin to absorb the moisture of the filling.

For storage longer than a few days, consider freezing. Nearly every cookie in this book can be frozen if treated properly. Freezing temperatures can suspend the staling process and keep cookies fresher for longer. To freeze baked cookies, we like to wrap several cookies together with plastic wrap or aluminum foil. Wrapped cookies are then sealed in airtight heavy-duty resealable freezer storage bags. Cookies can also do well when frozen in airtight containers, but it is difficult to remove the air from those containers so the cookies might be at increased risk for freezer burn over time. For custardy bars or cakey cookies, it's best to freeze on one single layer rather than stacking them. This might take up valuable freezer space, so plan accordingly. Kept frozen, most cookies will keep fine for at least 3 months. To thaw frozen cookies, remove the cookies from the freezer, but keep them in their packaging. Let the cookies thaw at room temperature. Once completely thawed, remove the packaging and serve or refresh in a warm oven if recommended in the recipe. Keeping the cookies wrapped prevents condensation from forming directly on the cookies while they thaw.

Most drop and slice-and-bake cookies can be frozen before baking. This means that these cookies can be baked on-demand from frozen portions of dough, allowing you and your guests to have the freshest cookies possible.

Modern Mincemeat Pockets

MAKES 3 DOZEN 3-INCH FILLED COOKIES

Unlike mincemeat of the Middle Ages that actually contained, well, *meat,* modern mincemeat mixtures are fully fruit and resemble a sweet compote more than beef stew. These comforting hand pies are based on a raisin-filled cookie that Chris enjoyed growing up in western Pennsylvania. Instead of just raisins, these soft pockets are filled with a warm mix of dried fruits and spices. They are perfect to nibble on during a fall walk to look at the changing leaves or to hide in your pocket for a light snack while picking out the perfect Halloween pumpkin. With a sprinkling of cinnamon-sugar, these homey cookies are pure autumn, but don't shy away from making them all year-round. Refer to page 137 for tips and techniques on preparing rolled cookies.

INGREDIENT	VOLUME	WEIGHT
DOUGH		
Unbleached all-purpose flour	5½ cups	780 grams
Baking powder	4 teaspoons	
Baking soda	1¾ teaspoons	
Salt	1 teaspoon	
Unsalted butter, at room temperature	16 tablespoons	227 grams
Granulated sugar	1½ cups	300 grams
Light brown sugar	Packed ½ cup	100 grams
Eggs, at room temperature	2 large	100 grams (weighed without shells)
Pure vanilla extract	2½ teaspoons	
Whole milk	1 cup	242 grams
MINCEMEAT FILLING		
Unsalted butter	1 tablespoon	14 grams
Apples, peeled, cored, and diced into ¼-inch pieces (see Note)	2 medium	
Orange zest, freshly grated	1 medium orange	
Salt	¼ teaspoon	
Raisins, dark, golden, or a mixture	1½ cups	227 grams
Light brown sugar	Packed ½ cup	100 grams
Granulated sugar	½ cup	100 grams

Dried apricots, diced into ¼-inch pieces	½ cup	64 grams
Orange juice, freshly squeezed	¼ cup	57 grams
Ground cinnamon	¾ teaspoon	
Ground nutmeg	¼ teaspoon	
Ground coriander	¼ teaspoon	
CINNAMON-SUGAR TOPPING		
Granulated sugar	2 tablespoons	25 grams
Ground cinnamon	2 teaspoons	

1. Make the Dough: Whisk together the flour, baking powder, baking soda, and salt in a large bowl; set aside.

2. Combine the butter, granulated sugar, and brown sugar in a stand mixer fitted with a flat beater, and cream together on medium speed until light and fluffy, 2 to 3 minutes. Scrape the sides of the bowl with a silicone spatula.

3. Beat in the eggs, one at a time, and vanilla until the eggs are incorporated and the mixture is creamy again.

4. Beat in half of the flour mixture on low speed until mostly incorporated. Stop mixing and scrape down the sides of the bowl and the beater. On low speed, slowly drizzle in the milk until incorporated, 20 to 30 seconds. Mix in the remaining flour mixture just until no dry flour is visible. Scrape the sides of the bowl. The dough will be soft.

5. Divide the dough into four equal pieces (about 435 grams each). Wrap each piece in plastic wrap and shape into a 6-inch disk. Refrigerate until cold and firm throughout, at least 2 hours or overnight.

6. Make the Mincemeat Filling: Melt the butter in a medium saucepan over medium-low heat. Stir in the apples, zest, and salt. Lower the heat to medium-low,

cover the pan, and cook for 5 minutes to soften the apples.

7. Remove the lid. Stir in the raisins, brown sugar, granulated sugar, apricots, orange juice, cinnamon, nutmeg, and coriander. Increase the heat to medium and bring the mixture to a boil, stirring constantly, and continue to cook until the syrup has thickened and begins to form strings when stirred and almost all of the liquid has evaporated, about 10 minutes depending on the juiciness of your apples. Transfer to a bowl and let cool to room temperature, about 1 hour. Don't rush it—if the mixture is too warm, it will melt the cookie dough before it bakes.

8. Make the Cinnamon-Sugar Topping: Whisk together the granulated sugar and cinnamon in a small bowl; set aside.

9. Position a rack in the center of the oven and preheat to 400°F. Line two 18-by-13-inch baking sheets with parchment paper or silicone baking mats.

10. Remove one portion of dough from the refrigerator. Roll to a ⅛-inch thickness on a well-floured surface. Be generous with the flour to prevent the soft dough from sticking.

(continued)

11. Cut eight 2½-inch circles from the dough and space them evenly across one of the prepared baking sheets, leaving about 2 inches of space between cookies. Portion 1 tablespoon of filling (we use a #60 scoop) into the center of each circle. If your filling dollop is domed, gently smoosh the filling with the back of the scoop or use a spoon to flatten. Top each with a second circle of dough. Make sure that the edges of the circles touch all the way around the edge, but you don't have to press or crimp them shut—they will seal as they bake. Sprinkle each cookie with a pinch or two of the Cinnamon-Sugar Topping.

12. Bake the pockets, one sheet at a time, until the cookies are a light golden brown, 9 to 11 minutes. Halfway through baking, rotate the pan from front to back. Remove from the oven and let cool for 5 minutes on the baking sheet before transferring to a wire rack to cool completely. Continue with the remaining dough, preparing the next pan while the previous sheet is baking. After using the two prepared sheets, make sure that the baking sheets have completely cooled, or prepare additional baking sheets. The dough scraps can be gently rerolled. Refrigerate the dough if it gets too soft to handle. After cooling, the cookies can be stored in a loosely covered (but not airtight) container at room temperature for several days. When properly stored in a heavy-duty resealable storage bag, these cookies freeze well for months.

NOTE: Use an apple variety that holds up well to baking, such as Golden Delicious, Granny Smith, or Jonagold.

MAKE AHEAD: You can make both the dough and the filling the day before baking. Store both in the refrigerator.

Perfect Manhattan Thumbprints

MAKES ABOUT 6 DOZEN (1½-INCH) FILLED COOKIES

Filled with the undeniably adult flavors of a Manhattan cocktail, these cherry-speckled cookies are filled with a boozy whiskey and vermouth glaze. While we find these cocktail-inspired gems to be flawless, in the cocktail world, a "perfect" Manhattan is made with equal portions of sweet (red) and dry (white) vermouth. There's no need for such precision here—some whiskey and either type of vermouth will work just fine. It's a perfect cookie, no matter how you make it. Refer to page 83 for tips and techniques on preparing drop cookies.

INGREDIENT	VOLUME	WEIGHT
AMARENA CHERRY COOKIES		
Amarena cherries, well drained, chopped	¼ cup (about 20 chopped cherries)	43 grams
Unsalted butter, at room temperature	16 tablespoons	227 grams
Granulated sugar	1 cup	200 grams
Salt	½ teaspoon	
Egg, at room temperature	1 large	50 grams (weighted without shell)
Unbleached all-purpose flour	1½ cups	213 grams
Rye flour (see Note)	1¼ cups	142 grams
MANHATTAN FILLING		
Confectioners' sugar, preferably made with tapioca starch (see "Starch Madness," page 115)	2 cups	227 grams
Rye whiskey	2 tablespoons	25 grams
Vermouth, sweet (red) or dry (white)	2 tablespoons	30 grams
Angostura bitters	⅛ teaspoon	
Salt	Small pinch	

1. Position a rack in the center of the oven and preheat to 325°F. Line two 18-by-13-inch baking sheets with parchment paper or silicone baking mats.

2. Make the Amarena Cherry Cookies: Blot the chopped cherries dry with paper towels and set aside.

3. Combine the butter, granulated sugar, and salt in a stand mixer fitted with a flat beater, and cream together on medium speed until smooth and creamy, 1 to 2 minutes. Beat in the egg until fully incorporated and the mixture is smooth.

(continued)

4. Beat in the flours on low speed until combined. Stop mixing and scrape down the sides of the bowl and beater with a silicone spatula. Stir in the chopped cherries.

5. Portion 2 teaspoons (11 grams) of dough, using a #100 scoop, and roll into a ball. Place the balls 2 inches apart on one of the prepared baking sheets (you can fit 24 on each pan; see page 86). Press an indentation into each ball, using a ball tool (see page 215) or the very tip of your index finger. The cookies will puff while baking, so the indentation can be fairly deep, but not so deep that it breaks through the bottom of the dough ball.

6. Bake for 10 minutes. Remove the pan from the oven and use a ball tool, metal measuring spoon, or some other heatproof tool to re-indent the dimple that has filled in during baking.

7. Continue to bake until the dough is no longer shiny and the edges of the cookies have just started to brown, an additional 10 to 12 minutes. While the first pan bakes, prepare the next sheet. Remove the baked cookies from the oven and let cool for 5 minutes on the baking sheet before transferring to a wire rack to cool completely. Repeat with the remaining dough once the baking sheets have completely cooled, or prepare additional baking sheets.

8. Make the Manhattan Filling: Once all of the cookies have baked and cooled completely, whisk together the confectioners' sugar, whiskey, vermouth, bitters, and salt in a medium bowl. The mixture should be thick like honey. If it's too loose, stir in more confectioners' sugar, one spoonful at a time, until the consistency looks right. If it's too dry, add more vermouth or more whiskey (your choice), ¼ teaspoon at a time.

9. Transfer the glaze to a disposable piping bag. Snip off the tip of the piping bag to create an approximately ⅛-inch hole. Pipe the glaze to fill the cookies, but do not overfill. You will need about ½ teaspoon per cookie. The cookies can be eaten right away, but the glaze will set firm in a few hours. It will always be a little soft, so be careful if you have to stack the cookies. The cookies can be stored in a closed (but not airtight) container at room temperature for several days. After several days, the glaze will begin to soften the cookie.

NOTE: These cookies can be made without rye flour by increasing the all-purpose flour to 2½ cups (354 grams).

COOKIE BYTE

Cherry Picking

Typical maraschino cherries—the bright red kind most commonly found in the supermarket—are too strongly enhanced with almond and are not the right flavor for these cookies. Instead, seek out Amarena cherries. Amarenas are small, tart, darkly colored cherries grown in Italy and candied in a thick, darkly sweet syrup. You can substitute Luxardo maraschino cherries if that's all you can find, but the Amarenas have the edge in this cookie. As a bonus, the Amarena cherry syrup is divine when gently warmed and drizzled over icy cold vanilla cream or stirred into a creamy latte. Because they are often used to garnish cocktails, they can be found where you buy liqueur as well as at specialty food stores, such as Trader Joe's.

Jelly Doughnut Dimples

MAKES 6 DOZEN (1-INCH) COOKIES

Jelly doughnuts are such a great invention, they appear in cultural traditions all around the globe. Secreting a sweet supply of jelly neatly inside a ball of fried dough allows the adept eater to get the right amount of fruit filling and fluffy foundation in every bite. In the spirit of continued confectionary conquest, we've reinvented the jelly doughnut as a thumbprint cookie. They are relatively simple and simply delicious. These two-bite treats—topped with a shower of confectioners' sugar, fragrant with grated nutmeg, and brightened with a ruby jewel of tart raspberry jam—are great treats for any time of year. Refer to page 83 for tips and techniques on preparing drop cookies.

INGREDIENT	VOLUME	WEIGHT
Unbleached all-purpose flour	2½ cups	354 grams
Ground nutmeg	2 teaspoons	
Salt	½ teaspoon	
Seedless raspberry jam	⅔ cup	200 grams
Unsalted butter, at room temperature	16 tablespoons	227 grams
Granulated sugar	1 cup	200 grams
Egg, at room temperature	1 large	50 grams (weighed without shell)
Pure vanilla extract	1½ teaspoons	
Confectioners' sugar, for sprinkling	About 1 cup	about 113 grams

1. Position a rack in the center of the oven and preheat to 325°F. Line two 18-by-13-inch baking sheets with parchment paper or silicone baking mats.

2. Whisk together the flour, nutmeg, and salt in a medium bowl; set aside.

3. Stir the jam in a small bowl until it has loosened and is no longer lumpy. Transfer the jam to a disposable piping bag (see Note).

4. Combine the butter and granulated sugar in a stand mixer fitted with a flat beater, and cream together on medium speed until smooth and creamy, 1 to 2 minutes. Beat in the egg and vanilla until the mixture is smooth and uniform.

5. Beat in half of the flour mixture on low speed just until combined. Stop mixing and scrape down the sides of the bowl and the beater with a silicone spatula. Mix in the remaining flour mixture on low speed just until no dry flour is visible. Scrape down the sides of the bowl and ensure that no clumps of flour remain.

6. Portion 2 teaspoons (11 grams) of dough, using a #100 scoop, and roll into a ball. Place the balls 2 inches apart on one of the prepared baking sheets (you can fit 24 on each pan; see page 86). Press an indentation into each ball, using a ball tool (see page 215) or the very tip of your index finger. The cookies will puff while baking, so the indentation can be fairly deep, but not so deep that it breaks through the bottom of the dough ball.

7. Bake for 10 minutes. Remove the pan from the oven and use a ball tool, metal measuring spoon, or some other heatproof tool to re-indent the dimple that has filled in during baking. Snip off the tip of the piping bag to create an approximately ⅛-inch hole. Pipe the jam to fill the dimples, but do not overfill. You will need about ½ teaspoon per cookie.

8. Continue to bake until the dough is no longer shiny and the edges of the cookies have just started to brown, an additional 10 to 12 minutes. While the first pan bakes, prepare the next sheet. Remove the baked cookies from the oven and let cool for 5 minutes on the baking sheet before transferring to a wire rack to cool completely. Repeat with the remaining dough once the baking sheets have completely cooled, or prepare additional baking sheets.

9. After cooling, use a fine-mesh sieve to sprinkle confectioners' sugar over the cookies. The sugar that lands on the jam will dissolve after several hours, leaving a snow-capped doughnut ring surrounding a center of jam. Stored in a closed (but not airtight) container at room temperature, the cookies will keep for several days.

NOTE: If you don't have a disposable piping bag, you can transfer the jam to a resealable plastic storage bag. Snip off a small bit at the corner to create a hole for piping. Otherwise, use a small spoon to fill the cookies with jam.

Pumpkin Spice Latte Thumbprints

MAKES 4 DOZEN (2-INCH) FILLED COOKIES

For many people, the arrival of the pumpkin spice latte (or PSL, for the true fans) at the corner coffee shop has become the official harbinger of autumn. Of course, picking up a hot coffee at a crowded café doesn't quite have the same natural beauty as the first robin of spring or winter's first snowflake. Regardless, the blend of hot coffee and autumn spices is actually a comforting and delicious cold weather combo. The pair is a natural for these coffee-boosted spice cookie thumbprints. A simple two-color latte art design sets these thumbprints apart. (P.S. There's no pumpkin in these. It's all about the autumn spices here!) Refer to page 83 for tips and techniques on preparing drop cookies.

INGREDIENT	VOLUME	WEIGHT
PUMPKIN SPICE COOKIES		
Unbleached all-purpose flour	2½ cups	354 grams
Ground cinnamon	1½ teaspoons	
Ground ginger	¾ teaspoon	
Salt	½ teaspoon	
Ground nutmeg	¼ teaspoon	
Ground cloves	¼ teaspoon	
Ground allspice	¼ teaspoon	
Unsalted butter, at room temperature	16 tablespoons	227 grams
Light brown sugar	Packed ⅔ cup	133 grams
Granulated sugar	⅓ cup	67 grams
Egg, at room temperature	1 large	50 grams (weighted without shell)
Pure vanilla extract	1 teaspoon	
LATTE ART FILLINGS		
Confectioners' sugar, preferably made with tapioca starch (see "Starch Madness," page 115)	1½ cups	170 grams
Strongly brewed coffee	4 to 6 teaspoons	
Salt	Small pinch	
Milk (any kind, or water)	2 to 4 teaspoons	
Brown gel food coloring (optional)		
White gel food coloring (optional)		

(continued)

1. Position a rack in the center of the oven and preheat to 350°F. Line two 18-by-13-inch baking sheets with parchment paper or silicone baking mats.

2. Make the Pumpkin Spice Cookies: Whisk together the flour, cinnamon, ginger, salt, nutmeg, cloves, and allspice in a medium bowl; set aside.

3. Combine the butter, brown sugar, and granulated sugar in a stand mixer fitted with a flat beater, and cream together on medium speed until smooth and creamy, 1 to 2 minutes. Stop mixing and scrape down the sides of the bowl with a silicone spatula. Beat in the egg and vanilla until fully incorporated and the mixture is smooth.

4. Beat in the flour mixture on low speed until combined. Scrape down the sides of the bowl and the beater to ensure that no clumps of flour remain.

5. Portion 1 tablespoon (17 grams) of dough, using a #60 scoop or tablespoon measure, and roll into a ball. Place the balls 2 inches apart on one of the prepared baking sheets (you can fit 24 on each pan; see page 86). Press an indentation into each ball, using a ball tool (see page 215) or the very tip of your index finger. The cookies will puff some while baking, so the indentation can be fairly deep, but not so deep that it breaks through the bottom of the dough ball.

6. Bake for 10 minutes. Remove the pan from the oven and use a ball tool, metal measuring spoon, or some other heatproof tool to re-indent the dimple that has filled in during baking.

7. Continue to bake until the dough is no longer shiny and the edges of the cookies have just started to brown, an additional 10 to 12 minutes. While the first pan bakes, prepare the next sheet. Remove the baked cookies from the oven and let cool for 5 minutes on the baking sheet before transferring to a wire rack to cool completely. Repeat with the remaining dough once the baking sheets have completely cooled, or prepare additional baking sheets.

8. Make the coffee-flavored (brown) Latte Art Filling: Once all of the cookies have baked and cooled completely, whisk together 1 cup (113 grams) of the confectioners' sugar, 4 teaspoons of brewed coffee, and the tiniest pinch of salt in a small bowl. The mixture should be thick like honey. If it's too loose, stir in more confectioners' sugar, one spoonful at a time, until the consistency looks right. If it's too dry, add more coffee, ¼ teaspoon at a time. Whisk in a drop or two of brown food coloring (if using) to create a desirable coffee color. Transfer the filling to a disposable piping bag and set aside.

9. Make the milk-flavored (white) Latte Art Filling: Whisk together the remaining ½ cup (57 grams) of confectioners' sugar, 2 teaspoons of milk, and the tiniest pinch of salt in a small bowl. The mixture should be thick like honey. If it's too loose, stir in more confectioners' sugar, one spoonful at a time, until the consistency looks right. If it's too dry, add more milk, ¼ teaspoon at a time. Whisk in a drop or two of white food coloring (if using) to create a brighter white color. Transfer the filling to a disposable piping bag and set aside.

10. Snip off the tip of the piping bag with the brown filling to create an approximately ⅛-inch hole. Pipe the glaze to fill about six cookies two-thirds full, but do not fill all the way. Snip off the tip of the piping bag with the white filling to create a very small hole (about ¹⁄₁₆ inch). Pipe a spiral of white icing over the brown

coffee filling in each of the six filled cookies. Use a toothpick to drag lines through the brown and white icings to create a latte art–style design. The icing will begin to crust over and dry immediately. Doing the cookies a few at a time prevents the icing from crusting over before the design is finished. The cookies can be eaten right away. The glaze will be soft for a few hours, so be careful if you have to stack the cookies. The glaze will harden after a few hours. The cookies can be stored in a closed (but not airtight) container at room temperature for several days. After several days, the glaze will begin to soften the cookie and the brown and white icing design will begin to fade as the colors bleed into each other.

Jam-on-Toast Thumbprints

MAKES 21 (2-INCH) COOKIES

The mere addition of some gentle heat transforms sliced bread into an aromatic brown landscape of crisp crevices and nubbins called toast. Toasted bread, with the addition of a thin coat of lightly salted butter and a generous dollop of a fruity spread, creates the perfect breakfast on a blustery fall day. Working those toasty and sweet notes into a cookie seemed like a great way to boost the profile of the ordinary thumbprint cookie. The addition of whole wheat flour (to lend a subtle nutty flavor) and a coating of toasted panko bread crumbs (for a welcomed crunch) evoke the flavor and texture of toast. Orange marmalade provides sticky sweet-tartness with subtle notes of bitter pith for a sophisticated finish to our buttery toast cookie. Refer to page 83 for tips and techniques on preparing drop cookies.

INGREDIENT	VOLUME	WEIGHT
Panko bread crumbs (unseasoned) (see "Crumb On" page 61)	¾ cup	43 grams
Unbleached all-purpose flour	½ cup	71 grams
Whole wheat flour	⅔ cup	104 grams
Salt	¼ teaspoon	
Unsalted butter, at room temperature	8 tablespoons	113 grams
Sugar	½ cup	100 grams
Eggs, separated, at room temperature	2 large	30 grams yolks About 70 grams whites
Pure vanilla extract	¼ teaspoon	
Orange marmalade, preferably fine-cut	½ cup	200 grams

1. Position a rack in the center of the oven and preheat to 350°F. Line two 18-by-13-inch baking sheets with parchment paper or silicone baking mats.

2. Toast the panko in a skillet over medium heat, stirring or tossing frequently, until light golden brown, about 5 minutes. Transfer to a small shallow bowl to cool completely.

3. Whisk together the all-purpose and whole wheat flours and the salt in a medium bowl; set aside.

4. Combine the butter and sugar in a stand mixer fitted with a flat beater, and beat together on medium speed until smooth and creamy, 1 to 2 minutes. Beat in the egg yolks and vanilla until the yolks are incorporated and the mixture is uniform. Mix in the flour mixture on low speed until no dry flour is visible. Scrape the sides of the bowl and the beater with a silicone spatula to ensure all of the ingredients are properly mixed in and no stray clumps remain.

5. Lightly whisk the egg whites in a separate shallow bowl to loosen them.

6. Portion 1 tablespoon (19 grams) of dough, using a #60 cookie scoop. Roll the dough between your palms into balls. Roll the balls in the egg white, let any extra egg white drip off back into the bowl, and roll the ball in the panko. Place the coated balls on one prepared baking sheet (13 per sheet). Press an indentation into each ball, using a ball tool (see page 215) or the very tip of your index finger. The cookies will puff some while baking, so the indentation can be fairly deep, but not so deep that it breaks through the bottom of the dough ball.

7. Bake the cookies for 12 minutes. Remove the pan from the oven and use a ball tool, metal measuring spoon, or some other heatproof tool to re-indent the dimple that has filled in during baking. Stir the marmalade in a bowl until it is loose and no longer lumpy. Fill the wells with 1 teaspoon of orange marmalade. Place the pan back in the oven to bake until the cookies are just browning at the edge, 13 to 15 more minutes. While the first pan bakes, prepare the next sheet. Remove the baked cookies from the oven and let cool for 5 minutes on the sheet before transferring to a wire rack to cool completely. Repeat with the remaining dough once the baking sheets have completely cooled, or prepare additional baking sheets. After cooling, the cookies can be stored in an airtight container at room temperature for several days.

NOTE: For slightly smaller cookies, portion the dough with a 2–teaspoon scoop and fill with ½ teaspoon of marmalade. This will increase the yield to about 30 cookies. Also, although we usually opt to fill thumbprint cookies with a piping bag, the pieces of citrus rind in marmalade make the use of a spoon preferable.

Coconut + Guava Sandwiches

MAKES 2 DOZEN SANDWICH COOKIES

We've noticed that most commercially produced coconut cookies, sadly, are all fairly similar. They are either plain coconut (yawn), or chocolate and coconut with the occasional caramel accent (delicious but done to death). Coconuts are tropical fruits! They deserve their place in the sun alongside their warm weather neighbors. Guava, another tropical fruit, is equally deserving of the spotlight, but its fragrant sweetness is often overlooked. Once peeled and seeded, the shells of the guava can be stewed into a chunky confiture, a spreadable preserve, or a thick sliceable paste. We've found the preserves (sold in jars like jam) to be the best suited for use as a cookie filling. Using a combination of toasted coconut flakes and cream of coconut, we made a cookie packed with coconut flavor. Sandwiched around some thickened guava preserves, it makes a tasty tropical treat. Refer to page 83 for tips and techniques on preparing drop cookies.

INGREDIENT	VOLUME	WEIGHT
Unbleached all-purpose flour	1 cup	142 grams
Cream of coconut, well stirred (see "Going Coconuts," page 76)	⅓ cup	100 grams
Sugar	⅓ cup	67 grams
Salt	¼ teaspoon	
Unsalted butter, at room temperature	8 tablespoons	113 grams
Egg yolk, at room temperature	1 large	15 grams
Sweetened shredded coconut, toasted and cooled (see page 22)	1⅓ cups	113 grams (weighed before toasting)
Guava preserves	⅔ cup	200 grams
Instant ClearJel (see "Modified Starch," page 258)	1 tablespoon	

1. Position two racks to divide the oven into thirds and preheat to 350°F. Line two 18-by-13-inch baking sheets with parchment paper or silicone baking mats.

2. Stir together ¼ cup (36 grams) of the flour and the cream of coconut in a large, microwave-safe bowl. Microwave the coconut mixture on high (100%) power, stirring every 30 seconds, until the mixture has thickened into a paste, 1 to 2 minutes (see "The Tangzhong Technique," page 125). If you don't have a microwave, cook the mixture in a small nonstick pan over medium heat for about 2 minutes, stirring constantly with a silicone spatula, and then transfer the paste to a mixing bowl. Depending on the capacity of your stand mixer, this might be more convenient to mix using an

(continued)

electric hand mixer. Add the sugar and salt and beat on medium speed to break up the coconut paste and incorporate the sugar. Allow this mixture to cool completely before proceeding, 10 to 15 minutes.

3. Beat in the butter on medium speed until smooth and creamy. Add the yolk and continue to mix until it has been incorporated.

4. Mix in the toasted coconut and the remaining ¾ cup (106 grams) of flour on low speed until no dry flour is visible. Scrape the sides of the bowl and the beater to make sure that all of the ingredients are incorporated.

5. Portion 2 teaspoons (11 grams) of dough, using a #100 cookie scoop. Roll the dough into balls between the palms of your hands and place them on the prepared baking sheets (13 per sheet; see page 86).

6. Bake until the edges of the cookies are set and just beginning to brown, 14 to 16 minutes. Halfway through baking, rotate the pans from front to back and top to bottom. Remove from the oven and let cool for 5 minutes on the baking sheets before transferring to a wire rack to cool completely. Repeat with the remaining dough once the baking sheets have completely cooled, or prepare additional baking sheets.

7. Whisk the guava preserves and Instant ClearJel together in a small bowl. Using a cookie scoop or measuring spoon, portion about 1 teaspoon of filling onto the surface of half of the cookies. Place a second cookie on top of the filling to form a sandwich.

8. The cookies can be stored in an airtight container at room temperature for several days.

Modified Starch

Instant ClearJel is a product familiar to most pie bakers. It is a modified starch that does not require heat to thicken liquids. (If you've ever made instant pudding from a box, then you're familiar with a similar form of modified starch.) Instant ClearJel dissolves and gels at room temperature. Adding a bit to the fruit preserves helps to prevent it from squishing out from between the cookies when it is used as a filling. If you don't use it, your jam filling will be much looser and likely to squish out when you take a bite. Instant ClearJel can be found in some grocery stores or online (see Sources, page 350). You can also use it to stabilize whipped cream to prevent it from weeping.

Modified starches are processed or treated in some way, sometimes with heat or an acid, to cause them to act differently than they usually would. Please don't confuse them with genetically modified starch that comes from genetically engineered plants.

Fried Green Tomato Sandwiches

MAKES 3 DOZEN (1¾-INCH) COOKIES

Who can resist a traditional fried green tomato, with its fried cornmeal crunch coating a slice of tart, juicy tomato? If you were to judge this cookie by its title, you might think that this recipe probably belongs in the Savory Cookies chapter. While the flavors of the O.G. F.G.T. were our inspiration for this cookie, this sandwich cookie is no savory side dish. Smooshed between two crisp cornmeal cookies, its green tomato jam filling is both sweet and delightfully complex, with the sheerest hint of black pepper. Remember—technically, even green tomatoes are fruits! Refer to page 177 for tips and techniques on preparing slice-and-bake cookies.

INGREDIENT	VOLUME	WEIGHT
TOMATO JAM		
Green (unripe) tomatoes	2 medium	About 300 grams (⅔ pound)
Granulated sugar	1 cup	200 grams
Salt	¼ teaspoon	
CORNMEAL COOKIE		
Unbleached all-purpose flour	¾ cup	106 grams
Finely ground cornmeal	½ cup	71 grams
Salt	½ teaspoon	
Black pepper, freshly ground	⅛ teaspoon	
Unsalted butter, at room temperature	8 tablespoons	113 grams
Granulated sugar	¼ cup	50 grams
Light brown sugar	Packed ¼ cup	50 grams
Egg, at room temperature	1 large	50 grams (weighed without shells)

1. Make the Tomato Jam: Remove and discard the stem and hard core at the top of the tomatoes. Roughly chop the tomatoes into chunks. Puree the tomato in the bowl of a food processor. Transfer the tomato puree to a small saucepan along with the granulated sugar and the salt.

2. Bring the mixture to a boil over medium heat. Adjust the heat to maintain a gentle boil, and continue to cook for about 20 minutes, stirring frequently with a silicone spatula, until the mixture reaches 220°F (104°C) on an instant-read or candy thermometer.

(continued)

Transfer the jam to a small bowl to cool. Store the jam in the refrigerator until ready to fill the cookies.

3. Make the Cornmeal Cookies: Whisk together the flour, cornmeal, salt, and pepper together in a medium bowl; set aside.

4. Combine the butter, granulated sugar, and brown sugar in a stand mixer fitted with a flat beater, and beat together on medium speed until smooth and creamy, 1 to 2 minutes. Add the egg and continue to mix until it has been incorporated into the mixture. Stop mixing and scrape the sides of bowl and beater.

5. With the mixer on low speed, add the flour mixture and mix until no dry ingredients are visible. Scrape the sides of the bowl to make sure that all of the ingredients are incorporated.

6. Place the sticky dough on a piece of parchment paper and roll the dough into a 10-inch log. Freeze the dough until it is cold and firm throughout, at least 2 hours.

7. Position two racks to divide the oven into thirds and preheat to 350°F. Line two 18-by-13-inch baking sheets with parchment paper or silicone baking mats.

8. Cut the logs into ⅛-inch slices, placing 18 on each baking sheet (see page 86). This dough softens quickly, so be sure to place the dough log back in the freezer while batches of cookies are baking. Once firm, you can continue slicing more cookies.

9. Bake until the cookies are just light brown at the edges, 9 to 11 minutes. Halfway through baking, rotate the pans from front to back and top to bottom. Remove from the oven and let cool for 5 minutes on the baking sheets before transferring to a wire rack to cool completely. Repeat with the remaining dough once

the baking sheets have completely cooled, or prepare additional baking sheets.

10. Portion about 1 teaspoon of tomato jam onto half of the cookies. Place a second cookie on top of the filling to form a sandwich.

11. The cookies can be stored in an airtight container at room temperature for several days.

Variation: Blueberry Cornbread Sandwiches

As long as we are riffing on southern classics, let's also take on cornbread. Swapping out the heat for a bit of spice helps this cornbread stand up to Georgia's number one agricultural crop, which is not the peach but the blueberry.

For the cookie, replace the black pepper with ⅛ teaspoon of ground cinnamon. For the filling, replace the tomato jam with a simple blueberry filling made by placing ¾ cup of blueberry preserves in a small food processor along with 2 tablespoons Instant ClearJel (see "Modified Starch," page 258). Process for about 30 seconds to mix it together and break up the blueberry pieces. The filling will thicken as it sits.

CHAPTER SIX

piped, shaped, molded, and no-bake cookies

This chapter is a menagerie of cookies made using several methods. Piped cookies are made with a piping bag and tip or a spritz press to create freestanding cookies with unique shapes and designs. Molded cookies are made using special pans to create unusual shapes or patterns. No-bake cookies don't require any baking at all! Usually, a few minutes cooking on the stovetop is all they need. No-bake cookies are great for when the heat of summer makes you dread the heat of the oven. Because this chapter uses tools and techniques that are each unique to only a few cookies, we don't include many techniques here because it's more efficient to include the specific techniques directly in the recipe.

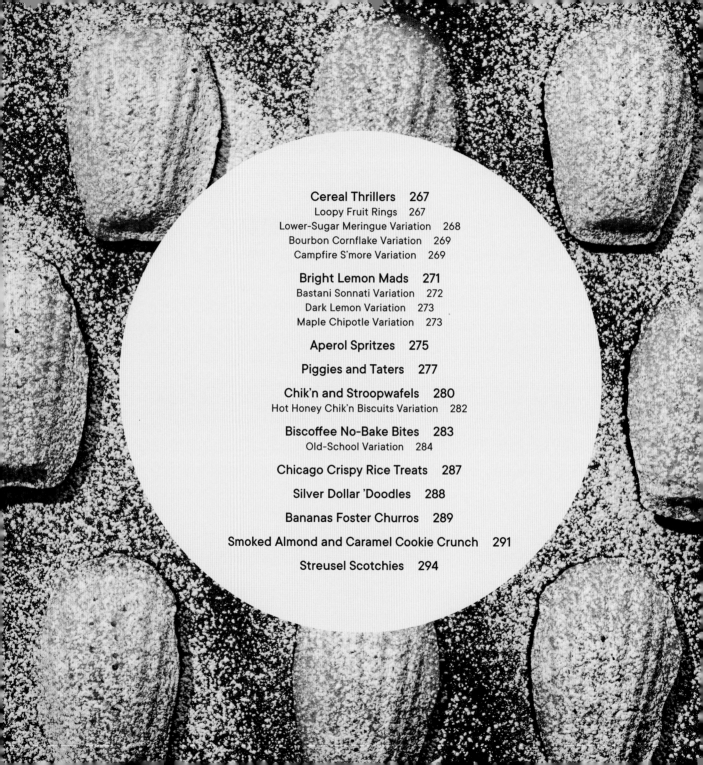

Helpful Tools

These tools are used in this chapter and are briefly described here. Because only a few recipes in each chapter use each tool, additional information on the use of the equipment is included in the individual recipe. Refer to Sources (page 350) for more information on where to purchase this equipment.

 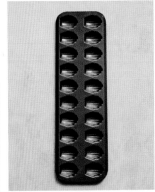

Spritz Cookie Press   Mini Madeleine Pan

- **Piping bags.** Plastic bags hold fillings so soft doughs and batters can be piped through a tip to create a shaped cookie. We prefer disposable piping bags made from plastic. Any type of plastic is fine, but we prefer bags described as "tipless" because the thinner plastic is easy to handle. If you don't have piping bags, a quart-size resealable plastic storage bag works, too. Just cut one of the bottom corners off and pipe the filling as directed. To easily fill a piping bag, fold the opening of the bag over by about 3 inches to create a cuff. Insert a pastry tip and cut off just enough plastic at the tip of the bag to expose the opening of the tip. Fill the bag about halfway full, unfold the cuff, and twist the top of the bag to keep the contents inside while you pipe.
- **Piping tips.** These help when you are looking to pipe cookie dough or batter to create a unique pattern.
- **Spritz cookie press.** It uses a trigger to deposit stiff cookie doughs in defined shapes that can't be easily re-created with a piping bag and tip. A piping bag and tip can be used instead, but spritz cookie dough can be stiff and difficult to pipe for some people.

- **Madeleine pan.** Metal pans with shell-shaped molds used to create the classic madeleine cookie. Pans come with wells in standard (3-by-2-inch) or mini (1½-by-1-inch) sizes. In the absence of madeleine pans, our madeleines will also bake nicely in mini muffin tins.
- **Mini muffin tin.** A smaller version of the classic muffin (or cupcake) tin, this is usually made with 24 cavities about 1 inch across.
- **Dent de loup pan.** French for "wolf tooth," this is a metal, accordion-pleated pan that bakes cookies into long wedges.
- **Pizzelle iron.** Think of this as a variation on a waffle iron. Batter is deposited onto preheated textured plates and cooked to create a thin, crispy pizzelle cookie with an intricate design. You can find irons with a variety of designs, including standard and mini sizes. We have always used electric pizzelle irons, but you can also find irons that cook using stovetop heat.

Cereal Thrillers

There's so much to love about meringue cookies. They're pretty easy to make, the base recipe is gluten-free, they keep for weeks when stored in an airtight container, and it's a practical way to use up all of those extra egg whites from your other baking projects. Unadorned meringues are *fine*, but we added breakfast cereal to bring some unexpected flavors to your cookie table.

Although we like to pipe our meringues with a piping bag, if you don't have piping bags and tips or the thought of piping cookies causes you distress, you can use a cookie scoop or even just a couple of spoons to portion small mounds of meringue onto your cookie sheet. They will still be thrillingly tasty.

Loopy Fruit Rings

MAKES 4 DOZEN MERINGUES

Did you ever eat Froot Loops cereal and convince yourself that the colorful rings all had different flavors? Well, it's not true. The orange ones don't really taste like oranges, the greens are *not* lime, and the reds are definitely not cherry. The flavor of the loops is sort of a mix of fruitlike flavors. While the flavors of actual fruits are not discernable, only Froot Loops can deliver that tutti-frutti toucan-tastic flavor of our childhood. Piping the crushed cereal–packed meringues into a ring shape is a fun wink to their loopy flavor.

INGREDIENT	VOLUME	WEIGHT
Froot Loops cereal	2½ cups	73 grams
Egg whites	4 large (½ cup)	140 grams
Sugar	1 cup	200 grams
Lemon juice, freshly squeezed	½ teaspoon	
Salt	⅛ teaspoon	
Pure vanilla extract	1 teaspoon	

1. Position two racks to divide the oven into thirds and preheat to 200°F. Line two 18-by-13-inch pans with parchment paper. Fit a large 18-inch piping bag with a sultan piping tip (see Note).

2. Finely crush 2 cups (59 grams) of the Froot Loops cereal, using a food processor. Alternatively, place the cereal in a resealable storage bag and crush the cereal to fine crumbs using a rolling pin or the bottom of a saucepan; set aside.

3. Combine the egg whites, sugar, lemon juice, and salt in the clean bowl of a stand mixer. (Make sure the bowl is spotless and grease-free, or your egg whites won't whip.) Place the bowl over a pot of barely simmering water to create a double boiler, making sure

(continued)

that the bottom of the bowl does not touch the water (see "Double Boiler: Toil and Trouble?" page 44). Cook the egg white mixture over the simmering water, stirring constantly with a silicone spatula, until the sugar dissolves and the mixture reaches 165°F on an instant-read thermometer; the mixture will become slightly frothy and opaque.

4. Transfer the bowl to a stand mixer fitted with a whisk attachment. Beat the mixture on medium-high speed until it holds stiff peaks and has cooled to room temperature. The bottom and sides of the bowl should no longer feel warm. Add the vanilla and beat until it is incorporated. Remove the bowl from the mixer and fold the crushed cereal into the meringue with a silicone spatula until incorporated.

5. Use a silicone spatula to transfer the mixture to the prepared piping bag. Pipe 1½-inch circles of the meringue mixture onto the prepared baking sheet, keeping at least ½ inch of space between rounds. Place the remaining ½ cup (14 grams) of Froot Loops in a small bowl and crush into approximately ⅛-inch pieces with your fingers. Sprinkle these pieces on top of the piped meringues.

6. Bake for 90 minutes. The outsides will crust over and become firm. Turn off the heat and leave the cookies to cool completely in the oven, about 4 hours. (The meringues need the residual heat from the oven, so resist opening the oven door before the time is up.) Remove the meringues from the baking pans. Store the cookies in an airtight container for at least 2 weeks.

NOTE: We like to use sultan piping tips that can pipe a ring of meringue all at once (see Sources, page 350). If you don't have a sultan piping tip, use any decorative tip and pipe the meringue batter into rings or another shape of your choosing, or use a spoon to portion into mounds instead.

Variation: Lower-Sugar Meringue

For a slightly less sweet meringue, the sugar can be decreased to ¾ cup (150 grams). The meringues will be a bit lighter and slightly more fragile.

Variation: Bourbon Cornflake

Unless you enjoy a very different kind of breakfast than we do, you might not have realized how great cornflakes and bourbon go together. The malty corn flavor of cornflakes cereal pairs perfectly with bourbon's caramel and oak notes. Best yet, these meringues don't have the boozy, burning mouthfeel or intoxicating effects that you get from sipping straight spirits.

Replace granulated sugar with an equal amount of packed light brown sugar and replace the lemon juice with ¼ teaspoon of white vinegar. Replace the vanilla with 1 tablespoon of bourbon. Replace the Froot Loops with 2⅔ cups (75 grams) of cornflakes cereal. Reserve ½ cup (14 grams) of the cornflakes for sprinkling on top of the meringues as is done in the original recipe. We piped these into shapes using a star-shaped piping tip, but you can pipe or scoop as desired.

Variation: Campfire S'more

Who doesn't love a s'more, with its chocolate and hot sticky marshmallow squished between two graham crackers? It's a great campfire treat, but we wanted to enjoy that same toasted marshmallow flavor without getting out the firewood and matches. We saw our answer when we saw Chef Joshua John Russell use a torch to toast meringue right in the bowl of a stand mixer. He incorporated the meringue into a toasted buttercream, and that technique works perfectly for meringue cookies as well. The toasted marshmallow flavor with shaved chocolate and Golden Grahams cereal folded into the meringue creates a crisp and perfectly portable s'more. Just so you know, we did try this recipe with crushed graham crackers instead of Golden Grahams cereal. The cereal actually had more flavor and held up better in the meringue.

Begin by shaving 2 ounces (57 grams) of bittersweet chocolate into a bowl, using a grater. Chill the chocolate in the refrigerator to keep it cold while you prepare the meringue. In Step 2, replace the lemon juice with ¼ teaspoon of white vinegar. To create the toasted marshmallow flavor, at the end of Step 4, remove the bowl from the stand mixer. Using common sense regarding fire safety, use a kitchen torch to toast the entire surface of the meringue until it is dark brown (not black). Add the vanilla and reattach the bowl to the mixer. The heat of the torch will cause the meringue to soften, so rewhip the meringue until it is stiff again. Fold in 1½ cups (60 grams) of finely crushed Golden Grahams (subbed for the Froot Loops) plus the cold shaved bittersweet chocolate. We like to pipe ours using a star-shaped piping tip, but you can pipe or scoop, as desired. No extra cereal is sprinkled on top of these meringues.

Bright Lemon Mads

MAKES 2 DOZEN FULL-SIZE MADELEINES (OR DOZENS AND DOZENS OF MINIS)

We don't often adhere to traditions with baking, and these are not traditional madeleines. These cakey, shell-shaped cookies have a wonderfully bright lemon flavor that comes from adding freshly squeezed lemon juice that is emulsified into the batter. A higher proportion of melted butter in the batter combined with low-protein cake flour both keep these mads rich and delicately tender with a tighter, finer crumb despite all of the mixing needed. Like the traditional madeleines, these mads are best enjoyed within a few minutes of baking. We offer three flavor variations for these, including a Dark Lemon version made with brown sugar and brown butter, for a wonderful contrast to this brighter lemon version.

INGREDIENT	VOLUME	WEIGHT
Bleached cake flour	1¼ cups	142 grams
Salt	1 teaspoon	
Baking powder	¾ teaspoon	
Granulated sugar	1 cup	200 grams
Eggs, at room temperature	3 large	150 grams (weighed without shells)
Almond extract	½ teaspoon	
Unsalted butter	16 tablespoons	227 grams
Lemon juice, freshly squeezed	¼ cup	56 grams
Confectioners' sugar, for dusting (optional, but highly recommended)		

1. Sift together the flour, salt, and baking powder into a medium bowl; set aside. Melt 12 tablespoons (170 grams) of the butter and set aside until it is cool but still pourable.

2. Depending on the capacity of your stand mixer, this might be more convenient to mix using an electric hand mixer. Combine the granulated sugar, eggs, and almond extract in a bowl. Beat these ingredients together on high speed for 1 to 2 minutes, until well mixed and lightened in color. Add the flour mixture and mix initially on low speed until most of the dry ingredients have been incorporated. Scrape the sides of the bowl with a silicone spatula, then continue to beat on high speed for another minute.

3. Beat in the melted butter, followed by the lemon juice, until the batter is smooth and creamy. Pour the batter into a disposable piping bag with an uncut tip. Twist the top of the bag closed and clip or tie it securely. Chill the piping bag in the refrigerator overnight. (If

(continued)

you're all out of piping bags, store the batter in a bowl with plastic wrap pressed directly on top of the batter.)

4. Melt the remaining 4 tablespoons (57 grams) of butter. Use a pastry brush to lightly coat the wells of full-size or mini nonstick madeleine pans (see Note) and place the pans into the refrigerator until the melted butter has hardened, 10 to 15 minutes. (Don't use all of the butter at once! The melted butter should be enough to rebutter the pans before baking the next round of mads.) Position a rack in the center of the oven. Place a baking sheet upside down on the center rack and preheat the oven to 400°F.

5. Cut off and discard the tip of the piping bag and fill the wells of the madeleine pan about three-quarters full. (If not using a piping bag, fill the wells with a spoon or scoop.) By weight, portion 25 grams of batter per well for full-size mads; 4 grams of batter for mini mads.

6. Place the madeleine pan on the inverted baking sheet and bake until the mads have puffed and risen and begin to brown at the edges (a toothpick inserted into the center of a madeleine will come out clean), 10 to 12 minutes for full-size cookies (5 to 7 minutes for minis). Remove from the oven and immediately unmold them onto a wire rack (or a folded tea towel if you want to avoid impression marks from the rack on the madeleine bottoms). Dust them with confectioners' sugar, if you like, and eat them instantly. If baking more mads, allow the pans to cool completely before brushing with more melted butter. Chill the buttered pan, portion, and bake as instructed.

7. Madeleines are at their absolute best when they are fresh from the oven and just cool enough to eat. If baked in advance, they can be warmed up and refreshed in a 350°F oven for 5 minutes. (Even frozen mads thaw and refresh well!) The batter lasts well in the refrigerator for about 3 days. After making some, fold over and clip the tip of the piping bag, and place the batter back in the refrigerator. You can make mads on-demand so they are always at their peak of freshness.

NOTE: In the absence of madeleine pans, our mads will also bake nicely in mini muffin tins. Fill the wells two-thirds of the way to the top with about 13 grams of batter and bake them for 9 to 11 minutes.

Variation: Bastani Sonnati Mads

The flavors of *bastani sonnati*, cold Persian ice cream flavored with rosewater, saffron, and pistachios, are sublime in these warm, cakey cookies. If you are not familiar with this divine flavor combo, please try it. Traditional bastani sonnati can also include pieces of frozen clotted cream, but even our inauthentic take on a West Asian treat is a fantastic twist on the traditional madeleine.

Finely chop or grind 1 cup (128 grams) of roasted unsalted pistachios. Add a pinch of high-quality saffron threads to the butter when melting it. Replace the almond extract with 1 tablespoon of pure vanilla extract and 3 tablespoons of culinary-grade rosewater. Omit the lemon juice and, instead, mix in the ground pistachios.

Variation: Dark Lemon Mads

With a couple of simple substitutions, these madeleines taste completely different than the original. For a real treat, try these alongside the Bright Lemon Mads to really appreciate the contrast. If you make a batch of each, you can pipe the two batters side by side in the madeleine pan wells for a two-tone lemon delight.

Substitute 1 packed cup (200 grams) of light brown sugar for the granulated sugar. Replace the 12 tablespoons of melted butter with brown butter (see "Better Baking with Brown Butter," page 19) by first melting 12 tablespoons (170 grams) of butter in a small saucepan with a light-colored bottom (so you will be able to see the butter browning) over medium heat. Continue to cook; it will start to bubble noisily as the water boils off. Once the bubbling begins to quiet down, swirl the pan constantly for about 1 minute, or until the milk solids at the bottom of the pan have turned golden brown, and the butter has a nutty aroma. Remove the pan from the heat and transfer the brown butter to a small bowl. Proceed with the recipe when the brown butter is cooled but still pourable.

Variation: Maple Chipotle Mads

The subtle heat of chipotle pepper from the American Southwest crosses the corn-growing fields of the Midwest to meet up with maple syrup from New England for a modern American fusion version of this traditionally French cookie. Chipotle chile powder is made from ripe jalapeño peppers that have been smoked, dried, and finely ground. It is a rich source of smoky chile flavor but not very hot. You can find it in the spice aisle of your grocery store.

Decrease the cake flour to 1 cup (113 grams). Whisk ¼ cup plus 2 tablespoons (60 grams) of finely ground cornmeal and ⅜ teaspoon of chipotle chile powder with the flour in Step 1. Replace the sugar with ¾ cup (234 grams) of pure maple syrup. Replace the 12 tablespoons of melted butter with brown butter (see "Better Baking with Brown Butter," page 19) by first melting 12 tablespoons (170 grams) of butter in a small saucepan with a light-colored bottom (so you will be able to see the butter browning) over medium heat. Continue to cook; it will start to bubble noisily as the water boils off. Once the bubbling begins to quiet down, swirl the pan constantly for about 1 minute, or until the milk solids at the bottom of the pan have turned golden brown, and the butter has a nutty aroma. Remove the pan from the heat and transfer the brown butter to a small bowl. Proceed with the recipe when the brown butter is cooled but still pourable.

Aperol Spritzes

MAKES ABOUT 8 DOZEN (2-INCH) COOKIES

During a recent visit, I found my mom's old cookie press while rifling around her cabinets in search of a pan. Unfortunately, the canister and spring are all corroded now, but the cookie disks are still in good shape. Comparing hers to our new press, the technology really has not changed over the decades, but the cookie disks have evolved. Although her vintage disks have a bit more fine detail, the modern disks are available in many more designs, including pets and other animals—even dinosaurs! Although spritz cookies have been a mainstay of cookie platters for decades, we modernized their often simple flavor to match these fun new shapes by infusing them with the flavors of an Aperol Spritz cocktail. The citrus and complex botanical flavors of this light and refreshing cocktail are perfect for a hot summer afternoon. —P.A.

INGREDIENT	VOLUME	WEIGHT
Sugar	1 cup	200 grams
Orange zest, freshly grated	1 medium orange	
Pink grapefruit zest, freshly grated	1 medium grapefruit	
Unsalted butter, at room temperature	16 tablespoons	227 grams
Egg, at room temperature	1 large	50 grams (weighed without shell)
Angostura bitters	1 tablespoon	
Salt	½ teaspoon	
Pure vanilla extract	½ teaspoon	
Unbleached all-purpose flour	2¼ cups	319 grams

1. Combine the sugar, orange zest, and grapefruit zest in the bowl of your stand mixer. To extract the most citrus flavor, rub the zest and sugar between your thumbs and fingertips until the sugar is fragrant, very light orange in color, and has a texture like wet sand (see "Live Your Zest Life," page 25).

2. Position two racks to divide the oven into thirds and preheat to 375°F. Gather at least two baking sheets, but do not line them with parchment paper or silicone baking sheets. (Really—you don't need parchment paper for these cookies. In fact, parchment paper will make piping these very difficult because the cookie dough is stiff and it is much easier to deposit the cookie directly on the pan. We've made almost a million of these, and they will not stick.)

3. Add the butter to the citrus-sugar, fit the mixer with a flat beater, and cream together on medium speed until light and fluffy. Add the egg, bitters,

(continued)

salt, and vanilla. Mix until uniformly incorporated. Finally, gently incorporate the flour into the batter, either with the mixer on low speed or by folding in with a silicone spatula.

4. Following the manufacturer's instructions, place a decorative disk in a spritz cookie press (see page 265). Fill the cookie press with dough and press the dough out onto the ungreased and unlined baking sheets. The very first and last cookies piped out of the press are often imperfect. Feel free to scrape these off your baking sheet. These cookies will puff but don't spread much in the oven, so place them as close as your cookie press will allow, leaving at least ½ inch between. This recipe makes eight dozen cookies, and they may have to be baked in several batches.

5. Bake until the cookies are light golden brown at the edges, 10 to 12 minutes. Halfway through baking, rotate the pans from front to back and top to bottom. Remove from the oven and use a thin spatula to immediately transfer the cookies to a wire rack to cool completely. Repeat with the remaining dough once the baking sheets have completely cooled, or use additional baking sheets. After cooling, the cookies can be stored in an airtight container at room temperature for several days.

COOKIE BYTE

Intro to Botany

Aperol has a complex flavor but one that would be lost by simply adding a tablespoon or two of it to a cookie dough. This Italian aperitif is a mixture of several plants and herbs, most notably rhubarb, gentian (pronounced jen-chin), and quinine (kwy-nine)—the source of the sharp notes of tonic water. To mimic these delicate flavors, we turned to a more concentrated and convenient source of gentian—Angostura bitters! Bitters are usually added a dash or two at a time to finish off such cocktails as an old fashioned, Manhattan, or Pisco Sour. Adding a tablespoon of bitters—much more than most would ever use in a single cocktail—brings a gentle bite of herbal sharpness and breathes new life into the classic spritz cookie.

Piggies and Taters

MAKES 2 DOZEN COOKIES

Sometimes inspiration for baking comes to us in the form of a delicious new flavor combination. Other times, it begins with a trip through a catalog, scouting for unusual baking supplies. When Chris purchased a dent de loup pan, I was intrigued because I had never heard of such a thing. The idea of cookies shaped like a wolf tooth (the English translation of the French *dent de loup*) got my attention. Also known as *wolfzahn* (depending on which side of the France-Germany border you are on), the dent de loup is an Alsatian butter cookie that is baked in an accordion-pleated pan and is said to look like wolf teeth (though I am skeptical). The flavor profile of the traditional wolf tooth cookie was fairly plain, and I began to think about what flavors might complement a wolf tooth–shaped cookie. My first thought was to go gory. Maybe blood orange? Nah, too much. Instead, I decided that my Big Bad Wolf cookies should be filled with some "Three Little Pigs" in the form of bacon! However, after making several batches of these cookies, I realized that they looked more like *pomme de terre* (potato) than dent de loup! The flat sides resembled fried potato wedges more than any wolf tooth. I embraced the shape and leaned into the idea by adding potato chips to the bacon to produce delightfully smoky cookies with a unique shape and a fantastic sweet and salty crunch. —*P.A.*

INGREDIENT	VOLUME	WEIGHT
Thick-cut bacon, uncooked	4 strips	About 150 grams
Unbleached all-purpose flour	1 cup plus 3 tablespoons	168 grams
Salt	¼ teaspoon	
Baking soda	⅛ teaspoon	
Light brown sugar	Packed ¾ cup	75 grams
Granulated sugar	¼ cup	50 grams
Unsalted butter, at room temperature	7 tablespoons	99 grams
Liquid smoke (see Note)	¼ teaspoon	
Egg, at room temperature	1 large	50 grams (weighed without shell)
Potato chips	About 40 chips	57 grams

(continued)

1. Position a rack in the center of the oven and preheat to 350°F. Spray the surface of a 12-inch square, 8-row dent de loup pan (see Additional Note) with nonstick baking spray.

2. Place the strips of bacon in a skillet over medium heat, flipping the strips periodically until cooked crisp, 8 to 12 minutes. Save 1 tablespoon of the rendered bacon fat. Remove the bacon from the pan, drain on paper towels, and let cool completely.

3. Whisk together the flour, salt, and baking soda in a medium bowl; set aside.

4. Place the bacon in the bowl of a food processor. Process in 1-second pulses until it is finely ground. Add the light brown sugar and granulated sugar and pulse several more times until well mixed. Add the butter and the tablespoon of reserved bacon fat. Process until the mixture is smooth and creamy. Add the liquid smoke and the egg and process until incorporated.

5. Add the flour mixture and the potato chips and pulse just until no dry flour is visible. Remove the blade and scrape the sides and bottom of the bowl to incorporate any stray ingredients.

6. Portion 1 tablespoon of dough, using a #60 cookie scoop or measuring spoon, and place two scoops 4 inches apart in each row of the pan.

7. Bake until the cookies are golden brown with set edges, 14 to 16 minutes. Halfway through baking, rotate the pan from front to back. Remove from the oven and let cool for 10 minutes in the pan before sliding the cookies out of the pan and onto a wire rack to cool completely. Let the pan cool and repeat with the remaining dough. After cooling, the cookies can be stored in an airtight container at room temperature for several days.

NOTE: Liquid smoke is a fun ingredient readily available in the condiment aisle of your grocery store. Smoke from hickory wood is collected and condensed into a liquid, giving pure smoke flavor. It is a great way to boost the bacon flavor in these cookies.

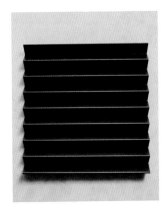

ADDITIONAL NOTE: This recipe calls for a piece of specialty equipment called a dent de loup pan). It looks like a metal pan that was folded into pleats. While it certainly makes these potato chip–infused cookies look like fried potato wedges (which is so cool!), it is not necessary. These cookies can still be enjoyed by scooping the recommended 1 tablespoon of dough (13 cookies per sheet) onto parchment-lined baking sheets and placing the sheets on the upper- and lower-middle racks of the oven, like making a standard drop cookie, then baking for the recommended time. Refer to page 83 for tips and techniques on preparing drop cookies.

Chik'n and Stroopwafels

MAKES ABOUT 1 DOZEN LARGE (4½-INCH) OR 2 DOZEN SMALL (3-INCH) SANDWICHES

These sweet cookie sandwiches are a fusion of two delightful foods from two very different places. The flavors are drawn from chicken and waffles, an any-time treat of hot, fluffy waffles topped with fried chicken and drizzled with maple syrup, ubiquitous in our adopted hometown of Atlanta, Georgia. (In our opinion, the best is made with spicy chicken and a warm maple syrup.) The cookie itself is our take on the Dutch *stroopwafel*—a thin yeasted cookie made in a special waffle iron and split in half to create a caramel-filled sandwich. Our version is made with thin, crisp pizzelle cookies. Each component is delicious in its original form, but this combination of savory spices sandwiched around a thin layer of rich maple caramel is divine. You will need a pizzelle iron to make these cookies. Note that malted milk powder contains gluten (from its origins in barley) and should not be included in cookies that need to be made gluten-free.

INGREDIENT	VOLUME	WEIGHT
PIZZELLE (WAFFLE COOKIES)		
Unbleached all-purpose flour	1½ cups	213 grams
Malted milk powder (see above)	1 tablespoon	
Baking powder	1½ teaspoons	
Cayenne pepper	⅛ teaspoon	
Unsalted butter, melted and warm but still pourable	8 tablespoons	113 grams
Chicken bouillon powder (see Note)	1 tablespoon	
Granulated sugar	¾ cup	150 grams
Pure vanilla extract	¾ teaspoon	
Pure maple extract	2¼ teaspoons	
Eggs, at room temperature	3 large	150 grams (weighed without shells)
MAPLE FILLING		
Light brown sugar	Packed 1½ cups	300 grams
Water	¾ cup	177 grams
Pure maple syrup	¼ cup plus 2 tablespoons	117 grams
Light corn syrup	3 tablespoons	63 grams
Salt	Pinch	
Unsalted butter, cut into 6 pieces	12 tablespoons	170 grams
Pure maple extract	¼ teaspoon	

1. Make the Pizzelle: Heat a pizzelle iron according to the manufacturer's instructions. Spray the iron with nonstick cooking spray or lightly brush with vegetable oil.

2. Whisk together the flour, malted milk powder, baking powder, and cayenne in a medium bowl; set aside.

3. Whisk the melted butter and chicken bouillon together in a large bowl. Whisk in the granulated sugar, vanilla, and maple extract.

4. Whisk the eggs, one at a time, into the butter mixture, adding each egg only after the previous egg is fully incorporated.

5. Fold (or gently whisk) in the flour mixture until no clumps of flour are visible. The batter will be thick but pourable.

6. Deposit portions of batter (about 1½ tablespoons for a 4½-inch pizzelle or about 2 teaspoons for a 3-inch pizzelle) on the pizzelle iron and cook according to the manufacturer's instructions until golden brown. As the pizzelle finish, remove them from the iron (a fork is helpful in removing the hot cookies, but be careful not to scratch the surface of the iron) and let them cool on a wire rack. They will be soft and floppy when lifted from the pizzelle iron, but will crisp as they cool. Keep on keepin' on until all of the batter is used. You will only have to oil the forms again if your pizzelle begin to stick.

7. Make the Maple Filling: Stir together the brown sugar, water, maple syrup, light corn syrup, and salt in a medium saucepan with a lid. Place the saucepan over medium-low heat and add the butter pieces. Stir the mixture until the butter has completely melted.

Seems Like a Lot of Salt

Chicken bouillon is a notoriously salty product, and this recipe calls for a whole tablespoon of it. On the surface, that may seem like an alarmingly large quantity of salt. Fear not! It is simply a somewhat large but correct amount of salt. We tested the four brands available in our supermarkets, and they all have a similar sodium content and tasted similarly salty. Repeated tests of the recipe with increasing amounts of bouillon revealed that 1 tablespoon was needed to get sufficient chicken flavor into the cookie. That amount of bouillon is the equivalent of about 1⅛ teaspoons of salt for the entire batch of cookies—yet the cookie does not taste salty. That salt is in balance with the other flavors and sugar in the cookie itself and with the maple filling.

8. Bring the mixture to boil, stirring constantly to dissolve the sugar. Once the mixture comes to a boil, cover and cook for 1 minute.

9. Remove the lid. If you have one, insert a candy thermometer (otherwise use an instant-read thermometer to check the temperature every few minutes). Increase the heat to medium and boil the mixture until it reaches soft ball stage, 234° to 240°F.

10. Remove the pan from the heat and add the maple extract, but don't stir it in yet. Leave the mixture in the pan and set aside to cool for 10 minutes. Stir the

(continued)

filling well to make sure that the mixture is smooth, and the butter and maple extract are fully incorporated. Continue to cool, if necessary, until the mixture is warm but not hot, and has the consistency of a caramel sauce. It should be thick enough to mound slightly when dropped from a spoon.

11. Use a spoon or scoop to portion 2 tablespoons of filling onto one large (4½-inch) pizzelle and sandwich with a second. For small (3-inch) pizzelle, portion 1½ teaspoons of filling. Kept in an airtight container at room temperature, the cookies will keep for several days.

NOTE: Don't be scared of the chicken bouillon powder in these cookies! It provides a bit of savory flavor, but it's nothing overwhelming or out of place. What's chicken and waffles without chicken?!

COOKIE BYTE

Picture-Perfect Pizzelle

Depositing the batter just slightly off-center toward the back of the form will result in a more evenly shaped pizzelle, as the batter is squished forward from the closing of the iron. Generally, pizzelle won't need to cook for more than 1 minute; some might be done after 30 seconds. You might have to experiment with portion sizes and cooking times to get them just right for your device. Immediately after the pizzelle are removed from the oven, they can be transferred to a cutting board and trimmed neatly with a metal cookie cutter. Otherwise, after they have cooled completely, gently use the side of your thumb to break off any unwelcome nibs or points.

Variation: Hot Honey Chik'n Biscuits

Fried chicken drizzled with spicy honey and served on a warm buttermilk biscuit is another delightful treat that can be enjoyed at any meal of the day. These spicy variations aren't actually made with chicken or biscuits—at least not the type of flaky biscuits that you might be thinking of. In this sense, we're referring to the British biscuit: cookies! For a spicy cookie, omit the maple extract and increase the cayenne pepper to ¼ teaspoon. For a hot honey filling, replace the maple syrup and light corn syrup with ½ cup plus 1 tablespoon (189 grams) of hot honey. Hot honey is simply honey that has been infused with chile peppers. Depending on your love of heat, you can also add up to ¼ teaspoon of cayenne pepper to the warm filling before portioning onto the pizzelle.

Biscoffee No-Bake Bites

MAKES ABOUT 3 DOZEN 1½-INCH COOKIES

These are our take on the aptly named cookies simply called no-bakes that I grew up with. Cooked quickly on the stovetop, they are great cookies for those hot summer days when you dread switching on the oven. They are flour-free and probably closer to a candy than a traditional baked cookie. The classic chocolate–peanut butter versions of these (see Variation) were a staple in my childhood home. In fact, several dozen would often make their way into care packages in my college dorm. Our revisited recipe with spiced cookie butter and crushed whole coffee beans appeals to those times when you want to enjoy a new take on a comforting favorite. If you're not a coffee drinker, you still might be into the bold crunch of crushed coffee beans. The whole beans have a deep, smoky flavor (like very dark chocolate) with less bitterness than brewed coffee. If coffee's *really* not your thing, you can substitute ¼ cup (30 grams) of cocoa nibs or ½ cup (57 grams) of chopped toasted pecan pieces. —C.T.

INGREDIENT	VOLUME	WEIGHT
Whole roasted coffee beans (see above)	¼ cup	18 grams
Unsalted butter, cut into chunks	8 tablespoons	113 grams
Granulated sugar	1 cup	200 grams
Light brown sugar	Packed ½ cup	100 grams
Whole milk	½ cup	121 grams
Salt	½ teaspoon	
Pure vanilla extract	1 teaspoon	
Speculoos cookie butter, such as Biscoff (see page 24)	½ cup	120 grams
Penzeys Baking Spice (see Note) or ground cinnamon	¼ teaspoon	
Quick-cooking oats	3 cups	267 grams

1. Place the coffee beans in a resealable storage bag and seal, removing most of the air from the bag. Lightly roll a rolling pin over the beans a few times to gently crush them. You don't want them ground to a powder, but you don't want whole beans, either; set aside.

2. Combine the butter, granulated sugar, brown sugar, milk, and salt in a medium saucepan. Heat the mixture over medium heat, gently stirring to melt the butter. Watch the mixture carefully and stir it constantly once it starts to bubble at the edges. When the first bubble breaks the surface in the center of the pot to indicate that the mixture is at a full boil, set a timer for 1 minute and continue to cook, stirring constantly,

(continued)

to prevent the mixture from sticking and burning on the bottom of the pan. After the full 1 minute, immediately remove the pan from the heat. Do not cook the mixture for longer than 1 minute because it will set with a crumbly texture instead of being smooth and fudgy. Stir in the vanilla, cookie butter, and baking spice until the mixture appears smooth and uniform. Stir in the oats and crushed coffee beans until the oats have been coated and no longer look dry.

3. Working quickly, portion the mixture into a silicone mold with 1½-inch square (½-inch deep) cavities (see Equipment Note). Press down on the top of each molded cookie with the back of a spoon to flatten and smoosh the mixture into the corners. The cookies will set as they cool, so work quickly to prevent the mixture from setting in the pan. If the mixture does set, gently reheat the pan over very low heat, stirring gently until the mixture is workable again.

4. Allow the cookies to cool and set until they reach room temperature. They will be firm and stackable. Kept in an airtight container, they will keep at room temperature for at least 1 week.

NOTE: We love Penzeys Baking Spice, with its blend of cinnamon and other spices, for these cookies. You can substitute ground cinnamon (or leave the spice out entirely), but ¼ teaspoon of spice adds a welcome warm note that pairs well with both the cookie butter, and coffee.

EQUIPMENT NOTE: We enoy the modern look of these cookies when they've been molded into fun, bite-size shapes using a silicone mold. If you don't have a silicone mold that would be appropriate, line an 18-by-13-inch baking sheet with parchment paper. Portion 1½-tablespoon (#40) scoops (or heaping tablespoons) about 1 inch apart onto the prepared sheet.

Variation: Old-School No-Bakes

If you're not familiar with these cookies at all, then the retro chocolate–peanut butter version is still a modern cookie to you. To make them the way Chris's mom does, omit the brown sugar and use a total of 1½ cups (300 grams) of granulated sugar, add ¼ cup (21 grams) of unsweetened natural or Dutch-processed cocoa powder to the butter mixture, substitute ½ cup (135 grams) creamy peanut butter for the cookie butter, and omit the baking spice. Portion using a 1½-tablespoon (#40) scoop or simply drop portions from a spoon, then cook as directed.

Notes on Oats

COOKIE BYTE

Nearly every other oatmeal cookie we make uses old-fashioned rolled oats rather than quick-cooking oats. So, why call for quick-cooking oats for these? First, it's important to know how they are different. Oats start as oat groats, or kernels, that are hulled. Steel-cut, or pinhead oats, are oat groats that have been cut into two or three pieces. These oats are processed the least, and the texture when cooked is very chewy. However, cooking steel-cut oats takes a long time, and most cookies do not bake long enough or contain enough moisture to properly cook them. Old-fashioned rolled oats, the kind we use most often for baking, are whole oat groats that have been steamed and flattened (i.e., rolled) so they are thin and cook faster than steel-cut oats. When baked in a cookie, old-fashioned rolled oats give a wonderful chewy texture. In these cookies, old-fashioned rolled oats would be too chewy with an assertive raw flavor. In contrast, quick-cooking oats are also steamed but rolled thinner, and those smaller pieces cook very quickly. We use quick-cooking oats in these no-bake cookies because the residual heat and moisture from the boiled mixture is just enough to cook the oats and provide a pleasing texture in the finished cookies.

Chicago Crispy Rice Treats

MAKES 16 (2-INCH) SQUARES

The first time we tried Chicago popcorn, a mix of cheese-coated and caramel popcorns, we thought we were in for a world of disappointment. We received the popcorn blend as a gift and wondered who thought it was a good idea to mix sweet caramel popcorn with powdered cheese–coated popcorn? Always up for a culinary adventure, though, we dug in for a few tentative bites. Wow—we were so wrong! The sweet-salty combination gives chocolate–peanut butter a run for its money. We applied those flavors to an old-timey Rice Krispies Treat, replacing the marshmallow goo with a caramel toffee matrix and adding crispy cheese-flavored puffs for a crunchy burst of that orange cheese stuff.

INGREDIENT	VOLUME	WEIGHT
Crunchy cheese-flavored snacks, such as Cheetos	1¼ cups	84 grams
Crispy rice cereal	2 cups	53 grams
Unsalted butter	5 tablespoons	71 grams
Dark brown sugar	Packed ½ cup	100 grams
Dark corn syrup	¼ cup	82 grams
Salt	1 teaspoon	

1. Line the bottom and sides of an 8-inch square baking pan with aluminum foil. Lightly spray the foil with nonstick cooking spray.

2. Gently break or crush the cheese snacks into ½- to 1-inch pieces and toss into a large bowl. Stir in the crispy rice cereal.

3. Melt the butter in a tall and wide saucepot (something large enough to comfortably stir in later) over medium-low heat. Stir in the brown sugar, corn syrup, and salt with a silicone spatula. Continue to beat the mixture, stirring constantly, until the sugar has dissolved and it starts to bubble at the edges, about 5 minutes. Stop stirring and check the temperature with an instant-read thermometer. When the mixture is bubbling all over and reaches between 230° and 235°F on an instant-read or candy thermometer, remove the pan from the heat.

4. Stir in the crispy rice mixture, using the silicone spatula. Continue to fold the mixture until everything is coated. Scrape out the mixture into the prepared pan. Press down on the top of the mix so that it reaches the edges and into the corners. Smooth the surface with the spatula. Set aside for several hours to cool.

5. Use the foil to transfer the squares from the pan to a cutting board. Peel the foil away before using a sharp or serrated knife to cut the bars into sixteen 2-inch squares. Store the bars in an airtight container at room temperature. The bars will begin to soften and lose their crunchy texture over time. They are best enjoyed within 3 days.

Silver Dollar 'Doodles

MAKES 2 DOZEN (2-INCH) COOKIES

Oh, the classic snickerdoodle! Soft, tender, and warm with its cinnamon-sugar goodness. Because our sugar-coated versions of classic cinnamon-sugar snickerdoodles are cooked on the stovetop, the direct heat of the griddle creates an enticing crown of caramelized bliss on both sides of the cookie that can't be re-created through traditional baking. Best of all, this miniaturized version of the classic cooks in less time than it takes to preheat your oven.

INGREDIENT	VOLUME	WEIGHT
Unbleached all-purpose flour	1½ cups	213 grams
Baking powder	½ teaspoon	
Salt	¼ teaspoon	
Unsalted butter, at room temperature	8 tablespoons	113 grams
Sugar	½ cup plus 2 tablespoons	125 grams
Egg, at room temperature	1 large	50 grams (weighed without shell)
Pure vanilla extract	1 teaspoon	
Ground cinnamon	2 teaspoons	

1. Whisk together the flour, baking powder, and salt in a medium bowl; set aside. Combine the butter and ½ cup (100 grams) of sugar in a stand mixer with a flat beater, and beat together on medium speed until smooth and creamy, 1 to 2 minutes. Beat in the egg and vanilla until the mixture is uniform. Beat in the flour mixture on low speed until combined. Scrape the sides of the bowl and the beater with a silicone spatula.

2. Roll the dough into a 6-inch log and wrap it in plastic wrap. Refrigerate the dough until it is cold and firm throughout, at least 2 hours or up to 3 days.

3. Stir together the remaining 2 tablespoons of sugar and the cinnamon. Unwrap the dough and slice into ¼-inch-thick disks. Dip and press both sides of each cookie into the cinnamon-sugar mixture.

4. If you have an electric griddle that reliably keeps a steady temperature, lightly spray it with nonstick cooking spray and heat it to 350°F. Otherwise, place a lightly sprayed flat nonstick skillet over medium heat on the stovetop. Once preheated, cook the cookies 3 minutes on the first side. Using a thin spatula, flip them over. They will puff slightly and should be lightly browned like a pancake. (If the cookies are too dark, lower the heat.) Touch the top of a cookie and try to wiggle it slightly from side to side. It is ready when it is resisting your wiggle, which should be after about an additional 3 minutes on the second side. Transfer the cooked cookies to a wire rack to cool slightly. They are fantastic to eat while still slightly warm and the sugar shell is at its crispiest, but they can be stored in an airtight container for a few days once they are cool.

Bananas Foster Churros

MAKES 2½ DOZEN (3½-INCH) CHURROS

Bananas Foster is that classic midcentury dessert that told everyone else in the room, "Hey, look at us, we're eating superfancy tonight!" Usually prepared tableside, bananas were sautéed in butter, brown sugar, and cinnamon until caramelized. The dish was finished with rum and banana liqueur, and lit on fire in a dazzling display of dining room pyrotechnics. Although that type of dining room theater has largely disappeared, we think those flavors are worth preserving. Fast-forward 70 years after the invention of the original, and we present the Bananas Foster Churros, with practically the entire dessert incorporated right into the dough. Instead of setting them on fire, though, we've added a warm, rum-laced dipping sauce. Still superfancy, but no need for reservations.

INGREDIENT	VOLUME	WEIGHT
CHURROS		
Unsalted butter	8 tablespoons	113 grams
Banana	1 medium	100 grams (weighed without peel)
Water	⅓ cup	79 grams
Dark rum	¼ cup	52 grams
Banana liqueur	¼ cup	56 grams
Turbinado sugar	¼ cup	50 grams
Salt	¾ teaspoon	
Ground cinnamon	1¼ teaspoons	
Ground cloves	Pinch	
Unbleached all-purpose flour	1 cup	142 grams
Eggs, at room temperature	3 large	150 grams (weighed without shells)
Vegetable oil, for frying		
Granulated sugar	2 tablespoons	25 grams
DIPPING SAUCE		
Dulce de leche	One 13.4-ounce can	380 grams
Dark rum	3 to 5 tablespoons	39 to 65 grams

(continued)

1. Make the Churros: Melt the butter over low heat in a medium wide-bottomed saucepot. Puree the banana in a small food processor and add it to the melted butter along with the water, rum, banana liqueur, turbinado sugar, salt, ¼ teaspoon of the cinnamon, and the cloves. Whisk the mixture until it is uniform.

2. Increase the heat to medium and bring the mixture to a boil. Once boiling, quickly stir in the flour with a stiff silicone spatula or wooden spoon. The mixture will thicken into a paste. Keep stirring the paste around the pan for a full 2 minutes and then transfer to the bowl of a stand mixer fitted with a flat beater.

3. Beat the paste on high speed for 1 minute to cool it down a bit. After the full 1 minute, add one egg and continue to beat on high speed until it is incorporated. Stop the mixer and scrape the sides of the bowl with a silicone spatula. Bring the mixer to high speed again and beat in each additional egg in the same way as the first, pausing to scrape the bowl between each egg.

4. Fit a large star piping tip, such as an Ateco #847, inside a standard piping bag. Fill the piping bag with the churro dough.

5. Pour a 2-inch layer of vegetable oil into a heavy saucepan, such as a Dutch oven, with tall sides for frying. Heat the oil and use a thermometer to determine when it has reached 375°F. While the oil is heating, stir together the remaining 1 teaspoon of cinnamon and the granulated sugar in a small bowl.

6. When the oil is ready, have the piping bag in one hand and a pair of kitchen scissors in the other. Squeeze out a 3- to 4-inch segment of dough over the oil and cut it away with the scissors, allowing it to drop into the oil. Depending on the diameter of your pan, you can fry three to six churros at the same time. When you see that the bottoms of the churros have turned medium brown, use a slotted spoon or spider strainer to flip the churros over. When they have turned a rich medium brown all over, remove them from the oil and place them on a paper towel–lined plate to drain. Use tongs to dredge the hot churros in the bowl of cinnamon-sugar. Repeat with the remaining dough.

7. Make the dipping sauce: Place the dulce de leche in a small, microwave-safe bowl. Heat it on high (100%) power for 20 to 30 seconds, until it is warm and softened but not boiling. Stir in between 3 and 5 tablespoons of rum, depending on how boozy you like your sauce.

8. Enjoy the churros while they are still warm. Uneaten churros can be refreshed in a 350°F oven for 5 to 10 minutes.

NOTE: If the thought of deep-frying these cookies is getting you down, there is an alternative. You can pipe the dough onto parchment-lined baking sheets and bake in a 350°F oven for 25 to 35 minutes (depending on the diameter of your piping tip and the resulting thickness of the cookie). The final product is a bit more éclairlike than a churro, but it's still delish.

Smoked Almond and Caramel Cookie Crunch

Packed with salty smoked almonds and creamy caramel chips, these sweet and salty cookies are the ultimate in crunchy cookie satisfaction. Baked as one large cookie, then cooled and broken into jagged pieces, these easy-to-make treats are perfect for those for whom only the crunchiest treats will do.

MAKES 2 TO 3 DOZEN IRREGULARLY SHAPED PIECES

INGREDIENT	VOLUME	WEIGHT
Unbleached all-purpose flour	1¾ cups	248 grams
White rice flour (see "Rice Flour Power," page 203)	¼ cup plus 2 tablespoons	60 grams
Salt	¼ teaspoon	
Sugar	1 cup	200 grams
Unsalted butter, at room temperature	12 tablespoons	170 grams
Pure vanilla extract	1 teaspoon	
Caramel baking chips (see Note)	1 cup	6 ounces
Smoked salted almonds, such as Smokehouse, coarsely chopped (see Note)	1 cup	142 grams

1. Position a rack to the lowest position in the oven and preheat to 350°F.

2. Whisk together the all-purpose flour, rice flour, and salt in a medium bowl; set aside.

3. Combine the sugar, butter, and vanilla in a stand mixer fitted with a flat beater, and cream together on medium speed until combined and even a little fluffy, about 1 minute.

4. Reduce the mixer speed to low, and mix in the flour mixture until combined. The mixture will be dry and sandy. Mix in the caramel chips and chopped nuts. The mixture will not come together to form a cohesive dough, but the dough will hold together when squeezed into a clump.

5. Scatter the mixture evenly across an ungreased 15-by-10-inch baking sheet. Press the dough mixture into the pan to make an even layer. The dough will not be much thicker than the chips or nut pieces.

6. Bake the cookie until the top is medium golden brown all over, 27 to 32 minutes.

7. Remove from the oven, set the pan on a wire rack, and let cool for 5 minutes. Run a thin metal knife around the sides of the cookie to loosen it from the pan. Invert the cookie onto a second wire rack. Invert the

(continued)

cookie again and let cool completely, right side up, 1 to 2 hours. After cooling, break the cookie into 2-inch-ish pieces. Store the cookie pieces in an airtight container at room temperature for up to 1 week.

NOTE: You can really use any kind of baking chips you like, but caramel chips pair wonderfully with the almonds. Do not substitute raw almonds for the roasted ones. Their flavor is essential to the cookie's taste and texture.

On the Level

COOKIE BYTE

Throughout the book, we instruct you to bake some cookies on higher or lower racks in the oven. We often also advise you to rotate your cookie sheets halfway through baking. The position of a ball of cookie dough relative to all of the sources of heat we mentioned will change the intensity of heat that it experiences and thus affect how the cookie bakes. Cookies closer to the heating element on the bottom of the oven will receive a higher dose of that direct heat energy on their bottoms. Some cookies, such as the Smoked Almond and Caramel Cookie Crunch, benefit from that attention and may end up undercooked in the middle if baked on a higher rack. Likewise, cookies that spend too much time near the top of the oven or near the edges may brown too quickly or intensely. Rotating the cookie sheets from back to front and top to bottom evens out the exposure across all of the cookies on the sheet. Keep in mind that oven sizes and configurations can vary considerably, from compact New York City apartment–style ovens all the way up to the cavernous gourmet kitchen ovens of TV celebrity chefs. Ovens with smaller cubic footage will bake differently than their larger cousins, even at the same temperatures, because of the differences in proximity to the sources of radiative heat at the top and bottom of the oven. The number of rack positions in the oven can vary as well. If you find yourself baking in an unfamiliar oven, do your best to adjust your oven racks to the positions needed for specific recipes and keep a close eye on that first batch of cookies. You may need to raise or lower your rack for round two.

Streusel Scotchies

MAKES ABOUT 4 DOZEN COOKIES

Oatmeal Scotchies are a classic back-of-the-bag recipe that is still a Christmas cookie mainstay at my mother's house. While Nestlé's recipe is always delicious, after 30+ years of enjoying them, I wanted to try something new. With its chewy oatmeal texture studded with butterscotch chips, the cookie was ripe for a remake. We deconstructed then reconstructed the cookie to keep all of the flavors of the original but give it a stylish spin. The cookie keeps all of the toffee flavors of butterscotch and brown sugar, but we removed the oatmeal from the cookie and added it to a nubbly, buttery streusel that browns in the oven to create a crisp top that's a modern take on a yesteryear treat. —C.T.

INGREDIENT	VOLUME	WEIGHT
DOUGH		
Unbleached all-purpose flour	3 cups	425 grams
Salt	¾ teaspoon	
Ground cinnamon	½ teaspoon	
Unsalted butter, at room temperature	16 tablespoons	227 grams
Granulated sugar	½ cup	100 grams
Light brown sugar	Packed ½ cup	100 grams
Egg, at room temperature	1 large	50 grams (weighed without shell)
Orange zest, freshly grated	Half of 1 medium orange	
Pure vanilla extract	1 teaspoon	
Butterscotch chips	2 cups	340 grams (12 ounces)
STREUSEL		
Unbleached all-purpose flour	1⅓ cups	189 grams
Old-fashioned rolled oats	1 cup	100 grams
Light brown sugar	Packed ⅔ cup	133 grams
Ground cinnamon	½ teaspoon	
Salt	¼ teaspoon	
Unsalted butter, melted and cooled but still pourable	12 tablespoons	170 grams

1. Position two racks to divide the oven into thirds and preheat to 350°F. Lightly spray the wells of two standard 12-cup muffin tins with baking spray.

2. Make the dough: Whisk together the flour, salt, and cinnamon in a medium bowl; set aside.

3. Combine the butter, granulated sugar, and brown sugar in a stand mixer fitted with a flat beater, and cream together on medium speed until smooth and creamy, 1 to 2 minutes. Beat in the egg, zest, and vanilla until the mixture is uniform.

4. Reduce the mixer speed to low and mix in the flour mixture until combined. Scrape the sides of the bowl and the beater with a silicone spatula and stir in the butterscotch chips.

5. Portion 1½ tablespoons of dough, using a #40 scoop or a slightly heaping tablespoon measure. Drop each portion of dough into a well of the prepared muffin tins. Press the dough down so that it is flat and touches the sides of the well.

6. Make the streusel: Stir the flour, oats, sugar, cinnamon, and salt together in a medium bowl using a silicone spatula. Add the melted butter and stir until all of the dry ingredients have been moistened and small nuggets of streusel are forming. Scoop and crumble 2 teaspoons of streusel on top of the dough in each well of the muffin tins.

7. Bake until golden brown at the edges, 16 to 20 minutes. Halfway through baking, rotate the pans from front to back and top to bottom. Remove from the oven and let cool for 5 minutes in the muffin tins. The cookies should slide out of the wells easily, but you can use an offset spatula or the tip of a butter knife if you need a bit of leverage to encourage them out of their cups. Place the cookies on a wire rack to cool completely. Using muffin tins that have completely cooled to room temperature, repeat with the remaining dough and streusel. After cooling, the cookies can be stored in an airtight container at room temperature for several days.

CHAPTER SEVEN
savory cookies

If you think cookies are just for desserts and kiddo b-day parties, then you'd be wrong. Stripping away a bit of the sugar opens up a whole lot of room for additional savory flavors. You might be thinking that savory cookies are just crackers (which are a savory cookie), but these cookies are more than that. Dorie Greenspan, in her book *Dorie's Cookies*, calls them cocktail cookies, and we think that is a great way to think about them: cookies that go marvelously as a snack with cocktails or a glass of wine. We love including savory cookies as part of predinner appetizers served along with cheese or hors d'oeuvres passed at a party. They are an especially welcome surprise during the winter holidays, when party guests are often on dessert overload and a small homemade bite of something savory really hits the spot.

Savory cookies come in all forms that sweet cookies do, including filled, rolled, or sliced and baked, and they are just as exciting. Less sweet and with flavors not usually seen in dessert cookies, these savory cookies will add new fresh ideas to your cookie-baking repertoire.

Cherry Chèvrons

MAKES ABOUT 3½ DOZEN COOKIES

In our book *The New Pie*, one of the most popular recipes is the Cheese Course pie. It has a walnut crumb crust, dried figs cooked in port, and a Gorgonzola cream topping. The flavor combination made some wonder if it was a savory pie, but the flavors work so well in a sweet dessert, it has become an instant classic with our friends. The cheese course after dinner is a convenient place to experiment with flavor pairings. More than just cheese and crackers, you'll find dried fruits, nuts, the occasional pickle, and often a glass or two of dessert wines, liqueurs, or digestifs to enjoy. For this cookie we paired earthy soft chèvre-style goat cheese with amaretto-soaked cherries and toasted pecans for a perfect cheese course bite. The dough fits flawlessly into a triangle-shaped pâté mold (see Sources, page 350), allowing us to make chevron-like shapes out of chèvre! Refer to page 177 for tips and techniques on preparing slice-and-bake cookies.

INGREDIENT	VOLUME	WEIGHT
Dried tart (a.k.a. sour) cherries, finely chopped	½ cup	71 grams
Amaretto liqueur	2 teaspoons	
Unbleached all-purpose flour	1⅓ cups	189 grams
Salt	1 teaspoon	
Baking powder	¼ teaspoon	
Unsalted butter, cold, cut into 8 pieces	8 tablespoons	113 grams
Soft goat cheese (chèvre), at room temperature	One 4–ounce log	113 grams
Sugar	2 tablespoons	25 grams
Egg yolks, at room temperature	2 large	30 grams
Pecan halves, toasted and cooled (see page 24)	½ cup	47 grams

1. Combine the chopped cherries and amaretto in a microwave-safe bowl. Cover the bowl with plastic wrap and microwave on high (100%) power for about 30 seconds, until the amaretto just starts to boil and steam. Keep the bowl covered and allow the cherries to cool completely, about 30 minutes.

2. Combine the flour, salt, and baking powder in the bowl of a food processor. Add the butter and pulse several times, until the mixture is a uniform sandy texture. Add the goat cheese, sugar, and egg yolks and pulse several times until evenly combined. Add the pecans and the cherries and pulse a few more times until they are fully mixed into the dough.

(continued)

3. Scrape the sides of the bowl to make sure that all of the ingredients are incorporated and no dry flour is visible.

4. Lightly spray the inside of a triangular pâté mold (or any shaped mold with a similar 25-cubic-inch or 1¾-cup capacity; see Note) with nonstick cooking spray and then line it with plastic wrap. (The cooking spray goes between the pan and the plastic wrap to help the removal of the dough log.) The mold we use is 11¾ inches long with 2¼-inch sloping sides. Roll the dough into an 11-inch log and press it into the lined mold. Chill the mold in the refrigerator until the dough is cold and firm throughout, at least 2 hours or up to 3 days.

5. Position a rack in the center of the oven and preheat to 350°F. Line an 18-by-13-inch baking sheet with parchment paper or a silicone baking mat.

6. Cut the chilled dough into ¼-inch slices and place the slices 1 inch apart on the prepared baking sheets (you can fit 13 on each pan; see page 86). Cover the pan with aluminum foil. Return the uncut dough to the refrigerator.

7. Bake for 25 minutes and then remove the aluminum foil. Bake until the cookies are golden brown at the edges, about an additional 5 minutes. Remove from the oven and let cool for 5 minutes on the baking sheet before transferring to a wire rack to cool completely. Repeat with the remaining dough once the baking sheets have completely cooled, or use additional baking sheets. After cooling, the cookies can be stored in an airtight container at room temperature for 3 days. They can be refreshed by reheating them in the oven for 5 minutes at 350°F.

NOTE: If you don't have the triangle-shaped pâté mold (see Sources, page 350), you can shape the round log of dough into triangles by hand (see page 177).

Cheese Course—The Other Dessert

COOKIE BYTE

Early in my graduate school career, I was invited to a dinner party at a colleague's house. It was my first "mixed company" party, which in academic circles refers to a mingling of university staff, graduate students, and both junior and senior faculty members. Not a formal occasion, but certainly not a time for bawdy jokes and poor table manners (unless, I have since learned, you are a senior faculty member). When the entrée course was finished, a plate of cheeses and fresh fruit was served. A cheese course was not something that I had ever really had before. It was a generous assortment of hard and soft cheeses plus a few utterly divine blues nestled on a plate with crackers, roasted nuts, and supremely fresh fruit. The cheeses were heavenly, with textures and flavors that I had never experienced before. However, as the evening wore on, the dessert wines were emptied, and the chatter wore down (along with the cheese wedges), I slowly began to realize that *this* was dessert. *This*. Cheese and nuts and grapes. *This*. Were there no forthcoming sugary sweets? No slices of lemon tart or warm, tender cookies? I remember the emotions ticking through my mind. Surprise, confusion, and—if I'm being honest—a little anger. *Was this my life now?* Enjoyable? Yes—but it was no chocolate cake.

Looking back, I realize that I simply didn't have the perspective to enjoy the cheese course for what it is. I didn't grow up with an appreciation of many types of cheese. At that point in my life, my tastes hadn't evolved to truly appreciate the enchanting beauty of a well-designed cheese platter. I don't mean to suggest that if you don't enjoy a cheese course (or cheese in general), you are unevolved. But for me, over time, my love of cheese has grown substantially. I've learned that I enjoy many types of cheese, from standard deli fare to the more obscure types with very soft textures or sharp, ripe aromas. In the bakery, we've both incorporated aspects of the cheese course into our more traditional forms of dessert, including cookies. The after-dinner cheese course is a very convenient place to experiment with flavor pairings. Some of the less forceful cheeses do pair marvelously with sweet flavors. Besides, the cheese course includes more than just cheese. The salty crackers, sweet fruits, crunchy nuts, sweet wine, and even the occasional briny pickle are all jumping-off points to use as inspiration for creating sweet and savory treats, including cookies. As die-hard bakers, we rarely feature a cheese course as dessert when we entertain. We prefer to enjoy cheese as a predinner treat that guests can gather around and chat before dinner begins, but for our post-dinner sweets, we aren't afraid to look to the cheese counter for inspiration. —C.T.

Wholly Moles

MAKES 3½ DOZEN (1¼-INCH) COOKIES

Pronounced moe-lay, *mole* refers to a number of Mexican sauces made with a variety of fruits, nuts, peppers, and spices. We took those flavors to make a savory chocolate cookie with a dark and alluring complexity. Because the flavors are balanced—not too spicy, chocolaty, or sweet—these fudgy cookies are a marvelous choice as an appetizer or to enjoy with after-dinner drinks. Don't be put off by the long recipe list. The spices are common enough that they are all sold in any decent grocery store. *Do we have to use them all?* Absolutely. Otherwise, they won't be wholly mole! Refer to page 83 for tips and techniques on preparing drop cookies.

INGREDIENT	VOLUME	WEIGHT
Unbleached all-purpose flour	½ cup	71 grams
Dutch-processed cocoa powder	2 tablespoons	10 grams
Chili powder	2 teaspoons	
Garam masala (see Note)	1 teaspoon	
Salt	½ teaspoon	
Baking powder	½ teaspoon	
Onion powder	¼ teaspoon	
Garlic powder	¼ teaspoon	
Unsalted butter, at room temperature	3 tablespoons	43 grams
Dark brown sugar	Packed ⅓ cup	67 grams
Granulated sugar	¼ cup	50 grams
Egg, at room temperature	1 large	50 grams (weighed without shell)
Unsweetened chocolate, melted and cooled but still pourable	4 ounces	113 grams
Cocoa nibs	3 tablespoons	23 grams
Dried currants	2 tablespoons	25 grams
Black sesame seeds (see Additional Note)	2 tablespoons	15 grams

(continued)

1. Position two racks to divide the oven into thirds and preheat to 350°F. Line two 18-by-13-inch baking sheets with parchment paper or silicone baking mats.

2. Whisk together the flour, cocoa powder, chili powder, garam masala, salt, baking powder, onion powder, and garlic powder in a medium bowl; set aside.

3. Depending on the capacity of your stand mixer, this might be more convenient to mix using an electric hand mixer. Combine the butter, brown sugar, and granulated sugar in a bowl and blend them together, using an electric mixer on medium speed, 1 to 2 minutes. Beat in the egg until fully combined. Beat in the melted chocolate.

4. Add in the flour mixture on low speed until just incorporated and no dry flour is visible. Scrape the sides of the bowl and stir in the cocoa nibs, currants, and sesame seeds.

5. Scoop 2-teaspoon (10-gram) portions onto the prepared baking sheets (18 per sheet; see page 86).

6. Bake until the cookies have puffed slightly, the edges are just set, and the tops are still a bit soft, 9 to 11 minutes. Halfway through baking, rotate the pans from front to back and top to bottom. Remove from the oven and leave on the baking sheets; they will continue to cook as they cool on the pans after removal from the oven. After 5 minutes, transfer the cookies to a wire rack to finish cooling completely. Repeat with the remaining dough once the baking sheets have completely cooled, or use additional baking sheets. After cooling, the cookies can be stored in an airtight container at room temperature for several days.

NOTE: Garam masala is an Indian spice blend and has nothing to do with traditional Mexican mole. Sort of. Although there are regional differences in garam masala throughout South Asia, common ingredients include cumin, coriander, cinnamon, bay leaf, and black pepper, which are also found in some moles, making it a convenient source of these flavors. If you can't find garam masala in your grocery store, use ¼ teaspoon each of freshly ground black pepper, ground coriander, ground cinnamon, and dried oregano.

ADDITIONAL NOTE: Black sesame seeds are covered by a dark hull that adds to their earthy and nutty taste. Once hulled, they become white sesame seeds, so you can substitute if you have to.

Pairing and Layering Flavors

COOKIE BYTE

I had a roommate in college who played the electric bass guitar. Nothing he ever played sounded at all recognizable (or even pleasant), and it made me wonder whether he could hear something I couldn't. I wondered why anyone would want to play an instrument that only produces repetitive and relatively monotonous thrums? Of course, he realized that the music he was playing was not supposed to be part of a solo performance. Outside of a few notable bass solos in rock music history, the bass is only one layer in a song, usually providing depth and beat to the more soaring sounds of music. This is not at all to suggest that bass guitars are unimportant. Far from it! While few people might want to listen to the bass by itself for extended periods of time, its presence would be sorely missed when listening to the music. It would sound thin and lack rhythm. Those deep bass notes provide needed structure and depth. It works the same way with flavors. While we think of baking as mostly sweet, the flavor notes of salty, sour, umami, and even bitterness all have roles to play in baked goods. The main flavors (those that are the most prominent flavors in a cookie) should work together harmoniously. When we begin to develop recipes, we start with single flavors or flavor combinations that are related (e.g., cherries and almonds), share similar characteristics (e.g.,

orange and pineapple), or have worked well together in the past (e.g., peanut butter and chocolate) and will complement each other like the notes in a harmonious chord. Even combining the ingredients that you have selected doesn't always get you what you think it should. Depending on how they are being used, you might have to go through a few rounds of trial and error to get the flavors you want. Even different forms of what appear to be the same ingredient are not the same. For example, a simple confectioners' sugar glaze made with freshly squeezed lemon juice will have a bright, sharp lemony zing. However, using lemon zest in a cookie dough provides lemon flavor but very little sharp brightness, despite being from the same fruit. These are differences that we have learned through time and experimentation. Once we've established primary flavor or flavors (melody), we begin the tweaking. Maybe another flavor or two (harmony) is added to round out the composition. Is it too sweet? Maybe introducing a little sourness or even bitterness can offset that. Too bitter? Sometimes a bit of salt can help. Finally, looking beyond those five basic tastes, we think about other flavor elements that can add the right interest (bass notes), such as cool herbs, warm spices, or peppery heat. Keep these tips in mind if you want to start experimenting with some of these recipes as you make them your own. —*P.A.*

Cucumber Cheesecake Everything Bagel Bars

MAKES 16 (2¼-INCH) SQUARES

How do you dress your bagel? This fairly simple food item is fraught with so many choices, starting with the actual bagel itself. New York versus Montreal style? Plain versus flavored? Toasted or not? Those choices alone are enough to stymie even the most decisive among us. But the real big choices are still to come, including dairy spreads, vegetables, pickles, and even fish. For this bagel-inspired cookie, we opted for a chewy everything bagel–inspired crust topped with cream cheese, slices of cucumber, and dill. Refer to page 39 for tips and techniques on preparing bar cookies.

INGREDIENT	VOLUME	WEIGHT
EVERYTHING BAGEL CRUST		
Unbleached all-purpose flour	1 cup	142 grams
Sugar	1 teaspoon	
Baking powder	1 teaspoon	
Coarse kosher salt	1 teaspoon	
Unsalted butter, cold	5 tablespoons	71 grams
Dried onion flakes	1 teaspoon	
Granulated garlic	1 teaspoon	
Sesame seeds	1 teaspoon	
Poppy seeds	1 teaspoon	
Water	⅓ cup	79 grams
Cider vinegar	1 teaspoon	
SAVORY CUCUMBER CHEESECAKE		
Seedless cucumber	1 small	About 85 grams
Unflavored powdered gelatin	1 teaspoon	
Cream cheese (full fat), at room temperature	One 8-ounce package	227 grams
Salt	Pinch	
Heavy cream	⅓ cup	77 grams
Fresh dill, finely chopped	1 tablespoon	

(continued)

1. Make the Everything Bagel Crust: Place the flour, sugar, baking powder, and salt in the bowl of a food processor. Pulse twice to mix the ingredients. Cut the butter into five pieces and add it to the flour mixture. Pulse the processor several times until the mixture is a uniform sandy texture.

2. Add the onion flakes, granulated garlic, sesame seeds, poppy seeds, water, and vinegar. Pulse several times until all of the dry ingredients have been moistened and incorporated into a dough. This can also be done by hand using a bowl and a pastry blender, if you prefer. Press the dough into a square, wrap in plastic wrap, and chill in the refrigerator until it is cold and firm, about 3 hours.

3. Position a rack in the center of the oven and preheat to 375°F. Line the bottom and sides of a 9-inch square baking pan with aluminum foil. Do not grease the foil.

4. On a lightly floured surface, use a rolling pin to roll the dough to an approximately 9-inch square. Lift the dough and place it in the prepared baking pan. Press the dough with your fingertips to make sure it evenly covers the pan from edge to edge, including the corners. Poke the dough all over with a fork to prevent it from puffing too much or unevenly while baking.

5. Bake until the surface of the crust is an even golden brown, 25 to 35 minutes. Halfway through baking, rotate the pan from front to back. Remove from the oven and keep the crust in the pan to cool completely before adding the cheesecake layer.

6. Make the Savory Cucumber Cheesecake: Place a box grater on a clean, lint-free kitchen towel. Grate the cucumber over the medium holes of the grater, catching the shreds on the towel. Wrap the towel around the shredded cucumber. Squeeze as much juice as possible

The Business of Blooming

Gelatin is protein that is used to thicken liquids into a soft, bouncy, sliceable gel. Sprinkling the gelatin over a liquid allows the gelatin to bloom or hydrate and soften so that it will melt easily and uniformly when heated. Once melted, it should be quickly dispersed into the liquid that is being gelled. As the mixture cools, the dissolved proteins reconnect into a network, trapping the liquid between the strands and forming the gel. In addition to the powdered gelatin that we have tested with this recipe, there are many other types and strengths of gelatin, vegan gelatin alternatives, and many other substances that can be used to form gels in modernist cuisine. While we have used some of these in other recipes, we have tested this recipe with both traditional supermarket unflavored gelatin (which is usually derived from pork) and unflavored fish gelatin. Both worked equally well.

from the cucumber, reserving 4 teaspoons of juice in a small, microwave-safe bowl. Set the squeezed shredded cucumber aside.

7. Sprinkle the gelatin over the cucumber juice and set it aside to soften and bloom for about 5 minutes. While the gelatin is blooming, beat the cream cheese and salt in a bowl on medium speed using an electric mixer for about 1 minute to loosen the cream cheese. Depending on the capacity of your stand mixer, this might be more convenient to mix using an electric hand mixer.

8. Microwave the gelatin mixture on high (100%) power for 10 to 20 seconds, stirring every 5 seconds, until the gelatin is just dissolved and starting to bubble at the edges. Beat the warm gelatin into the cream cheese.

9. Beat in the cream until the mixture is light and fluffy, 1 to 2 minutes. Slowly beat in the shredded cucumber and dill until the mixture is uniform.

10. Spread the mixture on the cooled crust and smooth the top with an offset spatula. Refrigerate the filled pan for at least 6 hours to allow the filling to set. When the cheesecake is set, use the foil to lift the filled crust from the pan and transfer to a cutting board. Slide the foil away before using a sharp knife to cut sixteen 2¼-inch squares (see "How to Cut a Batch," page 40) or cut each 2¼-inch square in half to create 32 party-perfect two-bite treats. Store the bars in an airtight container in the refrigerator for up to 3 days.

NOTE: You can replace the onion flakes, granulated garlic, sesame, and poppy with 4 teaspoons of a commercial everything bagel seasoning blend, which can sometimes be found in the spice aisle of your grocery store or specialty food shops. If your brand also contains salt, you can increase the blend measurement to 5 teaspoons and eliminate the added kosher salt.

Tuscan Crisps

MAKES ABOUT 6 CUPS OF (1-INCH-SQUARE) CRACKERS, ENOUGH FOR A NICE BIG BOWLFUL

Inspiration for cookie flavors is everywhere. We get ideas at the grocery store, tasting new cocktails, and even at our own dinner table. When not baking, we try to eat relatively healthy meals. To keep it interesting, we watch cooking shows, mine through our cookbooks, and read blogs, newsletters, and magazines to create fun and interesting dinner menus daily. While making Tuscan *rosticciana*, a recipe from our friends at *Christopher Kimball's Milk Street,* the house was filled with the aromas of fennel, garlic, rosemary, and peppers. We were inspired to build a savory cookie around this flavor combination. For this recipe, we packed all of the big bold flavors of the herbs and spices into a savory 1-inch cracker. The beautiful blend of flavors of Tuscany is outstanding in these crisp little snacks. Refer to page 137 for tips and techniques on preparing rolled cookies.

INGREDIENT	VOLUME	WEIGHT
Unbleached all-purpose flour	2 cups	284 grams
Light brown sugar	1 tablespoon	13 grams
Fresh rosemary, finely chopped	2 teaspoons	
Ground fennel (see Note)	1 teaspoon	
Baking powder	1 teaspoon	
Coarse kosher salt	¾ teaspoon	
Black pepper, freshly ground	½ teaspoon	
Red pepper flakes	½ teaspoon	
Garlic powder	½ teaspoon	
Unsalted butter, cold, cut into 6 pieces	6 tablespoons	85 grams
Olive oil	2 tablespoons	27 grams
Water	½ cup	118 grams

1. Combine the flour, brown sugar, rosemary, fennel, baking powder, salt, black pepper, red pepper flakes, and garlic powder in the bowl of a food processor. Process in 1-second pulses until the ingredients are just mixed. Add the butter pieces and continue to pulse until no large clumps of butter remain and the mixture has a coarse, sandy appearance.

2. Add the olive oil and water and pulse until a dough forms. Remove the dough from the bowl and knead it a few times into a ball to incorporate any remaining dry flour. Wrap the dough in plastic wrap and flatten it into a disk. Chill the dough in the refrigerator for several hours, preferably overnight, so the dough is cold and firm throughout.

3. Position two racks to divide the oven into thirds and preheat to 400°F. Gather at least two baking sheets, but you do not need to line them with parchment paper or silicone baking sheets.

4. Using a knife or bench scraper, divide the dough into three approximately equal pieces. Place the first portion on the center of a 16-by-12-inch piece of parchment paper. Lightly flour the dough to prevent the rolling pin from sticking. Roll the dough to a ¹⁄₁₆-inch thickness, to cover an area about 12 by 10 inches.

5. Poke the dough all over with a fork to dock the surface of the dough and prevent puffing. Cut the dough into 1-inch squares, using a fluted pastry wheel, pizza wheel, or a sharp knife (try not to cut through the paper!), but do not move the crackers. They can bake exactly where they are on the parchment. Place the parchment on an ungreased baking sheet. Repeat with the remaining dough, but don't bake more than two baking sheets at a time. Leave the dough at room temperature while the other sheets bake; it will be fine.

6. Bake until the crackers are all evenly golden brown, 10 to 16 minutes. Halfway through baking, rotate the pans from front to back and top to bottom. Remove from the oven and let cool completely on the baking sheets. After cooling, the crackers can be stored in an airtight container at room temperature for several days.

NOTE: If you don't have ground fennel, you can also use whole fennel seeds that you grind yourself, either in a mortar and pestle or an electric spice grinder.

Thin Crust Pepperoni Slices

MAKES 3 DOZEN (4-INCH) CRACKERS

How do you distill the essence of pizza into a thin and crispy treat? You have to start with real pizza ingredients! These savory crackerlike cookies are flecked with crisp nuggets of spicy pepperoni and traditional pizzeria herbs and spices, such as oregano, garlic, and a sprinkling of hot pepper flakes. The cheesy and buttery dough crisps in the oven to make a tender and flaky treat to tie all of the flavors together. Baked in rounds and cut into wedges, these savory snacks really do look, smell, and taste like your favorite pizzeria pie. Refer to page 137 for tips and techniques on preparing rolled cookies.

INGREDIENT	VOLUME	WEIGHT
Pepperoni slices (thinly cut slices work best)	15 slices	30 grams
Unbleached all-purpose flour	1 cup plus 1 tablespoon	151 grams
Parmigiano-Reggiano, finely grated	1⅓ cups	75 grams
Italian seasoning (see Note)	1 teaspoon	
Red pepper flakes (optional)	½ teaspoon	
Salt	¼ teaspoon	
Unsalted butter, cold, cut into ½-inch cubes	5 tablespoons	71 grams
Milk, cold (whole milk is preferred, but reduced-fat will work, too)	⅓ cup	81 grams
Flaky sea salt, such as Maldon	¾ teaspoon	

1. Prepare your pans. This recipe makes three 9-inch rounds. The easiest way to bake them is to roll them into 9-inch circles on sheets of parchment paper and bake them on baking sheets. For this, you will need four (yes, four!) 16-by-12-inch sheets of parchment paper. Trace a 9-inch circle in the center of one sheet of parchment paper, using a plate or cake pan as a guide. You will need to flip the parchment over so the pen/pencil/marker that you use doesn't touch the dough, so draw the circle as dark as you can so you can see it through the paper.

2. Position two racks to divide the oven into thirds and preheat to 375°F. Gather at least two baking sheets, but you do not need to line them with parchment paper or silicone baking sheets.

3. Line a microwave-safe plate with a double layer of paper towels. Arrange the pepperoni slices in a single layer on the paper towel. Microwave the slices on high (100%) power until they are crisp, dry, and all of the hissing and popping noises have ceased, about 1 minute. (Alternatively, cook the pepperoni slices in a nonstick skillet over medium-low heat until all of the fat has been rendered and the slices are very crisp. Set aside to cool.)

(continued)

4. Combine the flour, Parmigiano-Reggiano, Italian seasoning, red pepper flakes, salt, and crisped pepperoni slices in the bowl of a food processor. Process in 1-second pulses until the pepperoni pieces are finely chopped and dispersed throughout the flour.

5. Add the cold butter and pulse the mixture together just until the butter pieces seem to have disappeared and the dough appears sandy. Add the milk and process until the dough forms a cohesive ball in the food processor. Divide the dough into thirds (about 130 grams per portion).

6. Roll one portion of dough into a ball and press it into a circle in the center of a clean sheet of parchment. Place the parchment sheet with the circle drawn on it on top of the dough, being sure that the side with the circle drawn on it is not facing the dough.

7. Roll the dough into a thin 9-inch circle, using the circle as a guide. The round will be slightly thicker than 1/16 inch, but you can use 1/16-inch dough rolling guides (see page 138) to prevent the dough from being too thin. Once you are done rolling, peel off the top sheet of paper (with the circle drawn on it). Transfer the parchment sheet with the dough to a baking sheet.

8. Prick the dough circle all over with a fork. Score the circle into wedges by dragging a knife over the surface to divide the circle into quarters and then divide each quarter into thirds to mark 12 wedges. The dough is thin, but try not to cut it all the way through, as the dough is likely to shrink as it bakes. Sprinkle 1/4 teaspoon of flaky sea salt all over the circle. Repeat with the remaining two portions of dough.

9. Bake two circles at a time until the top is beginning to brown in places and the edges of the dough are golden, 13 to 16 minutes. Halfway through baking, rotate the pans from front to back and top to bottom. Immediately after removing from the oven, use the score lines as a guide to fully cut each circle into 12 wedges with a pizza wheel or sharp knife. Let cool for 5 minutes on the pans before transferring the wedges to a wire rack to cool completely. After cooling, the cookies can be stored in an airtight container at room temperature for several days.

NOTE: Italian seasoning is a mix of dried herbs and spices. The combinations and proportions vary by brand, but can include oregano, thyme, basil, rosemary, marjoram, savory, sage, or even garlic powder. We think Penzeys Frozen Pizza Seasoning hits all of the right notes, but if you have an Italian seasoning that you prefer, use that.

The Dangers of Cookie Cohabitation

COOKIE BYTE

Writing a cookie cookbook involves baking lots and lots (and lots!) of cookies. We have had days when the dining room table was covered, all visible counterspace was claimed by cookies, and every piece of Tupperware was filled with cookies. Maybe this sounds like you during a marathon Christmas cookie baking session those last weeks of December? When you run out of room or want to save space in your valuable storage containers, it's tempting to start storing different types of cookies together in the same containers. Please—avoid that temptation! Cookie cohabitation can often have a harmful impact on the taste, texture, and storage life of cookies. The aromatic compounds in some cookies (those chemicals that make them smell so darn good) can start to permeate into neighboring cookies that are sharing the same airtight space. Although it is possible that the interloping flavor can be a welcome addition, more often than not, such promiscuous flavor swapping is unwanted. You worked so hard on those chocolate chip cookies, why muddy the flavors of it with your deeply spiced gingerbread? Differences in moisture content can be just as important as flavor incompatibility. Placing stacks of thin and crisp shortbread next to moist and chewy brownies guarantees a shorter shelf life for both. The crisp cookies will soon morph into limp biscuits because they have wantonly drawn moisture from the brownies. The brownies are left drier and not nearly as fudgy as you had hoped when you reach for one days later. Both cookies are left prematurely stale and less appetizing by having unintentionally relinquished their texture to their bloodsucking bedfellows. These tragic tales can be easily avoided by chastely storing your cookies separately (and responsibly).

Smokeshow Cheese Coins

MAKES 5 DOZEN (2-INCH) COOKIES

Every December, we host an afternoon Christmas party at our house for our close friends. It's too early to serve dinner, but we serve a variety of hors d'oeuvres (both sweet and savory) for everyone to enjoy. We always plan lots of food and let our guests know that they can pop in and out when their schedule suits them. Besides a healthy offering of small desserts (including dozens of sweet cookies), one of our go-tos is a variety of cheeses with bread and assorted crackers. These thin, cheesy coins are phenomenal party fare. With smoked paprika and smoky sea salt, their flavor lingers and they can be enjoyed on their own, but they are exceptional with a thin slice of salty ham. If you can't find smoked flaky sea salt, substitute some other type of large sea salt (or even coarse kosher salt if that's what you have on hand). Do not skip it! Refer to page 137 for tips and techniques on preparing rolled cookies.

INGREDIENT	VOLUME	WEIGHT
Unbleached all-purpose flour	1 cup plus 2 tablespoons	159 grams
Smoked paprika	4 teaspoons	
Black pepper, freshly ground	½ teaspoon	
Parmigiano-Reggiano, cut into chunks (see Note)		113 grams (4 ounces)
Unsalted butter, at room temperature	10 tablespoons	142 grams
Sharp Cheddar, grated	½ cup (grated)	57 grams (2 ounces)
Smoked flaky sea salt, such as Maldon (see above)	1¼ teaspoons	

1. Whisk together the flour, paprika, and pepper in a medium bowl; set aside.

2. Place the Parmigiano-Reggiano in the bowl of a food processor and process until the cheese is finely ground (see Note). Add the butter and Cheddar and process until everything is well combined, using five to ten 1-second pulses. Add the flour mixture and process until a ball of dough forms.

3. Remove the dough from the processor and divide the dough in half (about 235 grams of dough per half).

Roll each half of the dough between two sheets of parchment or waxed paper to an ⅛-inch-thick, 12-by-8-inch rectangle. Stack the paper-covered sheets of dough onto an 18-by-13-inch baking sheet and refrigerate until cold and firm throughout, at least 2 hours or up to 3 days.

4. Position two racks to divide the oven into thirds and preheat to 300°F. Line two 18-by-13-inch baking sheets with parchment paper or silicone baking mats.

5. Release the dough from one sheet of parchment paper by peeling the paper from the top of one layer of chilled dough. Lay the paper back onto the dough and flip the whole dough sheet over so that loosened sheet of paper is now underneath it. Peel off the top layer of parchment paper. Prick the dough all over with a fork.

6. Cut 2-inch circles from the dough and transfer them to the prepared baking sheets, leaving about 2 inches of space between cookies. For 2-inch circles, you can fit 24 cookies on each baking sheet (see page 86). The dough can be rerolled, chilled, and cut to get about 12 more cookies.

7. Sprinkle ½ teaspoon of flaky sea salt over each sheet of 24 cookies. Bake until the cookies are set and beginning to lightly brown all over, 18 to 22 minutes. Halfway through baking, rotate the pans from front to back and top to bottom. Remove from the oven and let cool for 5 minutes on the sheet before transferring to a wire rack to cool completely. Repeat with the remaining dough once the baking sheets have completely cooled, or use additional baking sheets. Don't forget to prick rerolled cookies with a fork and sprinkle with the remaining ¼ teaspoon of flaky sea salt before baking! After cooling, the cookies can be stored in an airtight container at room temperature for several days.

NOTE: You can make this recipe using a stand mixer instead of a food processor. If using a stand mixer, finely grate the Parmigiano-Reggiano before adding it to the mixer in Step 2.

Variation: Lancelots

Growing up, we both ate our fair share of peanut butter on cheese crackers, marketed by such companies as Keebler and Lance. As kids, we really didn't think about the seemingly absurd pairing of orange cheese crackers and peanut butter. However, as adults, we questioned if the pairing worked with our (allegedly) more mature palate. Answer: Yes! We can't explain it, but the fusion of cheese cracker and peanut butter is still a winner. For a classic cheese cracker, substitute regular paprika for the smoked paprika and regular (nonsmoked) sea salt flakes for the smoked. Prepare and bake as directed. When cooled, sandwich two coins around a teaspoon of Peanut Butter Filling (page 338). Store at room temperature in an airtight container.

Frito Pie Cheese Coins

MAKES ABOUT 4 DOZEN (2-INCH) ROUND COOKIES

I had never *heard* of Frito Pie until I moved to Atlanta more than a decade ago. If you're not familiar, just get the notion of a traditional pie with flaky crust and tidy slices out of your head—it isn't that. Rip open a snack-size bag of corn chips, ladle hot beef chili over top, and garnish with cheese and maybe fresh diced onion or jalapeño slices. Boom—done. When done well, the salty, corny crunch paired with the spices and cheese is mind-blowing. These cheesy cookies (though not served hot) are loaded with chili spices, including cumin and chipotle powder, and topped with a crunchy layer of crushed corn chips. They're a great savory cookie for game day (or everyday!) snacking. Refer to page 177 for tips and techniques on preparing slice-and-bake cookies. —*C.T.*

INGREDIENT	VOLUME	WEIGHT
Bleached cake flour	1¾ cups plus 3 tablespoons	220 grams
Chili powder	2 teaspoons	
Chipotle chile powder	½ teaspoon	
Garlic powder	½ teaspoon	
Ground cumin	½ teaspoon	
Onion powder	½ teaspoon	
Black pepper, freshly ground	¼ teaspoon	
Salt	¼ teaspoon	
Sharp Cheddar, grated	2 cups (grated)	227 grams (8 ounces)
Unsalted butter, cold, cut into ½-inch cubes	8 tablespoons	227 grams
Tomato paste	2 tablespoons	33 grams
Corn chips, such as Fritos, finely crushed		120 grams

1. Combine the flour, chili powder, chipotle powder, garlic powder, cumin, onion powder, black pepper, and salt in the bowl of a food processor. Process the mixture for about 10 seconds to mix the ingredients.

2. Add the grated cheese and cold butter pieces. Process the mixture, using 1-second pulses, until the mixture looks sandy, like coarse cornmeal, and no large chunks of butter are visible. Add the tomato paste and 2 tablespoons of crushed corn chips. Process with 1-second pulses until a ball of dough forms, stopping and scraping down the sides of the bowl, if needed.

3. Roll each piece into a 10-inch log (see page 177). Tightly wrap the dough log in a sheet of parchment or waxed paper and refrigerate until cold and firm throughout, at least 2 hours or up to 3 days, or freeze the dough for up to 3 months (see page 178). Keeping the dough in a poster or paper towel tube (see page 177) will keep the bottom round while it chills.

4. Position two racks to divide the oven into thirds and preheat to 350°F. Line two 18-by-13-inch baking sheets with parchment paper or silicone baking mats.

5. Add the remaining crushed corn ships to a shallow bowl. Cut the logs into ¼-inch slices, rotating the dough to keep the log round, and press one side of each sliced cookie into the crushed chips. Shake off any loose chip bits and place, chip side up, 2 inches apart on the prepared baking sheets (you can fit 13 on each pan; see page 86). Return any dough to the refrigerator while the cookies bake.

6. Bake until the edges begin to lightly brown and the centers feel firm when gently pressed, 17 to 22 minutes. Halfway through baking, rotate the pans from front to back and top to bottom. Remove from the oven and let cool for 5 minutes on the baking sheets before transferring to a wire rack to cool completely. Repeat with the remaining dough once the baking sheets have completely cooled, or use additional baking sheets. After cooling, the cookies can be stored in an airtight container at room temperature for several days.

Pierogi Party Bites

MAKES ABOUT 3 DOZEN (2-INCH)
SAVORY HALF-MOON COOKIES

For many, pierogis are a quintessential comfort food. Buttered dumplings filled with potatoes, cheese, and onions check all of the requisite boxes for hearty home cooking. All the flavors of pierogis are packed into these smaller cookie versions. With a crisp outside and a soft and fluffy middle, these potato-packed party bites are perfect for a tailgate or pregame party when you don't want to pass out plates and forks. Refer to page 177 for tips and techniques on preparing slice-and-bake cookies.

INGREDIENT	VOLUME	WEIGHT
Baking potato (we prefer russet; see Note)	1 medium	170 to 227 grams (6 to 8 ounces)
Unbleached all-purpose flour	¾ cup plus 1 tablespoon	115 grams
Onion powder	¾ teaspoon	
Salt	½ teaspoon	
Black pepper, freshly ground	¼ teaspoon	
Unsalted butter, cold, cut into ½-inch cubes	4 tablespoons	57 grams
Sharp Cheddar, grated	1 cup	113 grams (4 ounces)
Whole milk	2 tablespoons	30 grams

1. Position a rack in the center of the oven and preheat to 350°F. Prick the potato all over with a fork and place directly on the center oven rack. Bake for 45 to 60 minutes, until a sharp knife can be easily inserted and removed (see Note). Transfer the potato to a heatproof surface and split in half lengthwise to allow the potato to cool faster. When the potato is cool enough to handle, scoop out the flesh into a bowl and mash with a fork. (If you have a potato ricer, it works great for this.) Weigh out 113 grams of potato (or lightly pack the potato into a ½-cup measure) and set aside.

2. Combine the flour, onion powder, salt, and pepper in the bowl of a food processor. Process in 1-second pulses until the ingredients are just mixed.

3. Add the cold butter cubes, cheese, and mashed potato and continue to process in 1-second pulses until the mixture looks like coarse cornmeal with no visible butter pieces.

4. Add the milk and continue to pulse the mixture until a soft dough forms.

(continued)

5. Remove the dough from the processor and roll into a 7-inch log. Wrap the log in plastic wrap and refrigerate until cold throughout, at least 2 hours but no longer than 1 day before you plan on cooking them. When chilled, this dough will be firm and sliceable but not rock-solid.

6. Preheat the oven to 200°F. Set a heatproof rack in an 18-by-13-inch baking sheet.

7. If you have an electric griddle that reliably keeps a steady temperature, lightly spray it with nonstick cooking spray and heat it to 350°F. Otherwise, place a lightly sprayed flat griddle or large skillet over medium heat.

8. Cut the dough into ⅓-inch (8 mm) rounds and cut each slice in half to create two half-moons. Cook the slices until the cookies are golden brown all over and lightly crisp, about 2 minutes on each side. If the cookies are darker than medium brown after 2 minutes of cooking, lower the heat. Cook as many cookies on your griddle as will fit with enough room left over to maneuver and flip the cookies over. Keep the remaining dough cold.

9. After each batch of cookies is finished cooking, serve immediately (our preference) or arrange in a single layer on the rack-topped baking sheet and keep warm in the oven until the last batch is cooked. If you have cookies left over, they can be frozen in an airtight resealable freezer storage bag or container for 1 month. Reheat them (from frozen) on an 18-by-13-inch baking sheet fitted with a heatproof wire rack in a 350°F oven for 5 minutes.

NOTE: You want a potato large enough to yield ½ cup of mashed potato. As an alternative to oven roasting, prick the potato all over with a fork and microwave at high (100%) power for 5 to 10 minutes (times vary based on microwave wattage), flipping the potato over after 3 minutes. Do not boil the potato, as this will add too much moisture to the potato and affect the texture of the cookie. Also, this dough should not be held in the refrigerator for more than 1 day, as the potato may be more prone to spoiling than other doughs.

Major Grey (Mango Chutney) Thumbprints

MAKES 56 (2-INCH) COOKIES

Looking at the ingredient list of curry powder, tangy Major Grey chutney, and crunchy cashews, some might think that these sweet-savory thumbprint cookies are traditional Indian treats. Absolutely not. In her seminal cookbook, *Classic Indian Cooking*, author Julie Sahni describes the corruption of *kari podi*, an Indian spice blend varying from region to region, into the standardized curry powder ubiquitous in the American supermarket spice aisle. Likewise, Major Grey chutney is a preserved mango relish purported to have been developed by a 19th-century British military officer (of the same name) during the time of the British Raj and colonial rule. While maybe not traditional Indian fare, the sweet-savory flavors are inspired by India's rich culinary flavors to add a modern twist to the classic jam-filled thumbprint cookie. Refer to page 215 for tips and techniques on preparing filled cookies.

INGREDIENT	VOLUME	WEIGHT
Unbleached all-purpose flour	1¾ cups	248 grams
Curry powder	1¼ teaspoons	
Salt	½ teaspoon	
Cayenne pepper (optional; see Note)	⅛ teaspoon	
Major Grey chutney	⅔ cup	203 grams
Unsalted butter, at room temperature	16 tablespoons	227 grams
Sugar	½ cup	100 grams
Eggs, separated, at room temperature	2 large	30 grams yolks About 70 grams whites
Cashews, roasted (preferably unsalted, but lightly salted is okay), finely chopped	1½ cups	170 grams (6 ounces)

1. Position a rack in the center of the oven and preheat to 325°F. Line two 18-by-13-inch baking sheets with parchment paper or silicone baking mats.

2. Whisk together the flour, curry powder, salt, and cayenne (if using) in a medium bowl; set aside.

3. Stir the chutney in a small bowl until it has loosened and is no longer lumpy. If your chutney has large pieces of fruit, spoon them out and give them a quick chop. Try to get pieces smaller than about ⅛ inch; anything too big could easily clog the piping bag. Transfer the chutney to a disposable piping bag (see page 216).

(continued)

4. Combine the butter and sugar in a stand mixer fitted with a flat beater, and cream together on medium speed until smooth and creamy, 1 to 2 minutes. Beat in both egg yolks until the mixture is smooth and uniform, about 30 seconds.

5. Beat in half of the flour mixture on low speed just until combined. Stop mixing and scrape down the sides of the bowl and the beater with a silicone spatula. Mix in the remaining flour mixture on low speed just until no dry flour is visible. Scrape the sides of the bowl.

6. Briefly whisk the egg whites in a shallow bowl until they have combined and begin to look frothy. Place the cashews in a second shallow bowl. Portion 2 teaspoons (11 grams) of dough, using a #100 scoop or heaping teaspoon measure, and roll into a ball. Roll the ball first in the egg whites, allowing any excess egg whites to drain off, then immediately roll in the chopped cashews. Place the nut-covered balls 2 inches apart on one of the prepared baking sheets (you can fit 24 on each pan; see page 86). Press an indentation into each ball, using a ball tool or the very tip of your index finger. The cookies will puff while baking, so the indentation can be fairly deep, but not so deep that it breaks through the bottom of the dough ball.

7. Bake for 10 minutes. Remove the pan from the oven and use a metal measuring spoon or some other heatproof tool to re-indent the dimple that has filled in during baking. Snip off the tip of the piping bag to create an approximately ⅛-inch hole. Pipe the chutney to fill the dimples, but do not overfill. You will need about ½ teaspoon per cookie.

8. Continue to bake until the dough is no longer shiny and the edges of the cookies are set and have just started to brown, an additional 10 to 12 minutes. While the first pan bakes, prepare the next sheet. Remove the baked cookies from the oven and let cool for 5 minutes on the baking sheet before transferring to a wire rack to cool completely. Repeat with the remaining dough once the baking sheets have completely cooled, or use additional baking sheets. Stored in a closed (but not airtight) container at room temperature, the cookies will keep for several days.

NOTE: If you are using a spicy (hot) curry powder or a particularly spicy chutney, you can skip the cayenne pepper.

Barbecuties

MAKES ABOUT 4 DOZEN COOKIES

So, what flavor is "barbecue"? One of the advantages of living in the American South is access to so many different styles of barbecue as you travel from state to state. For some, the flavor of barbecue is like a spicy ketchup, or very vinegary, or even mostly mustard. To make our barbecue cookie, we add our own dry rub of spices to the dough and then "sauce" them with a coating of salty sugar and more paprika just before baking. The flavor is reminiscent of barbecue-flavor potato chips but so much better! Even better is the crackling sugar crust on the cookies that gives them a wonderful sweet and smoky flavor and a delicate crunch. Refer to page 137 for tips and techniques on preparing rolled cookies.

INGREDIENT	VOLUME	WEIGHT
Unsalted butter, at room temperature	8 tablespoons	113 grams
Sour cream (full fat), cold	½ cup	121 grams
Sugar	¼ cup plus 1 tablespoon	63 grams
Salt	2 teaspoons	
Onion powder	1 teaspoon	
Smoked paprika	1 teaspoon	
Chili powder	½ teaspoon	
Garlic powder	½ teaspoon	
Unbleached all-purpose flour	1 cup plus 2 tablespoons	159 grams
Paprika	1½ teaspoons	

1.   Combine the butter and cold sour cream in a stand mixer fitted with a flat beater, and beat together on medium speed for about 1 to 2 minutes. The butter will break up into small (about ⅛- to ¼-inch) nuggets suspended in the cream (see "The Temperature of Ingredients" at right). Beat in 1 tablespoon of the sugar and 1 teaspoon of the salt along with the onion powder, smoked paprika, chili powder, and garlic powder on low speed until the mixture is well mixed. It will still have a somewhat nubbly texture with the butter

pieces. Add the flour and continue to mix on low speed until combined and no dry flour is visible. Scrape the sides of the bowl and the beater with a silicone spatula.

2.   Divide the dough in half. Roll each half of the dough to a ⅛-inch thickness (into approximately 12-by-8-inch rectangles) between two sheets of parchment or waxed paper. Stack the paper-covered sheets of dough on a baking sheet, and refrigerate until cold and firm throughout, at least 2 hours or up to 3 days.

3. Position two racks to divide the oven into thirds and preheat to 325°F. Line two 18-by-13-inch baking sheets with parchment paper or silicone baking mats. Stir the remaining ¼ cup of sugar together with the remaining 1 teaspoon of salt and the 1½ teaspoons of paprika in a shallow bowl.

4. Remove one packet of dough from the refrigerator and carefully peel back the parchment. Flip the exposed dough surface onto a lightly floured countertop and peel the parchment off the back. Using a sharp knife or pizza wheel, slice the dough into approximately 4-by-1-inch strips. Dip both sides of the strips into the sugar mixture and place on the prepared baking sheet, spacing them ¼ to ½ inch apart. The strips will shrink slightly when baking. You can fit about 24 barbecuties on each sheet. Repeat with the second packet of dough.

5. Bake until the edges are just starting to brown, 23 to 25 minutes. Halfway through baking, rotate the pans from front to back and upper to lower. Remove from the oven and let cool completely on the pans.

The Temperature of Ingredients

COOKIE BYTE

When listed as ingredients in our recipes, eggs, butter, and sour cream often have a temperature instruction next to them. We might specify that the eggs should be room temperature or that the sour cream should be cold from the refrigerator. We usually have a good reason if we took the trouble to specify a temperature. In general, these types of ingredients are more easily incorporated into batters and doughs when they are all at room temperature. In some recipes, such as the Salted Caramel Sugar Cookies (page 91), the cold ingredients are added after ingredients that have recently been heated and cooled. The addition of the cold ingredient to the one that is likely still warmer than room temperature will often bring the completed dough closer to the desired room temperature. In the case of the Barbecuties, when room-temperature butter is mixed into cold sour cream, it creates a suspension of little butter nuggets that contribute to the flaky texture of the cookie. For recipes that involve melting the butter, we usually don't specify a temperature—the butter will melt regardless.

fillings and other additional recipes

These recipes for fillings, icings, and glazes are used several times through-out the book. Refer to the instructions for individual cookies for the total amount of filling or icing needed. It might be less than the total yield of these recipes.

Cookie Decorating 101

For many people, decorated cookies remind them of holiday baking, with gingerbread men and little green Christmas trees coated in glittery sugar. Decorated cookies can be so lovely, and they shouldn't be relegated to the snowy days of December. Cookies can be decorated for any reason and any celebration! Birthdays, baby showers, divorce parties, dog weddings—all ideal cookie occasions. Going to your friends' housewarming party? Make them cookies painted like their new home! Bake up some fun decorated jack-o'-lanterns for Halloween. Just found out that your ex's boyfriend dumped him like he dumped you? Raise a toast to karma with some champagne bottle cookies! Whatever brings you joy and peace.

Decorated cookies also serve as more than food. Decorated turkey shapes can be used as Thanksgiving table place settings. Write a thank you note to share with a friend. Decorate some hearts as an edible valentine. You don't even need a holiday. Regardless of the occasion, a decorated cookie is a great channel to allow your artistic side to create something beautiful. If you've never decorated cookies before (or if you need a refresher), we have a few tips to help you make decorating cookies a success.

There are three basic mediums that we use to decorate cookies: glaze, royal icing, and rolled fondant. Glaze and royal icing have pourable consistencies and are usually piped onto cookies with piping bags. They can also be spread over cookies with an offset spatula, but that can be a little messier. Rolled fondant is a commercial product that you most likely know from beautifully decorated wedding cakes. Rolled fondant gets a bad rap because its soft, chewy texture is often a poor match with soft and fluffy American-style layer cakes. However, when paired with firmer cookies, the fondant texture is much more inviting. We most often decorate cookies with royal icing. That is simply our preference, but others prefer glaze or rolled fondant. All three can be used to make cookies that look stunning.

Royal Icing and Glaze

- Consistency is Queen! Learning the consistencies of icing that you prefer to use to decorate cookies (and then consistently achieving those consistencies) is one of the most difficult lessons to learn.

- In our opinion, the easiest way to decorate cookies is by using two consistencies of icing. To prevent icing from dripping off the edges of a cookie, thick icing is piped at the edge of the cookie to create a dam. For piping outlines and details, we use an icing that is thick but soft like toothpaste. Our royal icing recipe, as made, is very thick. We usually use this as our piping consistency. To check for the right consistency, use a spoon to lift icing from the bowl. The icing in the bowl should form a peak that flops over. If the icing holds a stiff peak, stir a little water into it to thin it down.

- For filling in (or flooding) shapes, we use a consistency similar to honey or shampoo. To create thinner consistencies, stir in water, no more than ¼ teaspoon at a time, until the right texture is achieved. If you accidentally make the icing too thin, you can thicken it back up by stirring in additional confectioners' sugar 1 tablespoon at a time.

- Many cookie decorators describe their icing consistency in terms of seconds. For example, we prefer to flood cookies with a 12-second icing. This means that if you spoon some of the icing from the bowl and let it dribble back, it should take 12 seconds (counting one Mississippi, two Mississippi . . .) before that dribbled ribbon disappears and the surface of the icing smooths out. Some cookie decorators flood with thinner 8-second icings, and some prefer thicker 15- or 20-second icings. There are no right or wrong answers. What consistency you prefer is learned over time as you decorate more and more cookies. No matter what consistency you choose, if the icing does not settle into a smooth layer on the cookie, it is probably too thick and needs a little bit more water mixed into it.

- We prefer gel, paste, or powdered food colors so that the consistency of the icing is not affected. Liquid food colors can make the icing too thin before the desired shade is achieved.

- We prefer to color the icing while it has a thick consistency. Since it can take several rounds of adding drops of color to get the perfect shade, mixing the icing when it's already thinned to a flooding consistency incorporates many unwanted air bubbles. Coloring the icing when it's thick allows both the thicker (piping) and thinner (flooding) consistencies to be the same shade.

- Portion icing into bowls before adding coloring it and adding water to thin it, if necessary.

- For beginners, it's easiest to decorate using metal piping tips. Tips are numbered to indicate their size and shape, and most numbers are about equal across manufacturers. A #2 round piping tip is a good size for piping outlines with piping consistency icing. A #3 round piping tip has a larger opening and is good for flooding cookies using thinner icing.

- To insert a piping tip into a disposable bag, snip off about ¼ inch from the tip of the bag. Drop the piping tip into the bag, tip down, and press the tip through the opening. The goal is for the tip opening to be free from plastic and to have no more than half of the piping tip sticking out of the bag. To prevent icing from leaking out as you fill, twist the bag just behind the tip and tuck the twisted plastic into the piping tip.

- To add icing to the piping bags, place a 12-inch disposable bag, point down, into a tall drinking glass (preferably a heavy-bottomed one so it's less likely to topple over). Pull about 3 inches of the bag over the rim of the glass to create a cuff. Add enough icing to fill the bag no more than halfway full. Twist the top of the bag closed.

- If you want to add some decorations, such as colored sugars or sprinkles, to your cookie, sprinkle them over your cookie immediately after flooding so the decorations will settle into the wet icing. When the icing dries, it will adhere to the sugar and sprinkles and prevent them from falling off.

- Leave cookies to dry, uncovered, at room temperature. The icing will take several hours to dry completely, but drying your cookies next to a fan on low speed can help speed up the process. Don't worry about the cookies drying out as they dry uncovered. The icing has created a great coating that helps to keep the cookie fresh. Once the cookies are dry, they can be stacked and stored in airtight containers. We have enjoyed cookies several weeks after they were made and found them to still be perfect.

Rolled Fondant

- You can certainly make your own using a variety of recipes found across the interwebs, but we most often rely on commercially made rolled fondant.
- Rolled fondant can be purchased in a variety of colors. You can also buy white fondant and color it yourself with gel, paste, or powdered food color. To color, add a small bit of color and knead it into a portion of fondant until the color is completely even throughout. Add more color until the desired color is achieved. Adding a lot of color to fondant to achieve deep shades of color can make it soft and difficult to work with. If you want a very dark color, such as deep red, purple, navy blue, or black, then we recommend purchasing fondant in that color.
- Before using rolled fondant, we knead the fondant on a smooth surface to loosen it up and make it more pliable. To prevent it from sticking, dust a rolling surface with confectioners' sugar or cornstarch (both will work). Don't add too much confectioners' sugar or cornstarch because it can dry the fondant out and make it difficult to work with.
- Roll fondant to an ⅛-inch-thick layer using a rolling pin. Cut out the fondant using the same cookie cutter that you used to make the cookie. Because our roll-out cookie recipes spread very little, the cut shape of fondant should cover most of the top of the cookie with a perfect fit.
- To apply the cut-out fondant, brush a small amount of corn syrup, piping gel, or even thin, strained jam over the surface of the cookie. Lay the fondant over the cookie and gently press to make sure it sticks.
- Rolled fondant can be textured with such tools as textured rolling pins or cookie stamps before it's cut and applied to the cookie. For additional flourishes, royal icing details can be piped on.
- Leave the fondant to set for several hours to begin to firm. For storage, we try to avoid stacking fondant-covered cookies if we can. The uncovered bottoms of the cookies can sometimes damage the fondant decorations. The fondant can still be dented if pressed too hard.

Cookie decorating is an art, and very few people become masters at it their first few times at it. We encourage you to seek out videos, read books, take classes, and practice, practice, practice! For cookie-decorating ideas, check out our Cookie Decorating Resources on page 353.

Royal Icing

MAKES ABOUT 6 CUPS

This creamy white icing dries hard with a delicate crunch. It is the ultimate building block for creating the perfect edible blank canvas. This recipe is one that we have been using for years to decorate cookies. It makes enough to cover at least three or four dozen medium cookies, plus some leftover for added details.

INGREDIENT	VOLUME	WEIGHT
Meringue powder (see Note)	⅓ cup	45 grams
Warm water	⅔ cup	157 grams
Confectioners' sugar	9 cups	1,025 grams
Light corn syrup	1 tablespoon	21 grams
Pure vanilla extract (see Flavor Options)	1 tablespoon	

1. Whisk together the meringue powder and warm water in the bowl of a stand mixer fitted with a flat beater until the meringue powder has dissolved. Add the confectioners' sugar and mix on low speed until all of the sugar is moist and is no longer in jeopardy of flying out of the bowl in a dusty white cloud.

2. Increase the mixer speed to medium and mix for 3 minutes, stopping after 1 minute to scrape the sides and bottom of the bowl with a silicone spatula.

3. Add the corn syrup and vanilla. Beat on medium speed for an additional 30 seconds. Immediately transfer the royal icing to a container with a tight-fitting lid. Press a layer of plastic wrap directly onto the surface of the icing to prevent it from crusting and drying out. When you are ready to start decorating, remove the plastic wrap and color as desired. Icing can be stored at room temperature for about 3 days, or in the refrigerator for up to 2 weeks. Royal icing can also be frozen. Bring to room temperature before using. Royal icing will separate over time, so stirring might be needed after icing has been sitting for more than a few hours.

NOTE: Meringue powder is basically dehydrated egg whites along with some stabilizers to help the meringue keep its structure. If you can't find it, substitute 3 egg whites (105 grams) for the meringue powder and water. For food safety purposes, we recommend using pasteurized egg whites. Pasteurized egg whites are usually sold in a carton (like heavy cream), or you can separate pasteurized egg whites from whole pasteurized eggs. In the United States, pasteurized eggs are stamped with a letter P on the shell. Do not confused pasteurized eggs with pasture-raised eggs. They are not the same. There will probably only be one brand (if that) of pasteurized eggs at your local grocery store. Meringue powder can be found online or in cake decorating or craft supply stores (see Sources, page 350).

Variations: Flavor Options

While we most often use pure vanilla extract as our flavor of choice, this recipe is easily adaptable to other flavorings. Stick to clear or lightly colored flavorings, or you risk coloring your icing too deeply. This could affect your ability to achieve certain colors in your icing, including a bright white. Strongly flavored extracts don't require as much as vanilla. For example, we use 2 teaspoons of lemon extract or only 1 teaspoon of peppermint or almond extract.

Glaze Icing

MAKES ABOUT 3⅓ CUPS

This recipe for an egg-free icing for decorating cookies is based very closely on a recipe from our friend Cameo Robinson, owner of CR Confections in Olathe, Kansas, near Kansas City. She, in turn, got her recipe from Pam Sneed, the wonderful innovator who created CookieCrazie.com. It's a great alternative if you don't want to use royal icing because of egg allergies or you can't find meringue powder. When made with organic confectioners' sugar (which is not processed with animal bone char), it can be made vegan-friendly as well. This glaze icing doesn't dry as fast as royal icing, so you have a little more time to manipulate it before it starts to crust over. The glaze also does not dry as hard as royal icing, so if you want an icing with a softer bite, this glaze is perfect.

INGREDIENT	VOLUME	WEIGHT
Confectioners' sugar	8 cups	907 grams (2 pounds)
Light corn syrup	½ cup	168 grams
Water	¼ cup plus 2 tablespoons	89 grams
Pure vanilla extract	2 teaspoons	
White gel food coloring (optional; see Note)		

1. Combine the confectioners' sugar, corn syrup, water, vanilla, and white food coloring (if using) in the bowl of a stand mixer fitted with a flat beater, and beat together on medium-low speed until all of the ingredients are combined and the mixture is smooth, about 2 minutes. Don't overbeat, or you will create air bubbles that might remain in the icing as it's applied to your cookie.

2. Portion and color the icing as desired. Gently stir in additional water for a thinner consistency, if desired. This glaze can be kept at room temperature for up to 3 days, or in the refrigerator for at least 2 weeks.

NOTE: Unlike royal icing, glaze icing can be slightly transparent. For a more opaque look, add about 10 drops of white gel food coloring (see Sources, page 350).

Salted Caramel Ganache

MAKES ABOUT 1 CUP

Pouring a rich, dark caramel sauce over bittersweet chocolate produces an intensely flavorful and creamy ganache. The warm ganache can be poured and spread over any 8-inch-square batch of brownies, blondies, or grahammies (double the recipe for a 13-by-9-inch pan). Once cooled, the ganache can be scooped as a decadent sandwich cookie filling, too.

INGREDIENT	VOLUME	WEIGHT
Sugar	¼ cup	50 grams
Unsalted butter, cut into 3 pieces	2 tablespoons	28 grams
Heavy cream	¼ cup plus 3 tablespoons	102 grams
Pure vanilla extract	½ teaspoon	
Salt	⅛ teaspoon	
Bittersweet chocolate, preferably 60 to 70 percent cacao, finely chopped		85 grams (3 ounces)

1. Place the sugar in a medium saucepan with high sides over medium-high heat. Once the sugar starts to melt, swirl the pan occasionally, encouraging any dry sugar to fall into the liquid parts until it has all melted and started to turn golden brown or caramelize. You can also stir the mixture with a long-handled silicone spatula instead of swirling, if you prefer. Let the caramelization go on until it is medium to dark brown.

2. Remove the saucepan from the heat and add the butter (the mixture might bubble ferociously—be careful). Once the butter is melted, after about 15 seconds, add the cream and whisk gently until all of the caramel is incorporated into a smooth sauce. Whisk in the vanilla and salt.

3. Place the chopped chocolate in a medium, heat-proof bowl. Pour the hot caramel sauce over the chopped chocolate and gently shake the bowl to ensure that the hot mixture is in contact with all of the chocolate. Set it aside for 30 seconds.

4. Whisk the chocolate and caramel sauce together until the mixture is smooth and uniform. If using to cover a pan of brownies, pour the ganache while it is still very warm and gently spread with an offset spatula. If using as a filling, allow the ganache to set at room temperature (about 3 hours) and portion the ganache with a small scoop.

Peanut Butter Filling

Perhaps the easiest recipe in the book, this cookie filling balances the sweet and salty sides of peanut butter.

MAKES ABOUT 1 CUP

INGREDIENT	VOLUME	WEIGHT
Creamy peanut butter	⅔ cup	180 grams
Unsalted butter, at room temperature	1 tablespoon	14 grams
Salt	¼ teaspoon	
Confectioners' sugar	⅔ cup	75 grams
Pure vanilla extract	¼ teaspoon	

1. Combine the peanut butter, butter, and salt in a medium bowl and beat together until smooth, using an electric mixer on medium speed. Add the confectioners' sugar and vanilla and start mixing on low speed.

2. As the mixture starts to come together, increase the speed until all the sugar has been incorporated into the filling.

Creamy Mascarpone Filling

Rich, creamy, and oh so versatile! This cookie filling is soft enough to easily pipe, with decorative star-shaped piping tips, like buttercream, yet it sets up just enough so that it resists squishing out from between the cookies when bitten.

MAKES ABOUT 2 CUPS

INGREDIENT	VOLUME	WEIGHT
Heavy cream	¾ cup	174 grams
Sugar	⅔ cup	133 grams
Mascarpone, cold	One 8-ounce container	227 grams
Pure vanilla extract	2 teaspoons	

1. Bring the cream to a boil in a small saucepan over medium heat. Alternatively, the cream can be heated to a boil, in a medium, microwave-safe bowl, in a microwave on high (100%) power. Stir in the sugar with a silicone spatula until the sugar is all dissolved. Cover and refrigerate the mixture until it is cold (at least 3 hours, or overnight).

2. Depending on the capacity of your stand mixer, this might be more convenient to mix using an electric hand mixer. Add the mascarpone and vanilla to the cold cream and beat on high speed until the mixture has thickened and holds stiff peaks, 3 to 5 minutes.

Variation: Cocoa Mascarpone Filling

When adding the sugar to the hot cream, also stir in 3 tablespoons (16 grams) of Dutch-processed cocoa powder and ½ teaspoon of instant espresso powder. Omit the vanilla.

Variation: Espresso Mascarpone Filling

When adding the sugar to the hot cream, also stir in 2 teaspoons of instant espresso powder. Replace the vanilla with 1 teaspoon of dark rum.

Variation: Berry Mascarpone Filling

Reduce the sugar to ½ cup (100 grams). Replace the vanilla with ½ cup of berry preserves, such as strawberry or black raspberry. Also sprinkle 1 tablespoon of Instant ClearJel (see "Modified Starch," page 258) over the chilled cream before whipping. Depending on the intensity of the color of the berry preserves, you may want to add a drop of gel food coloring to boost its berrylike hue.

flavor index

Are you in the mood for a chocolate cookie? What if you're craving something with a citrus kick? This table provides a quick reference to see the primary flavor(s) of each cookie regardless of its book chapter. Only the dominant flavors of each cookie are represented and are based on a recipe's main ingredients without substitutions. Not all flavors of each cookie are shown.

PAGE	RECIPE	CARAMEL, TOFFEE & BROWN BUTTER	CHOCOLATE	CITRUS	COCONUT	COFFEE	FRUIT	HONEY	MAPLE	NUT (EXCEPT PEANUT)	PEANUT AND PEANUT BUTTER	SPICE	SPIRITS	VANILLA	OTHER	CHEESE	SAVORY
49	Grahammies	●															
91	Salted Caramel Sugar Cookies	●															
210	Caramel Pretzel Rugelach	●															
294	Streusel Scotchies	●															
45	Streusel Crown Brownies	●	●														
87	Bronze Butter Chocolate Chip Cookies	●	●														
273	Dark Lemon Mads	●		●													
289	Bananas Foster Churros	●					●						●				

PAGE	RECIPE	CARAMEL, TOFFEE & BROWN BUTTER	CHOCOLATE	CITRUS	COCONUT	COFFEE	FRUIT	HONEY	MAPLE	NUT (EXCEPT PEANUT)	PEANUT AND PEANUT BUTTER	SPICE	SPIRITS	VANILLA	OTHER	CHEESE	SAVORY
147	Bronze Butter Pecan Cut-Outs	●								●							
291	Smoked Almond and Caramel Cookie Crunch	●								●							
287	Chicago Crispy Rice Treats	●														●	
43	Fudgy Cloud Brownies		●														
46	Infinity Brownies		●														
145	Deep Chocolate Fantasy Rolled Cookies		●														
217	OMGs (Our Marvelous Gobs)*		●														
234	Chocolocks*		●														
48	Midnight in Seville (Orange) Brownies		●	●													
64	Black-Bottom Lemon Squares		●	●													
228	Fig-Orange-Almond Fruity Newties		●	●			●										

PAGE	RECIPE	CARAMEL, TOFFEE & BROWN BUTTER	CHOCOLATE	CITRUS	COCONUT	COFFEE	FRUIT	HONEY	MAPLE	NUT (EXCEPT PEANUT)	PEANUT AND PEANUT BUTTER	SPICE	SPIRITS	VANILLA	OTHER	CHEESE	SAVORY
223	Old Fashioned Ice Cream Sandwiches		●	●									●				
54	Dandy Cake Bars		●			●											
45	Tuxedo Brownies		●				●										
165	Banana Pick-a-Chips		●				●										
229	Cranberry-Pomegranate Fruity Newties		●				●										
230	Ginger-Apricot Fruity Newties		●				●					●					
162	Mustachios		●							●							
57	Tandy Cake Bars		●								●						
150	Peanut Butter Cup Cut-Out Cookies		●								●						
239	Buckeye Snaps		●								●						
284	Old-School No-Bakes		●								●						
303	Wholly Moles		●									●					●

PAGE	RECIPE	CARAMEL, TOFFEE & BROWN BUTTER	CHOCOLATE	CITRUS	COCONUT	COFFEE	FRUIT	HONEY	MAPLE	NUT (EXCEPT PEANUT)	PEANUT AND PEANUT BUTTER	SPICE	SPIRITS	VANILLA	OTHER	CHEESE	SAVORY
108	Crispy Chocolate Five-Spice Oatmeal Cookies		●									●					
269	Campfire S'more		●												●		
153	Lemon Cheesecake Roll-Outs			●													
254	Jam-on-Toast Thumbprints			●													
271	Bright Lemon Mads			●													
131	Raspberry Lemonades			●			●										
184	Rum Puncharoos			●			●						●				
126	Golden Bites			●						●							
197	Grapefruit and Pistachio Stained-Glass Slices			●						●							
237	Mai Tai Cremes			●						●							
143	Orange Harvest Spice Cookies			●								●					
189	Tiger Tails			●								●					

PAGE	RECIPE	CARAMEL, TOFFEE & BROWN BUTTER	CHOCOLATE	CITRUS	COCONUT	COFFEE	FRUIT	HONEY	MAPLE	NUT (EXCEPT PEANUT)	PEANUT AND PEANUT BUTTER	SPICE	SPIRITS	VANILLA	OTHER	CHEESE	SAVORY
58	Whiskey-Lemon Sweet Potato Squares			●									●		●		
169	Stonewalls			●											●		
195	Orange Rosemary Bites			●											●		
275	Aperol Spritzes			●											●		
155	Coconut Cream Pie Roll-Outs				●												
257	Coconut + Guava Sandwiches				●		●										
103	Escapes (The Piña Colada Oatmeal Cookies)				●		●			●							
74	Thai Coconut Macaroon Bars				●					●					●		
159	Coffee Bean Crunchers					●											
51	Portland Pie Squares					●	●			●							
250	Pumpkin Spice Latte Thumbprints					●						●					
283	Biscoffee No-Bake Bites					●						●					

PAGE	RECIPE	CARAMEL, TOFFEE & BROWN BUTTER	CHOCOLATE	CITRUS	COCONUT	COFFEE	FRUIT	HONEY	MAPLE	NUT (EXCEPT PEANUT)	PEANUT AND PEANUT BUTTER	SPICE	SPIRITS	VANILLA	OTHER	CHEESE	SAVORY
221	Moonstrucks					●							●				
155	Cherry Chip Ice Cream Roll-Outs						●										
192	Fig and Maple Nut Slices						●		●	●							
113	Blush and Bashfuls						●			●							
179	Stollen Glances						●			●							
62	Where's Waldorfs						●			●					●		
299	Cherry Chèvrons						●			●						●	●
97	Speckle and Spice Softies						●					●					
100	Gingerbread Bogs						●					●					
248	Jelly Doughnut Dimples						●					●					
242	Modern Mincemeat Pockets						●					●					
323	Major Grey (Mango Chutney) Thumbprints						●					●					●

PAGE	RECIPE	CARAMEL, TOFFEE & BROWN BUTTER	CHOCOLATE	CITRUS	COCONUT	COFFEE	FRUIT	HONEY	MAPLE	NUT (EXCEPT PEANUT)	PEANUT AND PEANUT BUTTER	SPICE	SPIRITS	VANILLA	OTHER	CHEESE	SAVORY
72	Drunken Date Bars						●						●				
67	New-School Banana Puddin' Squares						●								●		
77	Mango Sunshine Bars						●								●		
261	Blueberry Cornbread Sandwiches						●								●		
101	Honey Whole Wheat Bogs						●	●									
110	Everybody Ryes							●									
282	Hot Honey Chik'n Biscuits							●				●					
280	Chik'n and Stroopwafels								●								
273	Maple Chipotle Mads								●			●					
105	Mocksies									●		●					
186	Badam Milk Bites									●		●					
272	Bastani Sonnati Mads									●		●					
205	Birthday Cake Rugelach Slices									●				●			

PAGE	RECIPE	CARAMEL, TOFFEE & BROWN BUTTER	CHOCOLATE	CITRUS	COCONUT	COFFEE	FRUIT	HONEY	MAPLE	NUT (EXCEPT PEANUT)	PEANUT AND PEANUT BUTTER	SPICE	SPIRITS	VANILLA	OTHER	CHEESE	SAVORY
70	Peanut Butter Humdinger Fingers										●						
94	Next-Gen Peanut Butter Cookies										●						
128	Peanut Satay Crunchers										●	●					
317	Lancelots										●					●	●
155	Cinnamon Roll Swirl Roll-Outs											●					
288	Silver Dollar 'Doodles											●					
122	Pumpkin Snickercrinkles											●			●		
306	Cucumber Cheesecake Everything Bagel Bars											●			●		●
313	Thin Crust Pepperoni Slices											●			●	●	●
310	Tuscan Crisps											●					●
326	Barbecuties											●					●
318	Frito Pie Cheese Coins											●				●	●

PAGE	RECIPE	CARAMEL, TOFFEE & BROWN BUTTER	CHOCOLATE	CITRUS	COCONUT	COFFEE	FRUIT	HONEY	MAPLE	NUT (EXCEPT PEANUT)	PEANUT AND PEANUT BUTTER	SPICE	SPIRITS	VANILLA	OTHER	CHEESE	SAVORY
201	Elderflower Dainties												●				
203	Pick-Your-Potion Glazed Butter Cookies*												●				
245	Perfect Manhattan Thumbprints												●				
269	Bourbon Cornflake												●		●		
93	Chewy Malted Vanilla Sugar Cookies													●			
121	Best Vanilla Bean Shortbread													●			
141	Very Vanilla Cookie Artists' Best Butter Cookies													●			
231	Goldilocks*													●			
119	Teatime Stamped Shortbread														●		
259	Fried Green Tomato Sandwiches														●		

PAGE	RECIPE	CARAMEL, TOFFEE & BROWN BUTTER	CHOCOLATE	CITRUS	COCONUT	COFFEE	FRUIT	HONEY	MAPLE	NUT (EXCEPT PEANUT)	PEANUT AND PEANUT BUTTER	SPICE	SPIRITS	VANILLA	OTHER	CHEESE	SAVORY
267	Loopy Fruit Rings														●		
277	Piggies and Taters														●		
321	Pierogi Party Bites														●	●	●
316	Smokeshow Cheese Coins														●	●	●

* The choice of filling or glaze might add additional flavors.

sources

Ingredients

Almond Paste
Solo Foods, www.solofoods.com

Amarena Cherries
Toschi, www.toschi.it
Fabbri, www.fabbri1905.com
Specialty food stores, liquor stores, and online

Chocolate
Guittard Chocolate Company, www.guittard.com
Callebaut, www.callebaut.com
Ghirardelli, www.ghirardelli.com
Grocery stores, online, and www.pastrydepot.com

Coarse Sanding Sugar
Wilton, www.wilton.com
Cake and cookie decorating supply stores, craft stores,
    and online

Cocoa Nibs
Valrhona, www.valrhona-chocolate.com
Specialty food stores and www.pastrydepot.com

Cocoa Powder
Black cocoa powder, www.kingarthurbaking.com
Bensdorp (Dutch-processed),
    www.kingarthurbaking.com
Droste (Dutch-processed), select grocery stores, and online

Dried Fruits
Grocery stores, online, and www.kalustyans.com

Flavors and Other Extracts
Nielsen-Massey, www.nielsenmassey.com
McCormick, www.mccormick.com
Grocery stores, specialty food stores, and online

Flour

BLEACHED CAKE FLOUR
Softasilk, www.pillsburybaking.com
Swans Down, www.swansdown.com
Grocery stores and online

GLUTEN-FREE FLOUR SUBSTITUTE
King Arthur Baking Company Gluten-Free Measure for
    Measure Flour, www.kingarthurbaking.com
Grocery stores and online

RYE FLOUR
The Old Mill, www.old-mill.com
King Arthur Baking Company Organic Medium Rye,
    www.kingarthurbaking.com
Grocery stores and online

UNBLEACHED ALL-PURPOSE FLOUR
King Arthur Baking Company,
    www.kingarthurbaking.com
Grocery stores and online

WHITE RICE FLOUR
Bob's Red Mill, www.bobsredmill.com
Grocery stores and online

WHOLE WHEAT FLOUR

King Arthur Baking Company,
   www.kingarthurbaking.com

Grocery stores and online

Freeze-Dried Fruits

Karen's Naturals, www.shopkarensnaturals.com

Grocery stores and online

Golden Syrup

Tate & Lyle, www.lylesgoldensyrup.com

Specialty food stores, grocery stores, and online

Guava Preserves

Conchita, www.conchita-foods.com

Select grocery stores and online

Hot Honey

Mike's Hot Honey, www.mikeshothoney.com

Specialty food stores, select grocery stores, and online

Instant ClearJel

Online and www.kingarthurbaking.com

Liquid Smoke

Colgin, www.colgin.com

Grocery stores and online

Maple Sugar

www.kingarthurbaking.com

Specialty food stores and online

Meringue Powder

Genie's Dream Premium Meringue Powder,
   www.creativecookier.com

Cake and cookie decorating supply stores, craft stores,
   and online

Nuts

Grocery stores, online, and www.kalustyans.com

Piping Gel

Wilton, www.wilton.com

Cake and cookie decorating supply stores, craft stores,
   and online

Red Curry Paste

Thai Kitchen, www.mccormick.com

Grocery stores and online

Red Tart Cherries (Canned)

Oregon Fruit Products, www.oregonfruit.com

Grocery stores and online

Rolled Fondant

Renshaw Ready to Roll Fondant,
   www.renshawamericas.com

Cake and cookie decorating supply stores, craft stores,
   and www.nicholaslodge.com

Salt

Maldon Sea Salt Flakes, www.maldonseasalt.com

Pretzel salt, specialty food stores, and online

Soft Gel Food Color

AmeriColor, www.americolorcorp.com

Chefmaster, www.chefmaster.com

Cookie Countess Gel Icing Color,
www.thecookiecountess.com

Genie's Dream Premium Gel Food Color,
www.creativecookier.com

Cake and cookie decorating supply stores, craft stores,
and online

Speculoos Cookie Butter

Lotus Biscoff Cookie Butter, www.lotusbiscoff.com

Grocery stores and online

Spices and Dried Herbs

Penzeys Spices, www.penzeys.com

Vanilla Extract and Vanilla Bean Paste

Nielsen-Massey, www.nielsenmassey.com

Groceries stores and online

Equipment

Ball Tool (¾– and 1–inch heads)

Ateco Double Ended Ball Tool, www.atecousa.com

Cookie Cutters

See Cookie Decorating Resources, pages 353–54.

Cookie Portion Scoops/Dishers

Winco, www.wincous.com

Specialty kitchen stores, restaurant supply stores, and online

Cookie Stamps

Nordic Ware, www.nordicware.com

Dent de Loup Pan (Wolf Tooth Cookie Form)

Gobel 11-by-12-by-1-inch pan with 8 forms

Online at www.jbprince.com or www.pastrychef.com

Food Processor

Breville Sous Chef 16 Pro, www.breville.com

Instant-Read Thermometer

Thermapen Mk4, www.thermapen.com

Kitchen Torch

Hardware stores, specialty kitchen stores, and at
www.williams-sonoma.com

Lady Lock Molds

Grama Joan's Cookie Forms,
www.gramajoanscookieforms.com

Madeleine Pans

Chicago Metallic Professional 12-Cup Non-Stick,
www.cmbakeware.com

Gobel Nonstick Mini Madeleine Plaque,
www.williams-sonoma.com

Specialty kitchen stores and online

Parchment Sheets (precut)

www.kingarthurbaking.com and restaurant
supply stores

Piping Bags and General Piping Tips

See Cookie Decorating Resources, pages 353–54.

Pizzelle Iron

Palmer Non-Stick Electric Pizzelle Iron,
    www.cpalmermfg.com
Chef'sChoice PizzellePro Nonstick Pizzelle Maker,
    Model 835

Plastic Knife

Zyliss Lettuce Knife, www.zyliss.com
Lindén Sweden Multi-Use Spreader,
    www.lindensweden.com
Grocery stores, specialty kitchen stores, and online

Rasp-Style Grater

Microplane Classic Zester/Grater,
    www.microplane.com

Rolling Pin Guides

Regency Evendough, specialty kitchen stores and online
Rose Levy Beranbaum Signature Series
    "Fast Tracks" Thickness Guide Rails,
    www.realbakingwithrose.com/apg

Scale

My Weigh KD8000 scale, www.myweigh.com

Silicone Baking Mats

Silpat Half Size Baking Mat, www.silpat.com
Mrs. Anderson's Baking Silicone Bread Crisping Mat
    (perforated), www.hickitchen.com

Silicone Rolling Mat

King Arthur Baking, www.kingarthurbaking.com
Tovolo Silicone Pastry Mat, www.tovolo.com

Silicone Texture Mat

Waffle Fondant Impression Mat, www.nycake.com
Other designs available

Slice-and-Bake Molds

Masterproofing Spam Musubi Double Size 8-by-2-by-
    2-inch Mold, www.amazon.com
Ateco Triangle Mold (Cone Shaped Bottom) Terrine Mold
    with Cover, www.atecousa.com

Spritz Cookie Press

Kuhn Rikon Cookie Press, www.kuhnrikonshop.com
Specialty kitchen stores and online

Sultan Piping Tip

de Buyer Stainless-Steel Sultan Nozzle,
    www.debuyer.com
Specialty kitchen stores, online, and at
    www.pastrychef.com

Cookie Decorating Resources
Tips, Tricks, Classes, and Inspiration

Andy Kay's Cookies, www.andykayscookies.com
Arty McGoo, artymcgoo.com
The Bearfoot Baker, www.thebearfootbaker.com
Chua Cookie, www.chuacookie.com
Clough'd 9 Cookies, www.cloughd9cookies.com

The Colorful Cookie, www.thecolorfulcookie.com

The Cookie Architect, www.thecookiearchitect.com

CookieCon Cookie Art Convention and Show,
    www.cookiecon.net

CookieCrazie, www.cookiecrazie.com

CR Confections, www.crconfections.com

Dany's Cakes,
    www.instagram.com/danyscakesbydanylind

Downtown Dough T.O., www.downtowndoughto.com

Four Peas and a Dog, www.fourpeasandadog.com

The Frosted Swirl Bake Shop,
    www.instagram.com/thefrostedswirlbakeshop

Funky Cookie Studio, www.instagram.com/jillfcs

The Hungry Hippopotamus,
    www.thehungryhippopotamus.com

Inspired to Taste, www.inspiredtotaste.com

Julia M. Usher, www.juliausher.com

Lila Loa, www.lilaloa.com

Sarah's Cookie Jar, www.sarahscookiejar.com

Sugar Dayne Cookies, www.sugardayne.com

SweetAmbs, www.sweetambs.com

Sweet Sugarbelle, www.sweetsugarbelle.com

The Floured Canvas, www.theflouredcanvas.com

Tunde's Creations, www.tundescreations.com

You Can Call Me Sweetie, www.youcancallmesweetie.com

Cookie Cutters

Ann Clark Cookie Cutters,
    www.annclarkcookiecutters.com

Bobbi's Cutters, www.etsy.com/shop/BobbisCutters

KalediaCuts, www.kaleidacuts.com

Killer Zebras, www.killerzebras.com

LizViz, www.lizviz.com

Semi Sweet Designs, www.semisweetdesigns.com

Sinful Cutters, www.sinfulcutters.com

The Sweet Designs Shoppe,
    www.thesweetdesignsshoppe.com

Sweetleigh Printed,
    www.etsy.com/shop/SweetleighPrinted

Truly Mad Plastics, www.trulymadplastics.com

Whisked Away Cutters,
    www.etsy.com/shop/WhiskedAwayCutters

Decorating Supplies

2T's Stencils, www.2tsstencils.com

Bee's Baked Art Supplies,
    www.beesbakedartsupplies.com

The Cookie Countess, www.thecookiecountess.com

Creative Cookier, www.creativecookier.com

The Flour Box, www.flourbox.com

How Sweet Is That?, www.howsweetisthat.ca

The International Sugar Art Collection by Nicholas
    Lodge, www.nicholaslodge.com

Lezlie Belanger/Canterbury Keepsakes Stencils,
    www.etsy.com/shop/cankeep

Stencibelle, www.stencibelle.com

SugarVeil, www.sugarveil.com

Sweet Southern Stencils,
    www.etsy.com/shop/SweetSouthernStencil

Yoli's Yummies,
    www.etsy.com/shop/YolisYummiesSupplies

acknowledgments

No book is created in a vacuum, and we are so thankful for the support and guidance we've received as we wrote this book. We are forever grateful for all our friends and family who have supported our baking over many years by providing words of encouragement and constructive criticism. This friendship and encouragement mean the world to us.

Our fantastic agent, Joy Tutela of the David Black Agency, is an integral part of our team. Joy, you are a much-needed truth-teller and an indispensable advocate and supporter. Thank you for doing everything you do to help us succeed.

Andrew Thomas Lee, our photographer, used his fantastic vision to create another stunning set of photographs. Andy, our books would not be what they are without your talent and creativity. Additional thanks to our prop stylist, Thom Driver, whose eye for details was so integral in helping to create such wonderful shots.

Many thanks to our brilliant team at The Countryman Press and W. W. Norton. Thank you to our magnificent editor, Ann Treistman, who believed in us from the beginning and allowed us the freedom to express our vision and create this book. We are so appreciative of Allison Chi, who designed the art for this book, and also designed a truly fabulous layout to complement our recipes and photographs. Thank you to Iris Bass, Jessica Murphy, and Devon Zahn for providing insightful and valuable edits. Additionally, many thanks you to our talented marketing and publicity team of Jessica Gilo and Rhina Garcia, for helping to promote this book and ensure its success. Finally, thank you to Isabel McCarthy and the rest of the team who work so hard behind the scenes to make the publishing process run so smoothly.

To all our baking and cookie friends, who are too numerous to name, thank you for all your love, support, and well wishes over the years. Learning from you, teaching you, sharing with you, and laughing with you have been some of the brightest spots in our baking careers.

A special thanks to Liz and John Adams for creating a community of friendship at McGooU, where cookie makers of all kinds can come to learn and laugh together. And to Mike and Karen Summers, many thanks for tirelessly working to develop, grow, and produce CookieCon, our wonderful annual getaway where we reconnect with old friends and never fail to make new ones. Your legacies will be in the families you created.

index